THE SYNTAX OF IMPERATIVES

The imperative clause is one of three major sentence types that have been found to be universal across the languages of the world. Compared to declaratives and interrogatives, the imperative type has received diverse analyses in the literature. This cutting-edge study puts forward a new linguistic theory of imperatives, arguing that categories of the speech act, specifically Speaker and Addressee, are conceptually necessary for an adequate syntactic account. The book offers compelling empirical and descriptive evidence by surveying new typological data in the critical assessment of competing hypotheses towards an indexical syntax of human language. An engaging read for students and researchers interested in linguistics, philosophy, and the syntax of language.

ASIER ALCÁZAR is Associate Professor of Spanish at the University of Missouri. His research interests include generative syntax and its interfaces with semantics and morphology, corpus linguistics, and typology.

MARIO SALTARELLI is Professor of Spanish at the Dornsife College of the University of Southern California. His research and teaching includes publications in Romance and Basque linguistics, with recent emphasis on deixis in a context-sensitive theory of syntax.

T0370771

In this series

Earlier issues not listed are also available

The Syntax of Imperatives

THE SYNTAX OF IMPERATIVES

ASIER ALCÁZAR
University of Missouri

MARIO SALTARELLI
University of Southern California

CAMBRIDGE
UNIVERSITY PRESS

Shaftesbury Road, Cambridge CB2 8EA, United Kingdom

One Liberty Plaza, 20th Floor, New York, NY 10006, USA

477 Williamstown Road, Port Melbourne, VIC 3207, Australia

314–321, 3rd Floor, Plot 3, Splendor Forum, Jasola District Centre, New Delhi – 110025, India

103 Penang Road, #05–06/07, Visioncrest Commercial, Singapore 238467

Cambridge University Press is part of Cambridge University Press & Assessment, a department of the University of Cambridge.

We share the University's mission to contribute to society through the pursuit of education, learning and research at the highest international levels of excellence.

www.cambridge.org
Information on this title: www.cambridge.org/9781009342445

First published 2014
First paperback edition 2022

A catalogue record for this publication is available from the British Library

Library of Congress Cataloging-in-Publication data
Alcázar, Asier.
The syntax of imperatives / Asier Alcázar, Mario Saltarelli.
    pages   cm. – (Cambridge Studies in Linguistics ; 140)
Includes bibliographical references and index.
ISBN 978-1-107-00580-8 (hardback)
1. Grammar, Comparative and general–Imperative.   2. Grammar, Comparative and general–Syntax.   3. Language and languages–Grammars.   I. Saltarelli, Mario.   II. Title.
P281.A44   2013
415´6.6–dc23
2013023444

ISBN   978-1-107-00580-8   Hardback
ISBN   978-1-009-34244-5   Paperback

Contents

Figures

Tables

Abbreviations

A	Absolutive agreement
AA	Allocutive agreement
ABS	Absolutive case
ACC	Accusative
AND	Conjunction
AUX	Auxiliary
COMP	Complementizer
D	Dative agreement
DAT	Dative case
E	Ergative agreement
ERG	Ergative case
ETH.DAT	Ethical dative
FEM	Feminine
FUT	Future
GER	Gerund
IND	Indicative
INF	Infinitive
IMP	Imperative
IMPF	Imperfective
INSTR	Instrumental
MASC	Masculine
NEG	Negation
NOM	Nominative
PART	Partitive
PAST	Past
PER	Perfective
PRED	Pre-dative
PRES	Present
PROG	Progressive
PROH	Prohibitive
PL	Plural
Q	Question marker

SG	Singular
SUBJ	Subjunctive
THV	Thematic vowel
VOSEO	*Voseo* form

1   *Introduction*

1.0   Chapter overview

This chapter begins with a discussion of the imperative clause and a review of earlier studies of imperatives in generative grammar (1.1). The imperative clause appears to require recourse to conditions seemingly outside the realm of narrow syntax, such as "the subject of the imperative clause must be the addressee." Faced with this challenge, earlier generative studies have struggled to provide a principled syntactic account of the imperative type.

We claim that an adequate account of the syntax of the imperative clause must represent the *context of utterance* (1.2). More narrowly, imperatives require access to *indexicality*: speaker, hearer, time and world of utterance. Such referential categories have not played a formal role in the computation of the clause in narrow syntax. Accordingly, computational compliance would call for a derivational interface between syntactic categories (*content*), such as the subject of the imperative clause, and its binding thematic categories (*context*), such as addressee.

Before this interface challenge, earlier generative studies attempted to provide a principled syntactic account of the imperative type with the performative hypothesis (PH) (Ross 1970). In the spirit of PH, our proposal (Chapter 4) may be considered a recasting of Ross's conceptual bases implemented within the minimalist program (Chomsky 1995–2008), but focused on the imperative clause. We propose that the speaker and addressee of the utterance are encoded in a phase-theoretic context-to-content perspective: CP(vP).

Beyond the imperative clause type, diverse phenomena argue that syntax may be context sensitive. For example, indexical shift (Schlenker 1999, 2003, 2004; Baker 2008), logophoric pronouns (Hagège 1974; Clements 1975), complementizer deletion in Italian (Giorgi 2010) and conjunct-disjunct systems (Hale 1980; DeLancey 1986, 1992) suggest that the speaker and addressee must be syntactically present.

Other scholars have put forward alternative proposals to represent indexicality in syntax by means of accounting for context-sensitive phenomena, but without specific attention to imperatives (Speas and Tenny 2003; Bianchi 2003; Sigurðsson 2004). For a comprehensive review of generative studies on imperatives the reader is referred to the extensive introduction by van der Wurff (2007b).

1.1   Imperatives in generative grammar

This section presents a succinct overview of the imperative clause (its characteristics are discussed at length in Chapter 2) along with previous generative studies.

Compared to declarative and interrogative clauses, imperative clauses have distinctive morphosyntactic properties that set them apart as a basic clause type (1.1.1). We broadly characterize the previous generative analyses in relation to working assumptions that have remained constant across generative syntax (1.1.2). Emerging typological data, nonetheless, suggests that a reassessment is in order. At the same time, new empirical data may lead to alternative hypotheses with enhanced descriptive as well as explanatory advantages.

1.1.1   *The imperative clause*

The imperative clause is a basic sentence type (Sadock and Zwicky 1985) along with the declarative and interrogative. Each type differs in its communicative function[1] (orders, statements, questions) and often displays salient morphosyntactic differences. Consider English for illustration. Imperatives need not express an overt subject ("go!"). Yes/no-questions display subject–verb inversion with certain verbs ("Are you the manager?") or do-support ("Do you carry this brand?"). Wh-questions, in turn, typically feature movement of the interrogative pronoun to a sentence-initial position along with do-support ("Who did you see?"), except in the case of echo-questions, where the wh-element remains in situ ("You saw who?"). Declaratives display neither subject–verb inversion nor the verb *do* in this auxiliary role, and the subject is in most cases obligatorily expressed ("Peter saw Mary."). These morphosyntactic differences help us recognize and identify basic sentence types in English.

A closer look at the morphosyntax of basic clause types reveals that the imperative clause has distinctive characteristics that set it apart from both declaratives and interrogatives (henceforth D&I). While this is also arguably true of each type, in the imperative these distinctive properties appear to resist principled syntactic or morphological explanation without recourse to specific pragmatic conditions, such as "the imperative subject must be second person." By contrast, subject–verb inversion and do-support in interrogatives can be studied independently of pragmatic considerations. In the remainder of this section, we are going to briefly examine some of these differences between imperatives, on the one hand, and D&I on the other.[2]

Perhaps the most salient characteristic of imperatives is that their subject must be the addressee of the speech act ("you/you guys/you all go!"). Other person and number combinations in English are normally disallowed (*"I/*he/*she/*it/*we/*they go!", but see Potsdam 1998; Zanuttini 2008 for exceptional cases; on *let* forms, see 1.1.2). By contrast, in D&I the subject can be any number and person combination. This first asymmetry appears to indicate a pragmatic constraint in the interpretation of the imperative clause. Because the grammatical category person cannot be first or third person, it may seem unnecessary or even redundant to express a subject (a rationale offered by many scholars, see van der Wurff 2007b).

A similar restriction holds of the tense of the imperative in that the grammatical category features fewer possible values. Imperative tense is limited to a present or (near) future interpretation ("do it now/tomorrow/next year!"); the past tense is not attested in English (*"do it yesterday!"). A counterfactual past imperative is possible in some languages (Spanish: *¡haber-lo hecho antes!* [have.INF-it do.PART] 'You should have done it before' (Bosque 1980); also in Dutch, Beukema and Coopmans 1989, and other languages, Aikhenvald 2010). A true imperative past is seemingly not attested. By contrast, D&I display rich tense paradigms that include reference to the factual past (declaratives: "You work/worked/will work."). While English imperatives can refer to the future, they lack a distinct verb form ("(*will) work tomorrow!"). The tense value of imperatives is thus limited to the present and future/irrealis. This gap could be grounded in context-sensitive constraints or historical evolution similar to the interpretation and optionality of the imperative subject. Mainstream proposals, on the other hand, have argued that imperatives lack tense (Zanuttini 1996), along with other grammatical categories (1.1.2).

These properties of imperative clauses (i.e., second person subjects, optionality of the subject, limited tense values) seem to suggest that the imperative subject and tense are sensitive to the context of the speech act. On standard assumptions, this would constitute a descriptive argument for extended functional phases of CP(vP) syntax. Hence, beyond narrow imperative syntax, reference to speaker and addressee makes context sensitivity a conceptual necessity (1.1.2).

With regard to morphology, imperative verbs can be bare roots or minimally inflected forms. In Romance, exceptionally for five verbs, bare roots constitute second person singular imperative forms (Spanish: *¡sal!* [get.out.VROOT] 'get out!'). More generally, the root is flanked by a thematic vowel (*¡cant-a!* [sing-THV] 'sing!', Rivero and Terzi 1995; Zanuttini 1997). These uninflected forms stand out in synthetic-fusional languages that feature rich paradigms for indicative and subjunctive forms. All person and number combinations in the subject may be distinguished for most tenses and moods (Spanish: *cant-a-s* [sing-THV-2SG] 'you sing (indicative form)'; *cant-e-s* [sing-SUBJ-2SG] 'you sing (subjunctive form)'). The prevalence of bare forms raises the question of whether the imperative verb is finite (i.e., whether it lacks a syntactic projection) in comparison to D&I. Platzack and Rosengren (1998) defend the view that imperative clauses are defective. Among other projections, they lack a finite phrase (Rizzi 1997).[3] As a result, imperative verbs are bare forms. More generally, the lack of morphological distinctions is attributed to the context-sensitive constraints of the imperative clause (van der Wurff 2007b), but with no attempt to implement context syntactically, and they are thus left unanalyzed.

Two important syntactic characteristics of imperatives concern resistance to negation and embedding. In some languages, negative imperatives require substitution with other moods or non-finite forms (called *surrogate* forms in the specialized literature) or special negators (cf. Rivero and Terzi, Zanuttini above). The Romance family is well studied on this issue. For instance, the negative of *¡cant-a!* [sing-THV] 'sing!' in Spanish is not *¡no cant-a!* [NEG sing-THV] 'don't sing!', but rather the subjunctive form *¡no cant-e-s!* [sing-SUBJ-2SG] 'don't sing!'). In the same languages, nonetheless, D&I verb forms can be negated (but see Zeijlstra 2006).

The second syntactic characteristic is that imperative clauses rarely appear in dependent clauses (*"Mary said that John/you go!", see Platzack 2007; Kaufmann 2012). Yet interrogatives can be indirect ("David wondered who came to the party.") and declaratives can function as complement clauses ("Mary said that it was a cold winter."). On the other hand, there are cases where imperative verb forms appear to serve other functions as well. However, these seem to be cases where imperative morphology does not express the same meaning expressed in root imperative clauses. A prominent example is the Russian dramatic past (a vivid rendition of an unexpected event (А он и побеги 'he suddenly run,' cf. Gronas 2006: 89, in-text example). These uses fall outside the scope of our proposal for they do not express the functional meaning of the imperative clause as an intentional expression of a speech act.

Imperative verbs additionally observe a restriction to controllable processes and require animate subjects (Xrakovskij 2001; Aikhenvald 2010), excluding wishes. For example, compare the felicity of the imperative "fall to the ground!" with "slip to the ground!" When predicates that denote non-controllable processes are used in imperatives, they tend to be coerced into controllable actions ("hear me now!" = "listen to me now!"). Such restrictions and coerced interpretations are not observed in D&I.

In sum, we have seen a representative sample of properties that uniquely define the imperative type. On first impression, the imperative clause seems impoverished (not fully grammaticalized). Alternatively, these restrictions may follow from the absence of some grammatical categories altogether (e.g., tense, mood, finite phrase). Negative imperatives may not exist. The syntactic distribution of the imperative clause is uniquely limited. Finally, predicates denoting non-controllable processes are normally banned. In the next section, we review previous accounts of imperatives in generative grammar. These earlier analyses may have fallen short at the interface by ignoring the alternative of syntactic access to context.

1.1.2   Earlier analyses

Research on imperatives can be characterized according to assumptions about the form of grammar that have remained relatively unchanged over the years. They share a methodological compromise that considers imperatives to be second person forms (to the exclusion of related forms where the performer of the action is not the addressee, such as "let them go!"). Beyond what constitutes an imperative, there is a lack of consensus concerning what exceptional characteristics are syntactically analyzable. In this conceptual conundrum, scholars have attributed the majority of divergent characteristics of imperatives to context restrictions (van der Wurff 2007b). The only exception is the incompatibility with negation, often considered a morphosyntactic phenomenon independent of context, which has led to a productive research program expanding over two decades. In the remainder of this section, we elaborate on the above-mentioned characteristics.[4]

Regarding the first research question "what constitutes an imperative?", in earlier work, the imperative clause is often reduced to the canonical imperative, that is, the second person form ("go!"). Other person and number combinations exist, however, contingent on the language. In English, these forms require the auxiliary *let*: third person singular and plural ("let him/her/it/them go!"), or first person plural (inclusive exhortation: "let's go!"). Following the term chosen in van der Auwera et al. (2004), first and third person forms can be grouped under the label *hortative* (although, as they note, in some traditions they are referred to as *imperative* forms, e.g., Azkue 1925 on Basque).

In previous analyses, hortatives are not considered to be imperative forms proper for the following reasons. Hortatives typically involve indirect address ("let them go!"); the addressee mediates between the speaker and a third party. Importantly, the subject of the lexical verb need not be second person in hortatives, which may be considered sufficient grounds for treating these expressions separately from imperatives. Birjulin and Xrakovskij (2001) and Aikhenvald (2010) observe semantic differences based on person between imperatives and hortatives, such as invitation in first person forms. Morphosyntactically, hortatives may be different from imperatives. This is the case in English, where hortatives require the auxiliary *let*. Alternatively, first and third person forms are considered related, but spared for further research, following an elucidation of the properties of the canonical paradigm. Consistent with this trend in generative syntax, Kaufmann (2012), a recent monograph on the interpretation of imperatives, is also concerned mainly with second person forms.

In recent typological surveys, by contrast, imperative sentences include hortatives (Xrakovskij 2001; van der Auwera et al. 2004, 2008; Aikhenvald 2010). Two implicational hierarchies of number and person markedness (cf. van der Auwera et al., Aikhenvald above) show that imperatives and hortatives behave as a group. For instance, if a language has hortatives it also has imperatives; if dual is distinguished in hortatives, so it is in imperatives. Consistent with these hierarchies, Aikhenvald notes that hortatives present fewer morphological distinctions than imperatives for various grammatical categories (e.g., tense, aspect). One challenging question concerns a reversal in person markedness. In hortatives, third person is often marked (Spanish: *¡que salga!* [COMP get.out.3SG.SUBJ] 'let him/her get out!') relative to second person in imperatives, which is unmarked, particularly in the singular (*¡sal!* [get.out.VROOT] 'get out!'). Semantically, Birjulin and Xrakovskij (2001) propose that imperatives and hortatives are rather homogeneous, if first person forms are excluded. Upon closer scrutiny, hortatives replicate most of the restrictions observed in imperatives, such as an irrealis temporal interpretation (*"let them go yesterday!"), or their resistance to serving as a dependent clause (*"John ordered let them go!").

Future generative studies face the task of elucidating a pivotal difference in the distribution of person: second person (imperatives), first/third person (hortatives). Hortatives featuring an auxiliary verb can also refer to second person with reflexives ("let yourself go!").

In addition to the lack of consensus on the ontological meaning of the imperative, there is a lack of consensus on what context-sensitive properties of the imperative clause are syntactically analyzable. Consider the second person restriction by way of example. This property is unanalyzed or it is presumed to follow from the (as yet undefined) meaning or nature of the imperative. Accordingly, van der Wurff concludes that this may be an irreducible property. Some scholars have attempted a formal analysis, however. For Jensen (2004a), it is a particular property of imperative tense, which can introduce a second person argument. For Zanuttini (2008), imperatives have a unique phrase, the Jussive Phrase, which has a second person specification and ordinarily forces agreement for second person with the imperative subject. For Portner (2004), the imperative subject in English may be an addressee logophoric pronoun in a root context. Among the issues discussed, the prevalent research line remains the study of negative imperatives, which will be discussed below.

In the absence of a consensus on the yet to be defined meaning of the imperative, legitimately valid but disparate accounts are available (see van der Wurff 2007b). Some share similar assumptions to do with the deficiency, defectiveness or uniqueness of the imperative type. The imperative clause may lack certain syntactic projections, or these may not be licensed by imperative verbs that are morphologically defective (Zanuttini 1996, 1997; Platzack and Rosengren 1998; Portner and Zanuttini 2003, among others). By way of example, Zanuttini (1996) proposes that negation must select tense and that imperatives are tenseless (but see Zeijlstra 2006; Alcázar and Saltarelli 2007b). Other researchers have proposed or assumed that imperatives should conform to structural uniformity (e.g., Potsdam 2007). While this may be a desirable result, the more challenging characteristics of imperatives are generally unaccounted for or unaddressed in these studies.

Various characteristics of imperatives point to strict observance of grammatical principles in syntax and morphology, and thus press for the need to give full consideration to their syntactic analysis. While imperatives do not ordinarily serve as a dependent clause, they participate in coordination ("hold the bat tight and hit the ball hard!"; paratactic cases also exist, but it is doubtful that these are imperatives).[5] Furthermore, the subject of imperatives may be restricted to the addressee, but from this position the reference of lower subjects can be obligatorily controlled (ADDRESSEE promise PRO$_{*1/2/*3}$ to visit Grandpa!). In the few apparently genuine cases where imperatives embed, the embedded subject must still be interpreted as the addressee of the utterance context (vs. the reported context, which could be different: Kaufmann 2012 on Germanic). This restriction is reminiscent of the behavior of indexicals, which are interpreted relative to the utterance context even in reported speech. Thus, in this particular way, the subject of imperatives behaves as is normally expected of indexicals (but see Schlenker 1999, 2003, 2004).

Regarding verbal morphology and finiteness, imperatives may be bare, uninflected forms, but they may also be complex. Basque is a good example. Basque imperatives can be verb stems with or without the infinitival mark (*etor(ri)!* [come-INF] 'come!'), similarly to Romance verb stems with or without the thematic vowel. But Basque imperatives can also be complex forms that require agreement for number and person with the subject, object and dative (*eman iezaizkiozu!* [give.INF AUX.2SG(S).3PL(DO).3SG(IO).IMP] 'give them to him/her!'), as root D&I forms do elsewhere in the language (*ema-ten diz-kiozu* [give-IMPF AUX.2SG(S).3PL(DO).3SG(IO).IND.PRES] 'you give them to him/her'). This indicates that the imperative clause may be finite, even if a strong preference across languages, including Basque, is to use bare or minimally inflected forms.

The characteristics discussed above invite a partially revisionist context-sensitive syntax of imperatives along the functional lines of the CP(vP) phase-theoretic derivational framework. This research program has already been staked out in generative syntax with the functional projection CP (Chomsky 1986) and the course extended into the left periphery (Rizzi 1997; Cinque 1999). In the next three paragraphs, we briefly define the phenomena of indexical shift, logophoricity and conjunct-disjunct person-marking systems, which suggest that properties of indexicality, specifically, speaker and addressee, have a legitimate role in syntax.

Consider the phenomenon of indexical shift (Schlenker 1999, 2003). In languages like Amharic (Semitic, Afro-Asiatic), first and second person pronouns are ambiguous in certain dependent clauses, where they can refer to the speaker and addressee (as in English), or to the speaker and addressee of the reported context. By way of approximation, in an utterance like "John said that I bought a car," "I" could be interpreted as "John," the speaker of the reported context. Indexical shift is not generally possible across dependent clauses; instead, it seems to be restricted to propositional attitude verbs – speech predicates, psychological predicates and verbs of direct perception, or only possible with the verb *say*: Zazaki (Anand and Nevins 2004). Hence, the reference of the indexical pronouns may be syntactic in the limited domain of propositional attitude verbs. Other languages with indexical shift include Navajo (Athabascan, Speas 1999), Catalan sign language (Quer 2005), and Indo-Aryan and Dravidian languages (Sigurðsson 2004: 21, fn. 40).

Logophoric pronouns in certain African languages (e.g., Mundang, Tuburi; Niger-Congo) are generally restricted to indirect discourse. Similarly to indexical shift, logophoric pronouns appear in the complement clause of propositional attitude verbs. They obey a pragmatic constraint as well: their antecedent must be the person whose speech, feelings or perspective is reported (Hagège 1974; Clements 1975). Logophoric pronouns most frequently refer to the subject of the main clause (Sells 1987; Culy 1994, 1997), the *speaker* of the reported context. But there are addressee logophoric pronouns as well (e.g., Banda Linda (Niger-Congo), Donno So (Niger-Congo), Ewe (Niger-Congo); see Culy 1997: 849–50 and references therein).

Conjunct-disjunct person-marking systems refer to verbal inflections whose interpretation is contingent on the epistemic authority of the speech act (Hargreaves 1990, 1991, 2005). In a declarative, the speaker is the epistemic authority because he or she takes responsibility for the information; while in an interrogative the epistemic authority is the addressee. A morpheme denoting first person in a declarative (the conjunct) is interpreted as second or third person in an interrogative. The morpheme denoting second person and third person in a declarative (the disjunct) is interpreted as second person in an interrogative. If the interrogative is rhetorical, however, the conjunct is interpreted as first person only, as in the declarative. Additionally, conjunct-disjunct morphology is used logophorically under propositional attitude verbs. Languages with conjunct-disjunct systems include Newari (Sino-Tibetan, Hale 1980), Northern Akhvakh (Nakh-Daghestanian/"languages," Creissels 2008) and Awa Pit (Barbacoan, Curnow 2002b).

The list of context-sensitive indexical phenomena is extensive (see Speas and Tenny 2003; Chapter 3). We contend that the imperative clause is a good fit as a context-sensitive phenomenon for descriptive as well as explanatory adequacy in syntactic analysis. In this volume, the cross-linguistic centrality of encoding the role of speaker and addressee is underscored by the interaction of imperatives with allocutive agreement in Basque (i.e., non-argumental second person agreement, Oyharçabal 1993; Chapter 5).

When the diversity of these phenomena is taken into consideration, pressure mounts for syntactic theory to provide a principled account of clause structure that is accessible to the context of utterance. The syntax of the imperative clause, we argue, is more precisely understood under this derivation scenario (Chapter 4).

As noted, the analysis of negative imperatives (e.g., Spanish *¡no com-a-s!* [NEG eat-SUB-2SG] 'don't eat!' vs. **¡no com-e!* [NEG eat-THV]) is the only exception to the absence of consolidated research lines. This is sometimes referred to as the ban on true negative imperatives. Two basic premises can be identified. The first is that a morphologically dedicated imperative verb form (or *true* imperative, like Sp. *come*) requires syntactic licensing of some kind. The second is that negation may prevent the verb movement necessary for this licensing to take effect. Starting with the contributions of Zanuttini (1994, 1997), Rivero (1994), Rivero and Terzi (1995), permutations on the theoretical execution of these assumptions and further probing into additional empirical data have led to a consolidated research line (see Chapter 2 for extensive discussion).

This consolidated line, however, needs to be reassessed in light of new data. Typological evidence has emerged (van der Auwera 2005, 2006, 2010; van der Auwera and Lejeune 2005b) that undermines the basic premises of the analysis. Under the above-mentioned assumptions, it is not expected that non-dedicated forms may also have to resort to surrogate forms, effectively creating a parallel ban on *false* negative imperatives. In addition, non-dedicated forms may also have a special negation, in the form of prohibitive constructions. Yet prohibitives may also retain the original affirmative dedicated imperative form.

The syntactic approach to the true negative imperative ban was developed prior to this data becoming available. Pending forthcoming revisions, the aforementioned premises may no longer be tenable. This state of affairs opens new avenues to consider for an analysis of the apparent incompatibility with negation. The current consensus has not considered that a path that splits affirmative and negative paradigms in imperatives is not (always) solely syntactic. Other explanations are possible.[6] Prohibitives are a major source of split paradigms. The bulk of these are verbs that make it unnecessary to negate the imperative (e.g., "see to it that this does not happen again!" vs. "don't do it again!") or lexically include it (Latin *noli* 'be unwilling to'). In Basque, certain processes of phonological reduction apply in the affirmative but not in the negative. Over time, the same imperative form becomes morphologically distinct in the affirmative paradigm in the spoken language. A problem for a syntactic analysis of split paradigms is that the true negative imperative ban respects the implicational hierarchy for person and number alluded to earlier. That is to say, we know of no case in Romance where imperatives do not surrogate under negation but hortatives do. If split paradigms signal a genuine failure of licensing conditions, they need not observe this hierarchy.

In conclusion, the typological surveys question the adequacy of focusing on imperatives to the detriment of hortatives. Hortatives appear to behave as a group with imperatives. They share most of their characteristics, but crucially differ in at least the person restriction and mediation. The pragmatic restrictions of the imperative clause have not been investigated in the broader context of the relationship of indexicality to structure. Also as a consequence of growing typological evidence, a long research thread invites a reconsideration of the main tenets of the hypothesis.

1.2   Proposal

In 1.2.1 we introduce a proposal to represent the context of utterance in the syntax of imperative clauses, which is developed, formalized and justified in Chapter 4. In preparation, Chapter 3 frames the analysis within the minimalist program and earlier proposals regarding the encoding of indexicality in syntax. A representative sample and discussion of context-sensitive phenomena is also presented in this chapter.

1.2.1   *The "light" performative hypothesis (LPH)*
The "light" performative hypothesis (LPH) proposes that, in contrast with D&I, the imperative clause is uniquely characterized by the presence of a functional "light" v. This auxiliary-like verb defines the imperative type as a "prescription" (with Birjulin and Xrakovskij 2001). In imperatives, the speaker prescribes that the addressee carry out a (virtual) action or activity (e.g., "go!"). In hortatives, the speaker prescribes that the addressee cause (or 'see to it that') somebody to carry out the prescription ("(you) let them go!"). We argue that hortatives are causative or proxy imperatives prescribed through the mediation of a light causative c, the various choices in imperative–hortative meaning determined by the *strength* of the prescription (à la Aikhenvald 2010).[7]

The C-selected light v projects a variable (subject theta role in specifier of vP). This variable is interpreted by the speaker as an A-bar binding operator in CP. In a parallel context-sensitive derivation "the Addressee is identified with the grammatical subject of the imperative clause." This is the proposed representation of indexicality in a CP(vP) phase-theoretic syntax.

LPH assumes that speaker and addressee are encoded in root clauses in imperatives. A generalization to other clause types is suggested as an empirical (and conceptual) necessity on consideration of the interaction of imperatives, interrogatives and allocutivity in Basque (Chapter 5).

LPH integrates hortatives within an account of the imperative type and provides a resolution to seemingly contradictory properties. The restrictions and distribution of the morphosyntactic category person follow as a consequence of LPH. In hortatives, the introduction of the causative light verb makes the causative subject absorb the thematic constraint that the subject be the addressee (4.1.3), rendering the subject of the lexical verb free from a second person restriction. Hortatives make the case that the so-called pragmatic restriction of second person subjects is syntactically localized. They appear to conform to a different paradigm in cases where the causative verb is independently realized.

As the name of our hypothesis suggests, LPH is, in some respects, a minimalist return to the PH of Transformational Grammar (Ross 1970, among others). In contrast to the "little v" hypothesis of LPH, PH assumed a "lexical V," where main clause types were complements to superordinate (lexical) performative verbs (*state*, *ask*, *order*) rather than root clauses (4.1.1). For other proposals on the encoding of the context of utterance in syntax, see Chapter 3 and Speas and Tenny (2003).

1.3   Preview of following chapters

Chapter 2 presents a revised empirical base for the study of imperatives. In his leading introduction to *Imperative Clauses in Generative Grammar*, van der Wurff (2007b) includes a wealth of cross-linguistic data and discussion. However, reference to typological literature is limited. Regarding current assumptions about imperative syntax, morphology and semantics, recent typological surveys confirm some of the early generalizations introduced by pioneer surveys such as those of Sadock and Zwicky (1985). Yet they also invite reconsideration of assumptions about the defectiveness of the imperative clause or imperative verb forms, and the presumed absence of morphosyntactic categories. New typological data also challenges the separation of hortatives from imperatives. A dedicated section reviews earlier syntactic analyses of split affirmative and negative paradigms in the light of new patterns and explores an alternative morphological account.

Chapter 3 discusses the minimalist program for linguistic theory (Chomsky 1995–2008), and the research approach known as the Strong Minimalist Thesis (or SMT). A strong research thesis invites the study of imperatives to an extension of the functional phase (CP) in interphase with the content phase (vP). In the spirit of SMT, indexicality (specifically person one (Speaker) and person two (Addressee)) is encoded in the functional phase or, more vaguely, in the left periphery of the syntactic component. Part of the chapter is dedicated to reviewing and assessing earlier proposals for the representation of context. Phenomena like indexical shift, logophoricity and conjunct-disjunct systems are evaluated.

Chapter 4 develops, formalizes and empirically justifies the "light" performative hypothesis of imperative clauses. Section 4.1 defines core assumptions: the role of functional v, matrix clausality, future-oriented temporality, irreflexivity of the Speaker>Addressee relation, and person values. Section 4.2 construes the functional meaning of the imperative clause on an LPH-based theory of imperative expressions. Section 4.3 defines the role of functional v in deriving the canonical hortative system, as well as the logical validity of the negative (prohibition) type. The section closes with an operator-variable binding theory for encoding indexical properties. Section 4.4 justifies LPH assumptions in the grammaticalization of the range of imperative clauses. Sections 4.5–6 argue for the little v hypothesis on the basis of imperative phenomena in Romance, Mandarin Chinese and Maasai, Badiotto, as well as other realizations of imperative expressions. A summary of the chapter is found in 4.7.

Chapter 5 focuses on Basque allocutive agreement. This unique morphological phenomenon references the addressee when he or she does not participate in the predicate-argument structure of the verb (*tren-a ailega-tu dek* [train-ABS arrive-PERF AUX.3SG(S).2SG.MASC(Addressee)] 'The train has arrived (male addressee)'). D&I require this form of agreement in non-honorific/familiar address. Because allocutive agreement represents a second person non-argument, this phenomenon constitutes important evidence for context to be present in D&I. This phenomenon has not been previously discussed with reference to imperatives or the representation of context in syntax (but see Ross 1970). As in other indexical phenomena, such as logophoricity or indexical shift, allocutive agreement is structure sensitive: it is not allowed in dependent clauses. A second restriction concerns second person arguments. In D&I, allocutive morphology is prevented when the addressee is an argument to the verb (i.e., there is no redundant second person mark). This phenomenon does not manifest in imperatives and hortatives. If the addressee is a syntactic argument to the verb in imperatives and hortatives, as LPH predicts, this restriction follows from the presence of a second person argument, as in D&I. At the same time, allocutive agreement suggests that declaratives and interrogatives are non-performative.

The Conclusion puts forward the conclusions of our study and offers directions for further research.

2 *Imperatives across languages*

2.0   Chapter overview

Until recent years, cross-linguistic examination of imperative clauses was limited to relatively modest data samples (Sadock and Zwicky 1985: 23 languages
(extended sample: 32), Zhang 1990: 46 languages).[1] Later typological surveys have tapped into larger pools of data. In a survey of 495 languages, van
der Auwera and Lejeune (2005a) investigate whether imperatives have dedicated forms (morphologically distinct from D&I). In a similar sample, van der
Auwera and Lejeune (2005b) and van der Auwera (2010) study the negation of
imperative clauses. On their part, van der Auwera et al. (2004) examine markedness relations in imperative-hortative paradigms in 376 languages.[2] Beyond
particular research questions, two volumes have broadly surveyed imperatives
and hortatives: the St. Petersburg survey (Xrakovskij 2001), an edited collection, and Aikhenvald (2010), arguably the most comprehensive typological
work to date.

Taken together, these volumes and articles provide new reference points for a
more exhaustive study of imperative syntax, morphology and semantics. Some
of the earlier observations have been confirmed. For instance, that imperative
subjects are optional. But a reassessment of some currently held assumptions
is necessary. According to Xrakovskij (2001), imperatives are the most morphologically complex form in some languages. Aikhenvald (2010) finds that
imperatives seem to have as many grammatical categories as D&I. Recall that
imperatives have been assumed to be defective (1.1.1) on account of imperative
verbs being bare roots or minimally inflected. Other important revisions in this
chapter include the study of hortatives, the ban on true negative imperatives,
and whether imperatives can lead to indirect speech act interpretations. These
questions were not raised in van der Wurff's (2007b) extensive review article,
which does not reference the aforementioned surveys (some were published at
a later date). Accordingly, this chapter serves to fill an empirical lacuna in the
generative literature.[3]

The current chapter is structured into six sections. Part I (2.1) groups generalizations drawn from preliminary samples that have been confirmed. Part II (2.2) discusses generalizations that have been brought into question. Part III (2.3) is concerned with differences in the interpretation of the typological evidence, namely whether imperatives can be embedded and whether hortatives are a type of imperative clause. Part IV (2.4) elaborates on similarities and differences between imperatives and hortatives. Part V (2.5) focuses on the semantics of imperatives and hortatives, and addresses whether context can override imperative meaning. Part VI (2.6) is dedicated to the negation of imperatives. It features a review of the generative literature on this topic and proposes an alternative morphological account. This chapter ends with a brief conclusion (2.7).

2.1   Part I: Confirmed generalizations

The current section groups four generalizations that have been confirmed in later surveys: imperative clauses are universal (2.1.1); imperative predicates are limited to controllable processes (2.1.2); imperative subjects are restricted to second person (2.1.3); and imperative subjects are optional (2.1.4).

2.1.1   *The universality of the imperative clause*
In their seminal paper on speech act distinctions in syntax, Sadock and Zwicky (1985) find the imperative clause to be one of three universal sentence types, together with D&I. Later surveys have confirmed this generalization, noting a few exceptions. In this section we examine some of the alleged counterexamples and find that some of these languages do in fact have an imperative clause.

In an extension of Sadock and Zwicky's original survey, König and Siemund (2007) report that some languages do not have an imperative clause distinguishable from a declarative: "For a few languages in our sample it has not been possible to identify a construction uniquely dedicated to the expression of directive force" (p. 311). The languages in question are Rapanui (Eastern Polynesian), Persian (Indo-Iranian), Hungarian (Uralic), Lango (Nilo-Saharan) and Maori (Austronesian). For König and Siemund, in the absence of an imperative type, some languages resort to indirection and employ the declarative type to render directive meaning. This discrepancy begs the question of whether the imperative clause is indeed universal.[4]

Some of the languages cited by König and Siemund turn out to have an imperative clause. Under closer scrutiny, syntactic, morphological and/or phonological evidence emerges. Maori, for instance, shows positive tests in clause union. If a certain adverbial clause ("to see whether...") is attached to a root declarative, the declarative is marked with the particle *ai*, but not so if the root clause is interpreted as an imperative (Bauer 1993: 73; ex. 307). If two imperative clauses or two declaratives are coordinated, the particle *ai* is also used. When one of the conjuncts is interpreted as a negated imperative clause, however, the particle cannot be used (Bauer 1993: 122; exs. 531–32). If, to express imperative meaning, Maori were using indirection only, the above facts regarding clause linking could not be explained. The claim that some languages lack an imperative clause thus requires more extensive vetting.

Xrakovskij (2001) features a section on "Languages without imperative paradigms," which comprises Vietnamese (Austro-Asiatic), Cambodian (Austro-Asiatic) and Bamana (Mande). Birjulin and Xrakovskij (2001: 10) presume that a distinctive intonation pattern is one of at least three universal characteristics of imperative clauses, but do not treat this aspect in the volume because of methodological challenges. Closer examination can reveal the presence of an imperative clause in these languages independent of intonation. According to Bystrov and Stankevič, in Vietnamese, the ambiguity between a declarative and an imperative sentence is only broken by the second person plural marker *các* used with kinship vocatives (a complex honorific system), which forces an imperative-only interpretation (2001: 463; ex. 5). Hence, on closer inspection, languages claimed not to have an imperative clause may in fact feature one, like Vietnamese.

Although the claim that some languages do not possess an imperative clause is sometimes premature, this is not tantamount to saying that all languages must have an imperative clause (*pace* Xrakovskij; König and Siemund). It seems plausible for languages to resort to indirection in lieu of an imperative. D&I can be interpreted as directive speech acts, as in "it's cold in here" (potentially implied meaning: "please, turn on the heating!") or "is it cold in here?" (potentially implied meaning: "please, turn on the heating!"; see Levinson 1983: Ch. 5; Newmeyer 1986: Chs. 4–5). More generally, context renders speech act distinctions in syntax superfluous, as basic sentence types need not be interpreted literally (cf. Sadock and Zwicky 1985; but see 2.5). That said, most surveyed languages have been found to possess an imperative type. Further examination of languages that seemingly lack such a type is necessary. At the same time, there is morphological evidence and evidence from first language acquisition that suggests that the imperative clause is universal.

König and Siemund (2007) and Xrakovskij (2001) touch on an important generalization. Imperative clauses are less marked than D&I. But this lack of markedness may follow from the morphological properties of the language. Van der Auwera and Lejeune (2005b) and van der Auwera (2010) find that having dedicated imperative verb forms is the norm (>75%). And this number does not include other means of identifying imperative sentences (e.g., Maori, Vietnamese; optionality of the subject in languages where subjects are obligatory, prosody, etc.). Importantly, many of the languages that depart from the norm are analytic. Hence, the general characteristics of the morphology of a language may be responsible for the apparent lack of an imperative type. From a theoretical perspective, the LPH assumes that the subject of the prescribed expression, the Addressee, cannot be first or third person, which further reduces the need for morphological contrast (see also Aikhenvald 2010 on loss of morphological distinctions in hortatives relative to imperatives).

An additional argument to entertain regarding the universality of imperatives concerns the possibility that imperative forms participate in the first stage of propositional language. According to Salustri and Hyams (2003), root infinitives (RI) play a central role in the acquisition of propositional language in Germanic (German, Dutch): "RIs are non-finite, non-agreeing forms that occur in root contexts ... First, RIs typically have a modal (or irrealis) interpretation expressing desires, intentions and needs." Secondly, RIs require the verb to be eventive (Salustri and Hyams 2006: 160–61). By contrast, Romance languages like Italian lack the RI stage (Guasti 1993). Salustri and Hyams (2006) propose that it is possible to find an analogue of the RI in the imperative clause for Italian, Spanish and Catalan, among other languages. "Prima facie, the imperative is a good candidate because it shares the essential RI properties: Imperatives have modal meaning, that is, they express obligation or volition with respect to some eventuality; they are restricted to eventive predicates; and they are tenseless (and arguably non-agreeing)" (p. 161). If Salustri and Hyams' imperative analogue hypothesis (IAH) were on the right track, the imperative clause could play a role in early propositional language.

While the IAH requires further research, some typological observations are a priori compatible with an early presence of imperatives in child language. Beyond the languages of Western Europe, Aikhenvald reports that children acquire imperative forms, the imperative clause or indirect strategies expressing imperative semantics very early (2010: 325–30). For Aikhenvald this follows from the type of interaction between caregivers and children, which is chiefly based on imperative expressions, as well as the simplicity of imperative verb forms (particularly second person singular). These facts are also amenable to a biolinguistic explanation where language acquisition proceeds stepwise and imperatives constitute an initial step towards propositional language.

Finally, concerning imperative marking, Aikhenvald notes parallelisms between spoken and signed languages, which also mark the imperative clause (p. 37). Another important observation is that spoken languages make use of paralinguistic resources, such as pointing and hand signaling, in imperative clauses (p. 321).

In sum, the majority of the world's languages feature dedicated imperative clauses. A minority apparently lacks them, but some of these counterexamples are not valid. Other seemingly genuine cases may be reduced to a lack of markedness, which would follow from the morphological properties of the language. A decisive example of a language without an imperative clause would require more extensive vetting, and must include a study of intonation across clauses.

2.1.2   *Predicates excluded from the imperative clause*

Birjulin and Xrakovskij (2001: 17) confirm earlier observations by Sadock and Zwicky (1985, inter alia) that imperative clauses have a restriction in the type of predicate they select: "they must denote controllable actions, i.e. actions which, in a given situation, can be performed (or not performed) in a controlled manner by any given person based on his/her own or somebody else's experience." This generally prevents stative predicates, non-volitive predicates and inanimate addressees from participating in imperative clauses (1–2).

(1)   a. look at me!
       b. *see me!

In (1a) the addressee is in control of the action and thus may comply with the directive expressed. In (1b) the verb *see* is a non-controllable action (in its literal meaning, see below) and it is infelicitous as a directive.

Birjulin and Xrakovskij stress that "there is no impenetrable wall between controllable and uncontrollable actions" (p. 17). Uncontrollable states may be the result of a series of controllable actions, as in falling ill, or getting thinner. Uncontrollable actions can be partially or temporarily controlled, for example, when breathing upon a doctor's request.

Aikhenvald observes the same exclusions and makes further observations about whether passives are acceptable as imperative forms (2010: 148–49). The passive is a valence-changing derivation that demotes the controller. But if the addressee can be understood to be in control of the action, passives are acceptable as directives in some languages. English is such a language (2: p. 149, exs. 4.63, 4.62).[5]

(2)   a. Be checked over by a doctor, then you'll be sure there's nothing wrong.
        b. *Be helped by Jill

Aikhenvald further notices that languages vary in the degree to which they allow non-controllable actions. If a suitable context can make the addressee appear to be in partial or temporary control, then non-controllable actions may be coerced into imperatives. For instance, the coercion of a control reading in uncontrollable predicates, such as perception verbs: "Hear!" (= "Listen!"; p. 152), or Spanish *¡Óye-me!* [hear-me] 'Listen to me!'. By contrast, in Tariana (Arawakan) stative verbs like *be cold, be sick* and *be afraid* cannot form imperatives. In Tukang Besi (Austronesian) *sleep* cannot form an imperative by itself (p. 151, but see our n. 8 in this chapter).[6]

This restriction against uncontrollable actions is one in a series of seemingly irreducible characteristics of the imperative clause. To our knowledge, no attempt has been made to derive this property syntactically, although semantic explanations have been proposed.[7] Some typological data suggests that this restriction can be overcome by means of an auxiliary verb. Comparable restrictions have been analyzed as syntactic constraints as well.[8]

All in all, imperative predicates must denote controllable actions. Languages vary in the degree to which predicates denoting non-controllable actions can be coerced. The LPH attributes this restriction to the imperative being a prescription due to the meaning of the performative (see Chapter 4). The animacy effect arguably follows from the restriction to second person. The LPH proposes that the second person restriction follows from the performative, which thematically identifies the grammatical subject of the imperative as the addressee.

2.1.3   *The subject of the imperative clause vs. vocatives*

This section shows that it is not possible to attribute the second person restriction to imperatives lacking a subject with the vocative being interpreted as the imperative subject. Imperatives have a subject position distinct from vocatives. An examination of vocatives across languages provides empirical support for the representation of the addressee in syntax. Additionally, vocatives can make reference to the speaker only or to both the speaker and the addressee. This is an important empirical argument in support of representing indexicality in the syntax.

As noted, the imperative in (3)[9] must be construed with reference to a second person subject, singular or plural.[10] It is not possible to interpret (3) with an underlying first or third person subject.[11]

(3)   Finish it!   Where the subject must be second person.

The second person restriction raises the question of whether imperatives have vocatives as subjects. Vocatives are nominal expressions that refer to the addressee of the utterance, directly ("John," "boy") or indirectly ("oh my"; cf. Hill 2007: 2079). Some languages have a special case for this type of expression (e.g., Latin) or special pronominal forms. Consider the following Basque examples, which can be glossed as 'hey': *ai-zu* hey-2SG.honorific, *aiza-k* hey-2SG.MASC. non-honorific, *aiza-n* hey-2SG.FEM.non-honorific. If imperatives lacked a syntactic subject, their second person restriction could follow from construal with a vocative. In fact, vocatives are not exclusive to imperative clauses.

Regarding this particular point, the generative literature argues that the imperative subject is to be distinguished from the vocative. A position has been identified that relates to the left periphery of the imperative clause (or right periphery, if the language is head final) that this noun phrase can occupy. Unlike vocatives, the noun phrase occupying this position cannot be detached from the clause (4a vs. 4b), bear vocative case (in the relevant languages) or occur clause finally (4c vs. 4d, exs. cf. Iatridou 2008: 5, exs. 15–16, 19–20).[12]

(4)   a. *Nobody, Romney withdrew from the race.
       b. Nobody move!
       c. *Move, nobody!
       d. John is sick, Fred.

Regarding whether the vocative is to be syntactically represented, Hill (2007, 2010) proposes to view certain vocatives with a narrow syntactic distribution in Romanian, Bulgarian and Umbundu (Bantu) as evidence for a syntax–pragmatics interface (building on Speas and Tenny 2003). Postulating such an interface presupposes that the speaker is also represented in the syntax. If that were the case, it would be conceivable that the world's languages had some form of first person vocative. Vocatives are often employed as a means of honorification ("sir/madam" vs. "you"). This task could be accomplished by honorification of the speaker as well, should something like a speaker-vocative exist.

As it turns out, the world's languages can include the speaker of the utterance as part of the vocative expression. This is the case in Amahuaca (Panoan, 4'a) and Lakhota (Siouian, 4'b, cf. Aikhenvald 2010: 123–24; in-text examples and table 4.2). Note that, in Lakhota, these vocatives additionally express meaning related to the imperative clause (command/permission; permission).

(4')   a. *-pu* 'male vocative' [for a male addressing another male]
       a'. *-u/-uu/-yu/-vu* 'female vocative' [for all other instances – i.e., a man addressing a woman, or a woman addressing a man or another woman']
       b. Woman speaking (command: *na*; permission: *ye'*, *we'* for singular addressee and *pe'* for plural addressee)

b'. Man speaking (command/permission: singular addressee *yo'*, *wo'* and *po'* for plural addressee)

Regarding *non-argumental addressee vocatives*, Antonov (2012: 3), additionally notes Malayo-Polynesian languages (Javanese, Sundanese, Madurese, Balinese, and Japanese, to a lesser degree; see references therein).

It is also possible, for the purposes of honorification, to choose to represent not the addressee, but rather the speaker of the utterance only. This is what happens with certain non-argumental speaker particles in Thai. Example (4″) is from Ross (1970: 260, ex. 19).[13]

(4″) a. *khaw   maa   khráp*
          he   come   1SG.MALE
          'He is coming.' (man speaking)
    b. *khaw   maa   kâ*
          he   come   1SG.FEMALE
          'He is coming.' (woman speaking)

Antonov mentions Thai and Burmese: "the gender of the speaker may optionally be encoded by (sentence-final) particles whose primary function is to convey 'politeness'" (see references in Antonov 2012: 3).

These lesser-known phenomena call for a new, preliminary nomenclature. Let us informally refer to them as speaker vocatives (Thai), speaker-addressee vocatives (Amahuaca, Lakhota), and addressee vocatives (English, Basque). It is possible to provide a rationale for these unfamiliar vocative expressions if the speaker and the addressee are represented in syntactic structure. Accordingly, vocative expressions provide additional empirical footing for a syntax–pragmatics interface (Chapter 3).

In sum, imperatives in world languages have a second person subject that is a different syntactic element from the vocative. Vocatives ordinarily refer to the addressee. In some languages vocatives refer to both the addressee and the speaker or only refer to the speaker (Aikhenvald 2010; Ross 1970).[14] The LPH proposes that the subject of imperatives is restricted to second person due to thematic identification from a higher predicate.

2.1.4   *Optionality of the imperative subject*

The subject of an imperative seems to be optional, even in languages that ordinarily need to express it, English being such a case (compare 5a, a declarative, with 5b, an imperative clause).

(5) a. *(You) will finish it by two.
    b. (You) finish it by two!

In (5a) omission of the subject renders the sentence ungrammatical.[15]

Birjulin and Xrakovskij (2001: 11) deem the optionality of the subject a frequent, yet not universal, feature. But there is no specific reference to which languages require an overt subject. Zhang (1990) initially reported that subjects must be overt in Luo and Hawaiian imperative clauses, but Potsdam (1998) later rebutted this claim. Aikhenvald (2010: 93) writes: "In the vast majority of the world's languages the subject of canonical imperatives – especially [the] ones with a singular addressee – does not have to be overtly expressed."

Realization of the imperative subject usually responds to pragmatic factors: (contrastive) focus, emphasis or politeness, among others (Potsdam 1998; Aikhenvald 2010; Hill 2010). This is similar to the realization of optional subject pronouns in languages with rich agreement systems, such as Spanish subjects (Silva-Corvalán 1982; Orozco and Guy 2008). The pragmatic effects between overt vs. non-overt subjects thus seem not to be imperative-specific.

The question of what empty category can represent the elided subject of imperatives – pro (finite) or PRO (non-finite), on standard assumptions – was unresolved in Government and Binding (see Beukema and Coopmans 1989 for the available options and argumentation) as was the specific mechanism by which the elided subject could be licensed in the absence of a syntactic antecedent. The challenge of implementing a pro subject lies in weak or nonexistent inflectional paradigms (NB: under the previously assumed empirical base). In turn, PRO would require a syntactic antecedent, which seems not to be available in the imperative clause. Most analyses have chosen pro over PRO (cf. Iatridou 2008: 8).

The following Spanish sentences illustrate syntactic environments for pro and PRO (6). Spanish is a language where subject pronouns are normally elided in finite contexts; they are recoverable from the inflection in the verb (6a: main clause, 6c: dependent clause). Infinitival complements in Spanish exemplify a syntactic environment for PRO (6b). The sub-indices indicate the referential dependencies between the elided pronouns and their antecedents. Depending on the characterization of imperatives as a finite or non-finite clause, the underlying pronoun could be pro or PRO (6d).

(6)   a. pro$_i$ *Llev-o$_i$*   *dos botellas de agua por si acaso.*
          carry-1SG.IND   two bottles of water for if perhaps
          'I am carrying two bottles of water just in case.'
       b. *Juan$_i$ quier-e*   [PRO$_{i/*k}$ *ir*   *a la India].*
          Juan want-3SG.IND   go.INF   to the India
          'Juan wants to go to India.'

c. *Juan$_i$ quier-e*   *[que* pro$_{*i/k}$ *vay-a*   *a la India].*
   Juan want-3SG.IND   that   go-3SG.SUBJ to the India
   'Juan wants him to go to India.'
d. *¡*pro$_{2SG}$/PRO$_{2SG}$ *Acáb-a-lo!*
                 finish-THV-3SG.ACC.MASC
   'Finish it!'

In Minimalism, it is open to debate whether control is to be viewed as a result of displacement (Hornstein 2001; Boeckx and Hornstein 2004, 2006a, 2006b, 2007) or as an agreement operation (Landau 2000, 2004, 2008; Reuland 2001, 2005), among other alternatives, but, to our knowledge, this question has not been raised regarding imperatives.

All in all, the imperative clause has an optional subject irrespective of whether the language in question is pro-drop. Whether the silent pronominal is pro or PRO is unresolved. It is possible that indexical elements, such as the speaker and the addressee, may be governed by different licensing/visibility conditions. Future studies on the syntax–pragmatics interface may in time help resolve this question.

2.2   Part II: Generalizations in need of review

This section discusses generalizations that have been brought into question. Imperative verbs can be morphologically complex (2.2.1). In some languages, the imperative is the most complex form. Imperative clauses can feature a similar range of grammatical categories to D&I (2.2.2–3). This leads to reconsideration of whether imperatives are non-finite and/or defective clauses.

2.2.1   *Imperative verb forms and morphological complexity*
As noted in the earlier samples, imperative verbs tend to be bare, minimally inflected forms. A plain verb stem is a typical manifestation, sometimes followed by an additional morpheme, such as a thematic vowel/consonant, infinitival marker or aspect morpheme. Here is a representative set of examples: Basque (7a: isolate, may drop infinitival mark), Dutch (7b: verb stem only), Italian, Lingala (Bantu), Norwegian (7c: verb stem only: drops infinitival schwa, among other strategies; see Rice 2003), Spanish (7d: verb stem + thematic vowel, or verb stem only), Tinrin (Austronesian), Zulu (Bantu) (7e: verb stem and final vowel *–a*).

(7)   a. *Etor(ri)!*
          come-INF
          'Come!'

    b. *Slaap!*
    sleep
    'Sleep!' (Zeijlstra 2006: 405–6, ex. 1b)
    c. *Gå   no!*
    go-IMP   now
    'Go now!' (Faarlund 1985: 150, ex. 3b)
    d. *¡Sal!*
    come.out.VROOT
    'Come out!'
    e. *Sebenza*
    work.IMP.2SG
    'Work!' (van der Auwera 2010: 6, ex. 11a)

We have seen a Basque example as a bare or minimally marked form (7a). If construed with an auxiliary, Basque imperatives indicate agreement for case, person and number for up to three verbal arguments (8a), as in indicative (8b) and subjunctive (8c) clauses (Zubiri and Zubiri 2000).[16]

(8)   a. *Eman   iezaiozu*
        give.INF   AUX.2SG(E).3SG(A).3SG(D).IMP
        'Give it to him/her!'
    b. *Eman   zenion*
        give.INF   AUX.2SG(E).3SG(A).3SG(D).IND.PST
        'You gave it to him/her.'
    c. *Opari-tu   dizut Jon-i   eman   diezaiozun*
        gift-INF   AUX   Jon-DAT   give.INF AUX.2SG(E).3SG(A).3SG(D).SUBJ
        'I gave it to you so that you give it to Jon.'

The complexity of imperative paradigms in Basque sharply contrasts with the equally valid alternative in the language of rendering imperative verb forms as bare stems. This indicates that there is far more complexity to imperative morphology than a barren paradigm would lead us to assume. It is by no means unusual for imperative paradigms to realize all number and person combinations (9: Kobon, Karam cf. Aikhenvald 2010: 49–50, table 2.10).

(9)   a. 1sg: *-in/in*   1dual: *-ul*   1pl: *-un*
        b. 2sg: *-Ø*   2dual: *-il*   2pl: *-im*
        c. 3sg: *-aŋ*   3dual: *-il*   3pl: *-laŋ*

Imperatives can be the most complex form in the language (Birjulin and Xrakovskij 2001). For instance, in Nivkh (Paleosiberian) imperative forms are marked obligatorily for person and number, in spite of person and number marking being optional elsewhere (10a: Gruzdeva 2001: 64, ex. 17) – "indicative finite verb forms do not agree with any of their arguments in person, but plural subjects are optionally coded" (p. 60), "the imperative paradigm in Nivkh distinguishes subjects by person and number [for all persons and number combinations, including dual]" (p. 64). In Klamath, person and number are marked exclusively in the imperative (Plateau Penutian, Stegnij 2001; 10b cf. p. 81, ex. 15) – "In contrast to the indicative mood, Klamath imperatives have a person and number paradigm, otherwise found only in personal pronouns" (p. 81). Mongolian is yet another example (Mongolic, Kuzmenkov 2001; 10c cf. p. 99, ex. 2) – "Mongolian verbs have no personal endings, but imperative verb forms appearing in various combinations do correlate with the person, and partially, number of the subject" (p. 98).

(10) a. *Nav-ux   taf-tox   vi-ja!*
          Now-LOC/ABL   house-DAT/AD   go-IMP:2SG
          'Go to the house now!'

      b. *sg-otG-i   ?ins!*
          act.upon.a.canoe-take.away-IMP.2SG   you.me
          'Take me over in your boat!'

      c. *Dorž-guaj!   Deesh-ee   suu-gtuj*
          Dorzh-HON   up-EMPH   sit-IMP2
          'Dear Dorzh! Take the place of honor!'

Imperative verb forms tend to be dedicated (exclusive to the imperative paradigm (van der Auwera and Lejeune 2005a; van der Auwera 2010), particularly in the affirmative. Considering data from the negation of imperatives, 276 languages with prohibitive constructions in the second person singular have a dedicated form in the affirmative (vs. 78 that have non-dedicated forms). In this sample, the ratio of dedicated to non-dedicated forms is higher than 3:1. The trend is stronger than the numbers suggest if we consider that many of the languages without dedicated forms are analytic.

Earlier we saw an example of dedicated forms in Spanish second person imperatives vs. indicative and subjunctive forms. A parallel example in Basque is given above (8). English is an example of non-dedicated forms ("go!"; "you go shopping all the time"; "did you go?").

In conclusion, languages like Basque, Nivkh, Klamath and Mongolian give rise to the possibility of viewing the imperative clause as finite, along with root D&I.[17] Platzack and Rosengren (1998) propose that imperative clauses lack the projections corresponding to tense, mood and finiteness. In particular, they attribute the resistance to embedding to the lack of FiniteP – they assume that subordination requires referring expressions anchored to time and space. As far as person, number and case are concerned, the above data casts doubt on the idea that imperatives are not finite clauses. That said, the prevalence of bare forms could also be interpreted to signal that imperatives have finite and non-finite manifestations. Under the LPH, both options are potentially compatible,

since the performative could select a finite or a non-finite clause as its complement – languages like Basque could be explained in this manner (see Speas
and Tenny 2003 for a similar idea – subcategorization of a higher predicate –
regarding syntactic typing of basic clause types).

2.2.2   Tense in imperative clauses and imperative verb forms

A commonly held belief that imperatives are tenseless structures or tenseless verb forms (Beukema and Coopmans 1989; Zanuttini 1996; Platzack
and Rosengren 1998) is brought into question by the marking of different
future values, already observed in languages such as Latin (Baldi 1999), but
which has turned out to be a common occurrence (North American Indian
Languages: Mithun 1999: 153–54 via Aikhenvald 2010: 129; South American
Indian Languages: Fox (Algonquian, 11a,b cf. p. 129, exs. 4.13–14), Tariana
(Arawakan), Tucano (Tucanoan, 11c,d cf. p. 130, exs. 4.15a, 415b), Tubatulaban
(Uto-Aztecan) cf. Aikhenvald 2010: 129–31).

(11)   a. *peteki   ina·ho*
           back   go+2impv
           'Go back!'
        b. *ini=meko e·šimeneki*
           that=EMPH say.thus.to.someone.+2.CONJUNCT.PARTICIPLE.OBLIQUE
           išawihkani
           do.thus+2FUT.IMPV
           'Do [later on] exactly what you are told.'
        c. *ba'á-ya*
           eat-IMPV
           'Eat!'
        d. *ba'á-apa*
           eat-FUTURE.IMPV
           'Eat (later)!'

Less frequent, but also more attested than previously thought, is the encoding of (counterfactual) past reference (Spanish (12): Bosque 1980; Dutch:
Beukema and Coopmans 1989 and further examples in Aikhenvald 2010: 159,
fn. 22). Aikhenvald states that "Past tense imperatives are cross-linguistically
rare." (p. 133).[18]

(12)   *¡Hab-e-r   ven-i-do   antes!*
        have-THV-INF   come-THV-PSTPART   before
        'You should have come earlier!' (a counterfactual imperative)

Zanuttini (1996) ingeniously exploits the absence of overt tense marking in
her Romance data to propose an account for imperative surrogates in negative
contexts: subjunctives (13: Spanish), indicatives, non-finite forms (14: Italian

infinitive). The imperative verb form, if unique to the imperative paradigm (i.e., morphologically dedicated (Zanuttini 1994; Rivero 1994), is ungrammatical in these contexts. Dedicated forms in the literature on negative imperatives are often referred to as *true* imperative forms.

(13)   a. *!Com-e!*
           Eat-THV
           'Eat!'
       b. **!No com-e!*
           NEG eat-THV
           'Don't eat!'
       c. *!No com-as!*
           NEG eat-2.SG.SUB
           'Don't eat!'

(14)   a. *Mangi-a!*
           Eat-THV
           'Eat!'
       b. **Non mangi-a!*
           NEG eat-THV
           'Don't eat!'
       c. *Non mangi-a-re!*
           NEG eat-THV-INF
           'Don't eat!'

Zanuttini (1991) shows that negation can be preverbal or postverbal. Preverbal negation heads a phrase immediately above tense. Postverbal negation is not a head but an adjunct. On the assumption that preverbal negation selects tense, and that true imperative forms lack tense, true imperative forms cannot be negated unless negation is postverbal. The proposal captures a general trend in Romance languages, where negation is preverbal and true imperative forms are not allowed in negatives. In languages with postverbal negation, such as Piemontese (15), Milanese (16) and Valdotain (17), true negative imperatives are allowed (exs. from Zanuttini 1997: 111, exs. 20a, 20b, 21a, 22a and references therein).

(15)   a. *Parla!*
           Talk
           'Talk!'
       b. *Parla   nen!*
           Talk   NEG
           'Don't talk!'

(16)   *Gèina-tè   pa*
           bother-you   NEG
           'Don't worry!'

(17)   *Guarda   minga i tosànn*
            look   NEG   the girls
            'Don't look at the girls!'

Within the confines of the Romance family, Zanuttini's analysis is rather successful. Unfortunately, the negation of imperatives is a more challenging task for a syntactic account than previously thought (2.6). The work of van der Auwera and Lejeune (2005b) and van der Auwera (2010) describes the Romance family as atypical with respect to negative imperatives (it is far more common to employ prohibitives, and after that to negate the imperative verb directly, without surrogation, as in English). In light of this, Zanuttini's analysis could still be preserved, perhaps for a minority of languages that express no tense and require surrogates. That said, Jensen (2004b) has argued for the need of a tense node to account for the felicity of temporal adverbial modification, such as "do it now/tomorrow" (via van der Wurff 2007b: 21). Also, depending on the theoretical role ascribed to tense in the licensing of phi-features, the presence of person, number and case may also warrant its presence in the imperative clause, as a theory-internal argument.

In summary, the reasoning to ascribe defectiveness to the imperative clause, or to imperative verb forms, arises from comparison with D&I and their verb forms. The absence of grammatical tense, or other categories, in some languages need not be taken as compelling evidence of their absence. The availability of morphologically simple and morphologically complex imperative clauses in Basque is a case in point. Similarly, the absence of tense marking in analytical or isolating languages need not be taken as evidence that in these languages tense is defective or absent. Having said that, the different temporal properties of imperative tense, and its poor marking or absence in more complex languages, needs an explanation. In the LPH, the comparative lack of markedness generally follows from indexical restrictions in the values of person and tense, which lead to a lower need for morphological contrast. However, reduced morphological contrast extends beyond these categories, as we will see next.

2.2.3   *Imperative clauses and generalized clause structure*

Birjulin and Xrakovskij (2001: 33) point out that other categories (in a broad sense) such as "reflexivity, reciprocality, causality and iterativity ... follow the same rules in both moods [imperative, non-imperative]." This suggests that there is a common core of syntactic operations that applies to various sentence types.

The presence of tense is a caveat against the widely held assumption that imperative clauses or imperative verb forms are defective (Culicover 1976;

Beukema and Coopmans 1989; Zanuttini 1997; Platzack and Rosengren 1998; Han 2000a; Rupp 2003; Zanuttini and Portner 2003; Zeijlstra 2006; Zanuttini 2008). In these analyses, imperative clauses lack one or multiple projections starting with tense and spanning to the left periphery, or the imperative verb form itself lacks certain features (tense cf. Zanuttini 1996; mood cf. Zanuttini 1997; Zanuttini and Portner 2003, on the revised assumption that sentential negation selects mood).

Tense is not the only unexpected category to surface in imperatives. Earlier we noted verbal agreement: person, number and case. Another example concerns evidentiality. Aikhenvald (2010: 138–41) notes that some languages, such as Tariana (18: p. 138, ex. 4.33), Tucano (19: p. 138, ex. 4.34) and Warlpiri (Pama-Nyungan), express reported information in imperatives. This appears to be the only evidential value that is available in imperatives. The interpretation is of an imperative by proxy, as Aikhenvald puts it.

(18)   *pi-ñha-pida*
        2SG-eat-SEC.IMPV
        'Eat (on someone else's order)!' (that is, eat-you were told to)

(19)   *ba'â-ato*
        eat-SEC.IMPV
        'Eat (on someone else's order)!' (that is, eat-you were told to)

Certain Romance imperatives that begin with a complementizer also relay previously uttered imperatives, as in example (20a) from Spanish and (20b) from Mallorquin (20b cf. Mónica Marcos-Llinás, p.c.). These forms may have been regarded previously as elliptical utterances ("(He told you to) do it!"). But in the context of (18) and (19), the same utterances can be read in a new light. Hortatives in Romance also adopt this form (i.e., subjunctives with overt complementizers) and, in this case, their origin is not necessarily elliptical. In effect, it is not unusual for imperatives and hortatives to have overt complementizers (Xrakovskij 2001; Aikhenvald 2010). That said, the speaker can also use the examples in (20) to repeat an imperative of his or her own. As a non-iterated form, (20a) can function as an angry, abrupt command, contingent on the dialect.[19] The form in (20c) is an equivalent example from Basque.

(20)   a. *¡Que   lo   hagas!*
            that   3SG.ACC   do.SUBJ.2SG
            '(He/she told you to) do it!'
        b. *¡Que   ho   facis!*
            COMP   3SG.ACC   do.SUBJ.2SG
            '(He/she told you to) do it!'

c. *Egi-teko!*
do-PURPOSE.CLAUSE
'(He/she told you to) do it!'

Another important category that imperative clauses feature and which, it would seem, no other clause types do, is a form of indexical category that Aikhenvald refers to as DISTAL: "Having special marking for distance in space is a unique property of imperative clauses which sets them apart from clauses of other types" (2010: 133). Distal imperatives (21a,b: Tariana p. 134, exs. 4.23–4) express the relative distance of the addressee to the speaker ("do here," "do there") or *extralocality*: the action is to be carried out in a different location (21c: Trio, Carib; p. 135, ex. 4.29). This is different from motion and directionality indexicals (e.g., *come, go*), which imperatives also feature.[20]

(21)   a. *pi-ñha-si*
2SG-eat-PROXIMAL.IMPV
'Eat here!' (close to the speaker)
b. *pi-ñha-kada*
2SG-eat-DISTAL.IMPV
'Eat over there!' (away from where the speaker is; addressed to people outside the house)
c. *ene-ta*
look-DISLOCATIVE.IMPV
'Look at it there!' (singular addressee)

Aikhenvald (2010) makes two observations that are relevant for a reassessment of whether imperative clauses and imperative verb forms are defective. The first is that tense, aspect, evidential and indexical elements figure prominently in the imperative clause (Ch. 4 in Aikhenvald). These categories can be interpreted as such (i.e., tense is interpreted as tense) or, alternatively, they can be reinterpreted as politeness markers, or elements that help articulate imperative semantics (2.5). Thus an immediate vs. non-immediate future can be reinterpreted as rude or polite, as a command or request in Nambikwara (Nambikwaran) and Yu'pik (Eskimo-Aleut, p. 131). Similarly, reported evidentials can soften commands in Warlpiri and Cavineña (Pano-Tacanan, pp. 139–40). Mood markers in imperatives seem to be interpretable only in this manner (but see Rivero and Terzi 1995; Isac and Jakab 2004; Hill 2010 on mood in the Balkan languages).

The second observation is that, under negation, imperatives usually display reduced paradigmatic choices in tense, aspect, person, number, distance in space and directionality, modality, reality status and transitivity marking (Ch. 5 in Aikhenvald). Far from being an imperative quirk, paradigmatic reduction under negation is a tendency previously observed outside imperative clauses for a multitude of categories (Aikhenvald and Dixon 1998 on gender, person, number, aspect, tense ...). The presence of these unexpected categories, or their particular interpretation, does not alter the exceptional characteristics of the imperative clause, nor do these seem to correlate with the particular strategy used to negate imperatives.

In sum, all of these findings favor the lesser-walked path of viewing imperatives as structurally on a par with D&I (Rivero and Terzi 1995; Potsdam 1998 and, to a degree, Jensen 2004a). The difference appears to lie not in the absence of grammatical categories, but in their less frequent morphological marking, particularly in negatives, and in the number of values distinguished for each category, compared to D&I. The LPH provides an explanation for a reduced need for contrast for person and tense. Aikhenvald's (2010) two generalizations discussed above can help explain on independent grounds why other grammatical categories too are reduced under negation and in hortatives.

2.3   Part III: Different interpretations of the typological evidence

This section examines whether imperative clauses embed (2.3.1) and whether hortatives are a type of imperative (2.3.2).

2.3.1   *The imperative as a dependent clause*
Earlier samples indicated that the imperative clause cannot serve as a dependent constituent. Example (22a) is an imperative clause in Spanish. Its dedicated form cannot resurface in a complement clause, even if the main predicate is a verb of saying (22b). The subjunctive is used instead (22c).[21]

(22)   a. *¡Ven   a   com-e-r!*
            come.VRoot   to   eat-THV-INF
            'Come eat with us!'
        b. **Te digo   que   ven   a com-e-r*
            2SG say.1SG   that   come.VRoot   to eat-THV-INF
            'I tell you to come eat with us.'
        c. *Te digo   que   vengas   a com-e-r*
            2SG say.1SG   that   come.SUBJ.2SG   to eat-THV-INF
            'I tell you to come eat with us.'

Some scholars have presented cases where imperative verb forms appear in dependent clauses.[22] Here we will follow the lead of van der Wurff's (2007b) article. The following examples of appositives are from Latin (24a), Ancient Greek (24b) and English (25a is from the Elizabethan period, cf. van der Wurff

2007b: 23, ex. 69; 24, exs. 70, 71; and references therein). An example of the conditional use of the imperative (23) precedes this set.[23]

(23)   Give me the football and I will throw it from here.

(24)   a. *multas   ad   res   perutiles   Xenophontis libri sunt;*
        many   for   things   very-useful   Xenophon's books are
        quos   legite   studiose
        which   read.IMP.PLU   carefully
        'Xenophon's books, which you should read carefully, are most useful for many things' (Cicero, Cat. M 59; Hopper and Trauggot 1993: 175)
    b. *krateres   eisin [...]   on   krat'   erepson*
        mixing-bowls are   whose   brims   crown.IMP.2SG
        'There are mixing bowls, whose brims you must crown.'
        (Soph. *Oed. Tyr.* 473; Rivero and Terzi 1995: 316 n.5)

(25)   a. Thursday next is Saint Iames day, against which time prepare thy selfe to goe with me to the faire.
        (T. Deloney, c.1600, *The Gentle Craft* 207.31–33: Ukaji 1978: 114–17)
    b. Space has sadly precluded any discussion of Wittgenstein's positive views on epistemology, for which see Wittgenstein (1969a)[24]
        (British National Corpus 1992).

Beyond matters of syntactic dependency/parataxis, to be discussed below, the crux of the issue is in justifying the logical validity of the cases of imperative verbs appearing in conditional clauses as constituting true directives (speaker/time/intention) as speech act expressions, hence bona fide imperative clauses: see Clark (1993), Fortuin (2000) and Han (2000a) – who concludes that "conditional imperatives are not actually imperatives" (cf. van der Wurff 2007b: 3.4; 4.5.4).

To settle the matter on whether imperative clauses can be "subordinate" (to a superordinate predicate verb 4.2.1), a resolution is needed as to the plausible paratactic status of non-restrictive relatives and purpose clauses (see van der Wurff 2007b: 22–27), which will have to be tackled on a language-by-language basis. Alternatively, the syntactic distribution of imperatives could be extending in these languages, as in the case of the distribution of logophoric pronouns in some languages (3.3.2), but retaining the context of utterance (e.g., imperatives and logophoric pronouns, respectively) or the reported context (logophoric pronouns) as the domain of evaluation. There is evidence for the former in embedded imperatives in Germanic (Kaufmann 2012).

Regarding the conditional use of the imperative verb we refer the reader to Boogaart (2004[Dutch], but cf. 4.5.4), via the English summary in van der Wurff (2007b: 29–30), who conjectures that this use could arise through pragmatic implicature. In a sequence of two imperatives the first may be inferred to be a precondition. Over time, the implicature strengthens and it becomes part of its semantics. In Dutch, imperative conditional clauses with past reference use a past tense form, which can be taken as evidence of a more advanced stage of reanalysis in the transition from an imperative to a conditional.

Boogaart's analysis can be extended as an aid to interpreting temporal reference in imperative clauses. As noted, imperatives refer to the present and to the future. On occasion, they also refer to a counterfactual past (but cf. 4.5.2 and 3). Reanalysis of the imperative clause as a conditional clause elucidates the emergence of counterfactual past reference. Adopting this extension of Boogaart's analysis, temporal reference in imperative clauses can be effectively reduced to present and future. The rarity of the counterfactual past would stem from reanalysis.

Other examples of unforeseen uses of imperatives involve harnessing imperative morphology for other purposes, such as imperatives meant as a past tense in declaratives, or to express a more general sense of obligation in D&I. Compared to the regular past tense, the past tense denoted by the imperative form is pragmatically and/or aspectually marked. By way of example, the Spanish root infinitive in (26) denotes that the speaker is emotionally involved or affected, but examples such as these do not necessarily fall under imperative speech acts.

(26) *Llegar a Atlanta, pasar tres horas por inmigración y los de Delta no me querían dar otro billete para San Luis.*
'I arrived [lit. to arrive] in Atlanta, I spent [lit. to spend] three hours going through customs, and Delta did not want to put me on the next flight to St. Louis.' [NB: the speaker is both angry and puzzled]

When consulted, many speakers initially reject them as ungrammatical utterances. Other examples outside Romance include Slavic (Gronas 2006), Maasai (Koopman 2001), and Haitian Creole (Flore Zéphir, p.c.), with other nuances of interpretation.[25]

Aikhenvald (2010: 248–52) proposes that imperatives need not be restricted to root clauses. In particular, she notes the parallelisms between imperatives and the Russian *dramatic* past, namely the speaker being "in charge" or in control of the action (cf. N. Nekrasov). But important asymmetries between the imperative clause and the use of the imperative verb as a past tense are not mentioned. These are, first, that the dramatic past does not require second person subjects and secondly, that such past uses are often found in mirative contexts, which denote unexpected, surprising information (as in А он и побеги 'he suddenly run' cf. Gronas 2006: 89, in-text example). Whatever the circumstances, these are outside the control of the speaker. In Spanish, Italian, French and Haitian Creole, root infinitives expressing a past tense can also be mirative (as in (26) for Spanish). Accordingly, neither the semantics, nor the morphosyntactic characteristics of the imperative clause are present in these uses. The question lingers of why an imperative verb can be used as a past tense, a valid and recurrent grammaticalization path. But this question is independent of the imperative clause as a speech act, and therefore it does not cast doubt on its use as a root clause.[26]

Regarding the use of imperative verb forms to render a more general sense of obligation, an example follows from Korean. Korean features a short preverbal negation (*an*) and a long postverbal negation (*ani* + *ha* [a light verb or little v]). Negative imperatives cannot be formed with the short negation (27b); they must use the long version. However, the morphological realization of long negation in imperatives is lexically different (*mal*, compare 27a and c).

(27)   a. **hakkyo-ey   ka-ci   ani   ha-yela.*
             school-to   go-Ci   NEG   ha-IMP
             'Don't go to school.'
       b. **hakkyo-ey   an   ka-la.*
             school-to   NEG   go-IMP
             'Don't go to school.'
       c. *hakkyo-ey   ka-ci   mal-ala.*
             school-to   go-Ci   NEG-IMP
             'Don't go to school.'

                                         (Han and Lee 2002: 59, ex. 2)

Han and Lee observe that *mal* can also be deployed to negate matrix declaratives and matrix interrogatives, as long as the sentence forms a "deontic modality context" (28). Accordingly, they see fit to separate the categories *imperative* and *deontic modality*.

(28)   a. *Cey-ka   hakkyo-ey   ka-ci   mal-kkayo?*
             I-NOM   school-to   go-Ci   NEG-Q
             'Should I not go to school?'
       b. *Na-nun   hakkyo-ey   ka-ci   mal-ayakeyss-ta.*
             I-TOP   school-to   go-Ci   NEG-IRREALIS-DECL
             'I should not go to school.'

                                         (Han and Lee 2002: 60, ex. 3)

Recognizing the above-mentioned syntactic and morphological uses is not tantamount to saying that there exist dependent imperative clauses. Outside root clauses, imperatives rarely convey imperative meaning, if ever, and they fail to impose the addressee subject requirement. This suggests that the morphology associated with the imperative paradigm is recruited to serve other ends.

In sum, the limitation of imperatives to root clauses seems a robust pattern. Imperative verbs can occur in certain dependent clauses that may turn out to be paratactic under closer analysis. At any rate, these clauses do not express the illocutionary force of the imperative clause. Few putative examples of embedded imperatives exist, and these seem to require total or partial agreement with the indexical values of the context of utterance, as well as imperative illocutionary force in the main clause. The use of imperative forms can change over time and undergo reanalysis. Earlier uses coexist with later uses (Hopper 1991). This leads to the appearance that imperatives can occur in dependent clauses more generally. Yet complement clauses, restrictive relative clauses and all sorts of adverbial clauses clearly reject imperative verbs in familiar languages. The LPH assumes a performative verb in the imperative clause that construes with indexical elements. Local licensing conditions restrict the occurrence of imperatives to root clauses. The exceptions occur under a main clause that is already an imperative – plausibly a licensing requirement of the performative – under propositional attitude verbs. Said verbs are shown to require a context of utterance in indexical phenomena across languages (see Chapter 3). Accordingly, a putative embedded imperative requires imperative illocutionary force in the main clause and a syntax–pragmatics interface in the dependent clause.

2.3.2   *Beyond second person imperatives: hortatives*
Generative studies generally agree that imperative clauses are limited to second person forms (see 1.1.2), to the exclusion of hortatives, whose subjects can be first or third person (e.g., "let me/them go!"). With a few exceptions focusing on English *let* (Sepännen 1977; Davies 1986; Clark 1993; Potsdam 1998), generative studies have concentrated on the canonical imperative type. With reference to the typological literature, two surveys propose that hortatives belong to the imperative paradigm (Birjulin and Xrakovskij 2001: 28; van der Auwera et al. 2004: 5–7). A third survey by Aikhenvald (2010) is, in our reading, somewhat ambivalent about including hortatives with imperatives. After all, Aikhenvald includes hortatives in her survey of imperative expressions. Eventually she argues against considering hortatives a type of imperative on formal and semantic grounds. This section discusses some of the main arguments presented in these surveys (2.3.2.2). Prior to this, we review the various forms that imperative-hortative paradigms adopt across languages (2.3.2.1).

2.3.2.1   Imperative-hortative paradigms
Hortatives can present an alternative morphosyntactic paradigm to the imperative. This they do in English (29: *let*), Spanish (overt complementizer plus

subjunctive: 30: *dejar* 'let') and Basque (overt complementizer plus subjunctive: 31: *utzi* 'let').

(29)   a. Finish your work!
        b. Let him finish his work!

(30)   a. *¡Acab-a   la tarea!*
           Finish-THV   the homework
           'Finish your homework!'
        b. *¡Que acab-e   la tarea!*
           That finish-3SG.SUBJ   the homework
           'Let him finish his work!'

(31)   a. *Etxekolan-ak   amai-tu   itzazu!*
           Homework-ABS.PL   finish-INF   AUX.2SG(E).3PL(A).IMPER
           'Finish your homework!'
        b. *Etxekolan-ak   amai-tu   ditza-la!*
           Homework-ABS.PL   finish-INF AUX.2SG(E).3PL(A).SUBJ-COMP
           'Let him finish his work!'

On the other hand, imperative-hortative paradigms can be homogeneous in
form, syntactically and morphologically, as well as complete for all persons
and numbers: Kobon (Karam, 32), Boumaa Fijian (Austronesian), Evenki
(Tungusic) and prominently in Uralic languages (cf. Aikhenvald 2010: 49–50,
table 2.10). In Old English, Old Spanish and Old Basque hortatives were synthetic, like the imperatives in these languages at the time (Azkue 1925; Visser
1966: 798–99, §842). In the Kobon paradigm below (32), repeated for the reader's convenience, second person singular is the unmarked form.

(32)   a. 1sg: *-ɨn/in*   1dual: *-ul*   1pl: *-un*
        b. 2sg: *-Ø*   2dual: *-ɨl*   2pl: *-im*
        c. 3sg: *-aŋ*   3dual: *-ɨl*   3pl: *-laŋ*

In the absence of a dedicated imperative form, its substitute may be suited to
express all person and number combinations (e.g., the future in Gooniyandi
(Bunuban) cf. Aikhenvald 2010: 51). At the same time, imperative paradigms
may miss specific person and number combinations, be altogether reduced to
second person, or construe first and third person forms differently. Germanic
and Romance languages are familiar examples in these last categories.

2.3.2.2   Are hortatives a type of imperative?

Various arguments are relevant to this question. Concerning morphology,
(i) imperative-hortative paradigms can be uniform and (ii) they constitute a
joint domain for a markedness hierarchy of person/number (2.4.1). In their

morphosyntax, (iii) hortatives reproduce the exceptional characteristics of the imperative type – person excepted. Lastly, (iv) the interpretation of hortatives seems to run parallel to that of imperatives – first person forms notwithstanding. This section discusses three of these arguments in detail (on (ii), see 2.5).

Because imperatives and hortatives can show complete paradigmatic uniformity, Birjulin and Xrakovskij (2001) and van der Auwera et al. (2004) take this as a formal argument to include hortatives with imperatives. Conversely, Aikhenvald (2010) separates canonical imperatives (second person) from non-canonical imperatives (first and third person) on the same formal grounds, stressing the existence of mixed paradigms, such as English ("go!" vs. "let me/ them go!").

In our view, the markedness hierarchy contributed by van der Auwera et al. (2004) and Aikhenvald (2010) is a compelling argument to regard hortatives as a type of imperative clause. Whether imperative-hortative paradigms are split or not, they still observe the same hierarchy. Furthermore, hortatives share most of the exceptional characteristics of imperatives discussed in the introduction. For example, hortatives cannot embed, their temporal interpretation is irrealis, they are restricted to controllable processes (wishes excepted) and, in analytical forms, their subject must be second person (e.g., "let[2] them go!"). This suggests a common morphosyntactic core to imperatives and hortatives. Consistent with these reasons, we consider the complete paradigmatic uniformity of imperative paradigms in some languages as an argument for hortatives to be regarded as a type of imperative. The LPH proposes that hortatives are a 'causative' or proxy imperative (see Chapter 4). The presence of an additional verbal head would account for the possibility for hortatives to present an extended paradigm in their realization across languages.

Aikhenvald proposes that the semantics of imperatives needs to be separated from that of hortatives and generally characterized according to differences in person, in light of meanings specific to these forms. In her own words (p. 75):

> While the canonical addressee-oriented imperative is expected to imply a straightforward command, orders directed at other people seem to develop meaning overtones which set them apart from canonical imperatives: first person commands may imply seeking a permission, while third person commands refer to wishes and indirect ways of inciting people to do things.

Aikhenvald (Ch. 6) dedicates a chapter to imperative semantics, where she provides exhaustive coverage of the various meanings of imperatives (orders, invitations, instructions, etc.). She proposes that imperatives be viewed as graded expressions in the strength of the command (Chapter 1, n.7). But Aikhenvald's chapter does not cover the meaning of hortatives, which present a similar range of interpretations, apparently not explored by the author. By contrast, Birjulin and Xrakovskij (2001:8) stress parallelisms between the semantics of imperatives and hortatives, if first person singular forms are excluded:

> Imperative sentences with third-person imperatives admit semantic interpretations similar to those of imperative sentences with second-person imperatives. The same is true for imperative sentences with first-person imperative verb forms both in the dual and the plural, except that they can express neither permission nor advice in situations where the speaker [=prescriptor] cannot be simultaneously the performer of the prescribed action. All other interpretations seem to be possible although these sentences appear to express invitation characteristic of their type.

The additional meanings of first person forms are seen to derive from a thematic separation of the addressee and performer argument, and the participation or exclusion of the speaker as the subject of the imperative verb.

Concerning the semantics of first person, Aikhenvald notes that singular forms are often employed to express "suggestion, proposition," "permission" (33), and "turn-taking" (Aikhenvald 2010: 74; 33: Manambu, Ndu, ex. 2.145).

(33)   *kwasa   wiya:r   yau*
        small+FEM.SG   house+LK+ALL   GO+1SG.IMPV
        'May I go to the toilet.'; 'Let me go to the toilet.'

When Aikhenvald compares imperatives with hortatives, she emphasizes the command or *strong* interpretation of the former, and the non-command or *weaker* interpretation of the latter (e.g., seeking permission; wishes). We disagree with this interpretation. If imperatives are graded expressions, imperatives can also be interpreted in a weaker form (e.g., a suggestion or a plea). In turn, hortatives can be interpreted as strong forms (e.g., in the military: "make them run 10 miles!"; parental commands "let your sister play with it!" etc.). It may be possible that imperatives and hortatives differ in the frequency with which they convey stronger or weaker interpretations in actual use. But we are not aware of studies that look into this possibility. This difference would be quantitative. As with the argument of paradigmatic uniformity, Aikhenvald seems to be stressing the differences over the similarities between imperatives and hortatives.

For Aikhenvald, third person hortatives tend to express wishes. Again, this is possibly intended as a quantitative or frequency argument. Our objection is that imperatives can express wishes too, as the following sentences from English suffice to demonstrate (34).[27]

(34)   a. Have a good time!
        b. Enjoy your reading!

In Spanish, wishes are expressed either as second person imperative morphology (35a) or as second person subjunctives preceded by an overt complementizer (35b), with no apparent difference in meaning. The overt complementizer form with subjunctives is the form assumed, in the second person, by strong, self-iterated, or reported commands. Either frame can express wishes.

(35)   a. *¡Pas-a-d-lo*   *bien!*
           Pass-THV-2PL.IMP-3SG.ACC   well
           'Have a good time!' (plural addressee)
       b. *¡Que   lo   pas-éis   bien!*
           COMP   3SG.ACC   pass- 2PL.SUBJ   well
           'Have a good time!' (plural addressee)

If imperatives and hortatives share a similar semantics (with Birjulin and Xrakovskij), it would make sense that they also share a similar syntax. Third person hortatives may have an overt second person addressee (the mediator). A second person is usually overt with causatives, although this is not observable in English.[28] Spanish shows a paradigmatic distinction in person (36), while Basque (37) and other languages overtly mark second person singular in hortatives (with overt causatives).

(36)   a. *¡Déj-a-les   sal-i-r!*
           let-THV-3PL   come.out-THV-INF
           'Let them come out!'
       b. *¡Dej-a-d-les   sal-i-r!*
           let-THV-2PL-3PL   come.out-THV-INF
           'Let them come out!'

(37)   a. *Utz-i   iezaie-zu*   *atera-tzen!*
           let-INF   AUX.3SG(A)3PL(D)-2SG(E)   come.out-IMPF
           'Let them come out!'
       b. *Utz-i   iezaie-zue*   *atera-tzen!*
           let-INF   AUX. 3SG(A)3PL(D)-2PL(E)   come.out-IMPF
           'Let them come out!'

Sometimes the addressee and the performer can be ascertained in contexts without an explicit causative verb (38a: Latin; 38b: Finnish, cf. Jensen 2004a: 160, (22–3) in that two sets of person and number features are present.[29]

(38)   a. *Aperi-te   aliquis!*
           open-IMP-2PL   someone-NOM-[3]SG
           'Someone open!'
       b. *Maista-kaa   joku*   *keitto-a*
           taste-IMP-2PL   someone-NOM-3SG   soup-PART
           'Someone taste some of the soup!'

To recapitulate, typological surveys include imperative expressions beyond second person forms. Certain semantic differences can be observed in the thematic separation of the addressee from the performer role and in the inclusion or exclusion of the speaker as the subject of the lexical verb. Two of the three surveys mentioned a joint hypothesis of imperatives and hortatives. Imperatives and hortatives abide by a markedness hierarchy, share the same core of morphosyntactic exceptional characteristics and similar semantics. Aikhenvald presents a partially dissenting view and we have addressed her arguments. Further arguments for the unity of imperative-hortative paradigms are offered in the next section. The LPH proposes that hortatives are a causative or proxy imperative, which explains the exceptional characteristics that hortatives share with imperatives and provides room for different paradigms that make the causative explicit.

2.4 Part IV: Further similarities/differences in imperatives-hortatives

This section elaborates on similarities and differences between imperatives and hortatives. These concern the observance of a markedness hierarchy (2.4.1). In spite of the observance of the hierarchy, a seemingly universal exception is found in a reversal in person markedness (2.4.2).

2.4.1 A markedness hierarchy in imperative-hortative paradigms

Van der Auwera et al. (2004) provide a semantic map of markedness relations that demonstrates that hortatives cannot exist in a language without that language also featuring imperatives. If all languages possess an imperative clause, as appears to be the case, this argument in itself does not prove that hortatives must be treated as a type of imperative clause. Nonetheless, when both imperatives and hortatives exist in the same language, a number of markedness implications follow. For example, if a hortative marks a distinction in plural, so does the imperative, but not vice versa.[30] They conclude that imperative-hortative paradigms are formally homogeneous, surface morphosyntactic appearances notwithstanding.

Aikhenvald (2010: 76) also contributes a person and number hierarchy of attested imperative forms (39):

(39)   1sg and/or 1pl exclusive > 3sg or pl > 1 pl inclusive; non-singular > 2pl
(sg, pl, or non-singular)

The existence of a form in the hierarchy implies the existence of all other forms to its right. Aikhenvald's hierarchy agrees with that of van der

Auwera et al. Aikhenvald does not explicitly state that hortatives must coexist with imperatives – unless we inadvertently missed it in our reading – although this is implied in her hierarchy.[31]

No hierarchy seems to be without exception (hierarchies can be construed as strong preferences, see Bobaljik 2008). A counterexample, although rather minor, comes from the study of suppletive stem forms (such as *go* vs. *went* for tense) in imperative-hortative paradigms. Veselinova (2005: 323) reports the following distribution for a sample of 193 languages (40).

(40)   a. A regular and suppletive form alternate: 8 languages
        b. Imperative suppletion: 29 languages
        c. Hortative suppletion: 2 languages
        d. Imperative and hortative suppletion: 1 language
        e. No suppletion in imperatives or hortatives: 153 languages

Two languages would seem to feature suppletion in hortatives but not in imperatives (40c). Unfortunately, we do not know the identity of these particular languages in order to probe the matter further. That said, the overall picture does conform to the proposed hierarchy, since imperatives outnumber hortatives in the number of suppletive forms.[32]

To recap, imperatives and hortatives abide by a markedness hierarchy for person/number. The LPH predicts this behavior in that hortatives are conceptualized as a causative imperative. Nonetheless, there is an important exception within this hierarchy, which we discuss next.

2.4.2   *A person-markedness reversal*

A puzzling exception to the markedness hierarchy, and one that is seemingly pervasive across languages, is found in the reversal of person markedness within the particular domain of imperative-hortative clauses. Third person is marked, while second person is often unmarked, particularly in the singular (Portner 2004; Aikhenvald 2010; an anonymous referee) – as in the above example from the Kobon imperative paradigm for all persons and numbers, including dual. The following set of examples illustrates this person-markedness reversal with exhaustive examples for Spanish and Basque (41–48).

The next dataset presents subject–verb agreement morphology in Spanish for all persons in the singular, in the present tense of the indicative mood, for declaratives (41), subjunctive clauses (41') and root polar interrogatives (42). Note that the third person singular form is unmarked in indicative forms of D&I (13c, 42c), consisting of the verb root and thematic vowel, while the corresponding subjunctive form is marked (41'c), yet not distinguishable from first person singular (41'a).

(41)   a. *Cant-o.*
sing-1SG.IND
'I sing.'
b. *Cant-a-s.*
sing-THV-2SG.IND
'You sing.'
c. *Cant-a.*
sing-THV
'She sings.'

(41')   a. *Juan quier-e   que pro cant-e*
Juan want-THV   COMP   sing-1SG.SUBJ
'Juan wants me to sing.'
b. *Juan quier-e   que pro cant-es*
Juan want-THV   COMP   sing-2SG.SUBJ
'Juan wants you to sing.'
c. *Juan quier-e   que pro cant-e*
Juan want-THV   COMP   sing-3SG.SUBJ
'Juan wants her/him to sing.'

(42)   a. *¿Cant-o?*
sing-1SG.IND
'Do I sing?'
b. *¿Cant-a-s?*
sing-THV-2SG.IND
'Do you sing?'
c. *¿Cant-a?*
sing-THV
'Does she sing?'

The data in (43) presents subject–verb agreement in imperatives. In contrast to non-imperative sentences (41, 42), canonical imperatives make use of an unmarked form, the verb root plus thematic vowel, which in this case is interpreted as second person singular (43a). The honorific second person form is built on indirection, as a third person form is used to convey social distance or reverence (43a'). The third person form is inflected with a fusional morpheme expressing third person subjunctive.

(43)   a. *¡Cant-a!*
sing-THV
'Sing!'
a'. *¡Cant-e!*
sing-3SG.SUBJ
'Sing!' (honorific)

Other forms of indirection are plurality in the second person in French and Russian, or reinterpretations of tense and other categories. Honorificity can be encoded directly in the second person. In Basque, for instance, pronouns and verbal agreement have paradigmatic choices in honorificity.

When the performer of the imperative is third person, the same third person form is used (as in 43a'), without an honorific interpretation (43b). Alternatively, the verb takes on an infinitival form if embedded under a causative verb (43b'). The latter option being analytical, it is even more marked.

(43)　　b.　*¡Que cant-e*　　　*Juan!*
　　　　　　　that sing-3SG.SUBJ　Juan
　　　　　　　'Let Juan sing!'
　　　　b'.　*¡Déj-a-le*　　　　*cant-a-r*　　　*a*　*Juan!*
　　　　　　　let-THV-3SG.DAT　sing-THV-INF　to　Juan
　　　　　　　'Let Juan sing!'

The infinitive is also employed as an imperative verb form in Spanish (not as a substitute form under negation, as in the relevant Italian example, but as a different paradigmatic option for second person). The infinitive is unmarked for person. It can be used for a second person singular or plural addressee (44a). If a preposition precedes the infinitive, the speaker is imposing the command on the addressee (44b), and similarly the gerund (44c; Haverkate 1976). The latter two can also be used indistinctively for singular or plural addressees.

(44)　　a.　*¡Cant-a-r!*
　　　　　　　sing-THV-INF
　　　　　　　'Sing!' (singular or plural addressee)
　　　　b.　*¡A　cant-a-r!*
　　　　　　　to　sing-THV-INF
　　　　　　　'Sing!' (singular or plural addressee)
　　　　c.　*¡Cant-a-ndo!*
　　　　　　　sing-THV-GER
　　　　　　　'Sing!' (singular or plural addressee)

It is noteworthy that the use of non-finite forms (44), even if unmarked for person, precludes an interpretation where the performer is first or third person. By contrast, an analytical infinitive can also be used for the overt causative strategy, in which case a second person interpretation for *sing* is excluded (45).

(45)　　*¡Dej-a-r*　　*cant-a-r!*
　　　　　let-THV-INF　sing-THV-INF
　　　　　'Let me/us/them/him/her sing!'

Since (45) is an analytical form, it remains a step up in markedness. Second person singular is consistently unmarked in the Spanish imperative paradigm.

Thus Spanish presents three markedness patterns: $1 \neq 2 \neq 3$ and $2 \neq 1/3$, where third person is unmarked or one of the least marked forms, but also a 1

≠ 2 ≠ 3 pattern where the least marked form is second person. This last pattern of markedness in imperative clauses is not language particular, but seemingly systematic in imperative paradigms, as noted.

A similar paradigm obtains in Basque (46–48). Third person singular ergative case is a zero morpheme in indicative (46c) and subjunctive clauses (46′c), while first (*-t/-da-*) and second person are marked (*-zu*). This is not to be confused with Ø in the detailed Basque gloss below, which we use to denote that *d-* is not a morpheme but possibly a phonological filler. As in Spanish, the verb form in declaratives (46) is the same as in root polar interrogatives (47).

(46)   a. *Abes-ten   d-u-t.*
             sing-IMPF   Ø-AUX.HAVE-1SG(E)
             'I sing.'
      b. *Abes-ten   d-u-zu.*
             sing-IMPF   Ø-AUX.HAVE-2SG(E)
             'You sing.'
      c. abes-ten   d-u.
             sing-IMPF   Ø-AUX.HAVE.3SG(E)
             'She sings.'

(46′) a. *Abes d-eza-da-n*   *nahi   d-u.*
             sing Ø-AUX.EZAN-1SG(E)-COMP want Ø-AUX.HAVE.3SG(E)
             'He/she wants me to sing.'
      b. *Abes d-eza-zu-n*   *nahi   d-u.*
             sing Ø-AUX.EZAN-2SG(E)-COMP want Ø-AUX.HAVE.3SG(E)
             'He/she wants you to sing.'
      c. *Abes d-eza-n*   *nahi   d-u.*
             sing Ø-AUX.EZAN.3SG(E)-COMP want Ø-AUX.HAVE.3SG(E)
             'He/she wants me to sing.'

(47)   a. *Abes-ten al d-u-t?*
             sing-IMPF Q Ø-AUX.HAVE-1SG(E)
             'Do I sing?'
      b. *Abes-ten al d-u-zu?*
             sing-IMPF Q Ø-AUX.HAVE-2SG(E)
             'Do you sing?'
      c. *Abes-ten al d-u?*
             sing-IMPF Q Ø-AUX.HAVE.3SG(E)
             'Does she sing?'

Morphologically complex imperatives in Basque indicate agreement for all arguments of the verb (48a), as noted in an earlier example. Alternatively, an infinitive can be used for singular and plural addressees (48a′). By contrast, third person is marked in that, along with an overt complementizer, a finite form is used (the subjunctive: 48b) – third person ergative marking remains a zero morpheme in the singular for the subjunctive form as well.

(48) a. *Abes-tu   eza-zu!*
       sing-INF   AUX.EZAN-2SG(E)
       'Sing!'
    a′. *Abes-tu!*
       sing-INF
       'Sing!' (singular or plural addressee)
    b. *Juan abes-tu   d-eza-la!*
       Juan sing-INF   Ø-AUX.EZAN.3SG(E)-COMP
       'Let Juan sing!'
    b′. **Juan abes-tu!*
       Juan sing-INF
       'Let Juan sing!'

As in the above example for Spanish, if third person is expressed by means of an overt causative verb (*utzi* 'let'), it is possible to dispense with the auxiliary. The subject then is interpreted as first or third person, singular or plural, depending on the context. It is not possible to interpret the subject of *sing* as a second person.

(48) c. *Utz-i   ieza-i-o-zu*   *abes-ten*
       let-INF   AUX.EZAN-PRED-3SG(D)-2SG(E)   sing-IMP
       'Let her sing!'
    c′. *Utz-i   abes-ten*
       let-INF   sing-IMP
       'Let me/us/them/her/him sing!'

While a comprehensive account of imperative clauses must include hortatives, a successful analysis must at the same time elucidate why there exists a person-markedness reversal. A related question in this regard is why second person tends to be realized separately from first and third person. This separation is brought about by the Spanish and Basque infinitival data in imperatives (*1/2/*3) and hortatives (1/*2/3). The LPH proposes that the grammatical subject of imperatives is thematically restricted to be the addressee. In hortatives the subject of the (underlying) causative verb meets this restriction, which allows for the lexical verb to have first/third person subjects and, in some cases, reflexive second person subjects as well.

2.5   Part V: The semantics of imperatives in root clauses

Earlier sections have discussed other uses of imperatives outside root clauses (e.g., conditionals, Russian dramatic past) and have drawn broad semantic comparisons between the semantics of imperatives and that of hortatives. This section in turn focuses on imperative semantics in root clauses. Imperative semantics appear to be homogeneous across languages. Paradigmatic choices

exist for imperatives interpreted as commands, suggestions, permission grant-
ing, pleas or exhortations, among other meanings (2.5.1). Such options undermine earlier views in pragmatics that saw imperative meaning as strongly
deontic, other interpretations being analyzed as indirect speech acts (2.5.2).
Finally, certain interpretations of imperatives, such as imprecatives, need to be
separated from core imperative meaning for they constitute different speech
acts (2.5.3; i.e., minor speech acts: Sadock and Zwicky 1985).

2.5.1   *Paradigmatic choices subdividing imperative meaning*

An important blueprint contributed by typological research, which also confirms the findings of the earlier samples, is found in the homogeneity of the
interpretation of imperatives in root clauses. Imperatives can be interpreted
as commands, requests, wishes, preventatives, demands, pleas, invitations,
instructions, advice, and can be used to request and grant permission. Some
of these interpretations may be expressed with specific paradigmatic forms
within the imperative clause but, more commonly, a few forms represent
clusters of (closely related) interpretations. For example, Alpatov (2001)
provides a matrix of Japanese imperative expressions (and a few indirect
speech acts – the negative interrogative) based on whether they can express
commands, demands, requests, advice and permission. For each expression,
Table 2.1 indicates whether the interpretation is available (Alpatov 2001:
121; table 1).

The table shows a multiplicity of options to express commands, demands,
requests, advice and permission. While some of these forms can cover most,
if not all of these interpretations (e.g., *–tamae*), other forms represent smaller
clusters, such as commands and demands (e.g., *o-kure*) vs. requests and advice
(e.g., *o...kudasai*) vs. permission (e.g., *narai*).[33] Many of these options carry
specific honorific restrictions. For example, adults use *–te/de* to indicate that
they put their addressee at their own social level; while in child language
usage these imperatives address both adults and other children (p. 108). The
forms *–e*, *–ero*, *–yo*, and *–i*, by contrast, are used to address people of lower
social standing, and must be flanked by polite and "super polite" forms when
etiquette demands it (p. 107).

Aikhenvald (2010) offers examples of languages that have rather specific
paradigmatic forms: "Many of the imperative-specific directive meanings
identified for English acquire formal realization in other languages" (p. 201).
For instance, Tuyuca (Tucanoan) has special verbal suffixes to express invitation (50a), permission (50b) and warning (50c).

Table 2.1 Japanese imperative markers and the meanings they express (+)

Imperative affix/ verb	Command	Demand	Request	Advice	Permission
-e, -ro, -yo, -na	+	+	−	−	−
o-kure, -yare	+	+	−	−	−
o-kure	+	+	−	−	−
-tamae	+	+	+	+	−
nasai, kuretamae, choodai	+	+	+	+	−
-te/de, o-...-i/Ø	+	+	+	+	−
nasai + o-	+	+	+	+	−
-te kudasai	+	+	+	−	−
O... kudasai	−	−	+	+	−
kudasaimase, asobase	−	−	+	+	−
Negative interrogative	−	−	+	−	−
ii, yoi, yoroshii, narai, ikenai	−	−	−	−	+

(49)   a. *Waá-co*
         go-INVITATION.IMPV
         'Let's go!'
       b. *Waá-ma*
         go-PERMISSIVE.IMPV
         'Let (me) go!'
       c. *Naa-ri*
         fall-APPREHENSIVE.IMPV
         'Make sure you don't fall! You might fall (lest you fall)'

Aikhenvald shows that strategies to soften commands (including honorification and reinterpretation of grammatical categories) help articulate imperative semantics and distribute said meanings over a discrete set of forms. As noted, she proposes that most of the above meanings (from commands to pleas) are related in the strength of the "command." Birjulin and Xrakovskij (2001) also seek to capture uniformity in the interpretation of imperatives and adopt the general term *prescription*, also to be interpreted in a social, interactive context. We remarked in an endnote in the introduction that these subdivisions within imperative paradigms resemble to a degree semantic parameters invoked for causative constructions (Comrie 1985b; Dixon 2000). For example, a prepositional infinitive in Spanish is used in orders (from a higher ranking officer to a private, from a teacher or parent to a child), but also in lullabies (*¡a dormir!*,

¡a dormir! [to sleep-THV-INF to sleep-THV-INF] 'Sleep! (idiomatic)'). Arguably, the semantic parameter in this case is that the addressee cannot refuse the prescription. Similarly, in causatives, some choices encode whether the causer can "resist" the causer. We leave this matter for further research.

2.5.2   What counts as an indirect speech act for imperatives?

A review is in order regarding consolidated ideas in pragmatics that view imperatives as a strong deontic speech act – a command or order – with the consequence that all other interpretations must necessarily arise from context as indirect speech acts. By way of example, Levinson (1983: 275) quotes Bolinger (1967) to show that imperatives have various indirect interpretations, which outnumber their literal uses.

> Imperatives are rarely used to command or request in conversational English (see Ervin-Tripp, 1976), but occur regularly in recipes and instructions, offers (*Have another drink*), welcoming (*come in!*), wishes (*Have a good time*), curses and swearing (*Shut up!*) and so on (see Bolinger 1967) [...] just about all the actual uses of imperatives in English will therefore have to be considered ISAs [indirect speech acts].

Similarly, König and Siemund (2007: 277) quote Clark (1996) and assume that imperatives have indirect interpretations in the range of speech acts that they can represent:

> A simple imperative like "Sit here," for instance could be used as a command, request, offer, advisory or exhortation, depending on the context, as is shown by the following potential responses: "Yes, sir" (command), "Okay" (request), "No thanks" (offer), "What a good idea" (advisory), "Thank you" (exhortation). (cf. Clark 1996: 213)

There exist paradigmatic choices in rich imperative paradigms for most of these alleged ISAs (cf. Japanese, Tuyuca, Spanish). Therefore, these are literal interpretations, read from the sentence type and the verb form, not from context. The idea that the interpretation of D&I is contingent upon context is most certainly correct.[34] Note that, when a declarative is used as a promise or a challenge, an imperative or an interrogative, among other examples, there is no change in verb form. It is context that furnishes these interpretive possibilities. Furthermore, some of the alleged ISAs are minor sentence types (see next section for discussion).

Under the prevailing pragmatic view of the imperative clause (Bolinger 1967; Levinson 1983; Clark 1996; König and Siemund 2007), it is not predicted that certain imperative forms are interpreted as commands and as commands alone (e.g., the prepositional infinitive in Spanish: Haverkate 1976). It is also unexpected that non-literal interpretations, such as invitation, permission and warning (e.g., Tuyuca), or clusters thereof, preclude the so-called literal (i.e., command) interpretation.

The pragmatic view may have been misled by too much reliance on English and similar languages without paradigmatic choices, or with few, ambiguous choices. A version of the performative hypothesis (Austin 1962; Searle 1969; Ross 1970) is extended to account for ISAs (Sadock 1974, inter alia). Accurate and legitimate criticism of this extension involved the crucial role of context in the interpretation of D&I. While context determines the interpretation of D&I in spite of their syntactic type, the same conclusions were presumed to hold for imperatives. The set of alleged non-literal interpretations is, in the light of cross-linguistic evidence, reduced to actual linguistic expressions, either as part of the imperative paradigm as a universal clause, or as minor sentence types (Sadock and Zwicky 1985; see 2.5.3). It is yet to be reexamined whether imperative clauses can be sensitive to context like D&I. It is not clear at this point what interpretations are left to conduct this research. Imperative clauses appear to be deterministic in interpretation. This may be related to their integration with the syntax–pragmatics interface (Chapters 3–4); a form of syntactic typing similar to the PH, but limited to the imperative clause.

Most recent generative analyses bank on the idea that imperatives constitute a strong deontic speech act, which legitimizes the exclusion from the second person paradigm of forms not interpreted as commands, further reducing the empirical data under consideration (but see exceptions in Poletto and Zanuttini 2003; Pak, Portner and Zanuttini 2008, among others). The extent to which the strong deontic view of imperatives is widespread should not be underestimated. By way of example, the survey on sentence types of König and Siemund (2007) also embraces this view, as seen in the above quote.

On the opposite side, another strong trend has envisaged imperatives more generally as irrealis or potential events, among other similar labels (see van der Wurff 2007b: 30–33 and references therein), trying to bring imperatives under a broad umbrella with infinitives and subjunctives. In consideration of the recurrent interpretations of the imperative clause across languages and its role as a universal sentence type, the latter approach falls short of recognizing imperatives as a distinct and independent semantic unit and does not furnish specifics regarding the mapping from these wide-ranging ideas to their concrete semantics.

2.5.3   *Core imperative meaning vs. minor sentence types*

Other uses of imperatives seem to fall off imperative semantics proper and are better seen as minor sentence types instead (in the sense of Sadock and Zwicky 1985, i.e., non-universal types). Imprecatives, threats or challenges are minor sentence types that can be derived from the imperative clause type, but they are not an imperative speech act. While Basque has imprecatives that look like imperatives, their use seems a conspicuous calque of French and Spanish, rather than a native development. Since the relevant examples are inelegant, we will spare them here. In Spanish, challenges (50a) and threats (50b) can begin with a root prepositional complementizer.

(50)   a. *¡A que   te   gan-o!*
           to that   2SG   win-1SG.IND
           '(I bet you that) I will beat you'
        b. *¡A que   te   part-o   la cara!*
           to that   2SG   break-1SG.IND   the face
           '[threatening] I am going   to beat you up'.

Their origin is likely an earlier performative utterance (*te apuesto a que...* 'I bet you that...'), not an imperative speech act, that has undergone phonological reduction (e.g., consider English 'betcha') and eventually disappeared – although the selected preposition and complementizer linger in Spanish (*A que* ...). In much the same way as exclamatives can be based on declaratives (51a,b) or interrogatives (51c,d cf. Sadock and Zwicky 1985: 162–63; (31–34), the imperative can also serve as a basis for minor types.

(51)   a. That's *so* tacky!
        b. She's *such* good syntactician!
        c. How tacky that is!
        d. What a good syntactician she is!

These minor interpretations are to be separated from the core meaning of the imperative clause in its role as a universal speaker intentional speech act type.

In sum, imperatives across languages present paradigmatic choices that align with particular semantic interpretations, casting doubt on the idea that imperatives have indirect speech act interpretations. The core of imperative semantics needs to be separated from other minor speech acts. The LPH proposes that imperative meaning is syntactically typed by a performative verb. The semantic choices articulating prescriptions may not be imperative-specific, but follow from more general subject–object/predicate relations (Chapter 1, n. 7; 4.4.3). Detailed examination of causative constructions (Dixon 2000) across languages may prove to be a good proving ground for testing this hypothesis.

2.6   Part VI: The negation of imperative clauses

This section is dedicated to the negation of imperative clauses. It reviews the main assumptions and mechanics of current syntactic analyses (2.6.1) and gradually exposes these to the new typological findings (2.6.2–3). As it turns out, a syntactic analysis of surrogate imperatives does not seem viable when faced with new typological data (2.6.4).

2.6.1   The negative imperative puzzle: the ban on true negative imperatives
The negation of imperatives has been the most studied characteristic of this clause type in generative linguistics. Its central role came to focus in the last two decades, particularly since the introduction of additional functional categories, to include negation, and the growing interest in Romance languages, where substitute forms arise (Laka 1990; Zanuttini 1991, 1994, 1996, 1997; Rivero 1994; Rivero and Terzi 1995; Potsdam 1998; Platzack and Rosengren 1998; Han 2001; Zanuttini and Portner 2003; Zeijlstra 2006, individual papers in van der Wurff 2007b and references therein). In this section, we will adopt the specialized term surrogate form or surrogate to refer to the substitute forms and surrogation to refer to the process of substitution. The negative imperative puzzle was illustrated with examples earlier in (13–14), which we repeat here for the reader's convenience as (52–53). Subjunctives are surrogates in Spanish (52c) while Italian uses infinitives (53c).

(52) a. *!Com-e!*
         Eat-THV
         'Eat!'
      b. **!No com-e!*
         NEG eat-THV
         'Don't eat!'
      c. *!No com-as!*
         NEG eat-2SG.SUBJ
         'Don't eat!'

(53) a. *Mangi-a!*
         Eat-THV
         'Eat!'
      b. **Non mangi-a!*
         NEG eat-THV
         'Don't eat!'
      c. *Non mangi-a-re!*
         NEG eat-THV-INF
         'Don't eat!'

The negation of imperatives splits imperative verb forms into two paradigms: one for affirmative sentences and one for negative sentences. The above syntactic accounts aim to provide an explanation for this morphological split.

Most of these analyses assume that the imperative verb must reach a higher clausal position (the complementizer area or left periphery, Rizzi 1997) to license an IMP (imperative) feature that identifies the clause as a directive speech act. This movement seems warranted in light of differences in the position of clitic pronouns in Romance (Kayne 1992) and other languages (e.g., Maasai: Koopman 2001). For example, Spanish direct and indirect object pronouns are enclitic in affirmative imperatives (54a). Elsewhere in the language these pronouns are proclitic on finite verbs. Negative imperatives with a surrogate show proclisis (54b).

(54)   a. *¡Dá-me-lo!*
            give-1SG.DAT-3SG.ACC.MASC
            'Give it to me!'
       b. *¡No me   lo   des!*
            NEG 1SG.DAT 3SG.ACC.MASC   give.2SG.SUBJ
            'Don't give it to me.'

Maasai features a set of portmanteau morphemes indicating combinations of agreement with more than one argument (e.g., *áa*: subject 'I', object 'you'; *kɨ*: subject 'he/they', object 'you'; *áá* subject 'I', object 'you'). These morphemes must precede the verb in all tensed forms (55a,b cf. Koopman 2001: 1, ex. 1) with the exception of the affirmative imperative (55c cf. Koopman 2001: 7, ex. 20), where the morpheme must follow.

(55)   a. *áá –   náp*
            I-you-   carry
            'I will carry you' (non-past)
       b. *kɨ-   tá-náp- a*
            He-you   ta-carry-a
            'He carried you' (past)
       c. *tánàp-á   kɨ*
            ta-carry-a you-me
            'Carry me'

In the above analyses, when the verb is a true imperative form, it is taken to be a reflex of the IMP feature, which requires licensing through a feature-checking operation (although auxiliaries escape this requirement, see Zanuttini 1997). The dedicated imperative verb form must move to the complementizer area to check off its IMP feature. In affirmative imperatives, nothing stands in between the verb and that position. In negative imperatives, preverbal negation may target the same position as the true imperative verb, or it may stand as a barrier to movement, while postverbal negation, being not a head but a phrase, does not (Laka 1990; Zanuttini 1991, 1994 and many of the analyses referenced above, which build on these proposals). Alternatively, the imperative verb form is defective and cannot license a tense phrase or a mood phrase (Zanuttini 1996, 1997, Zanuttini and Portner 2003). By contrast, as surrogates do not have an IMP feature, they do not require licensing by the complementizer, and thus need not move (cf. 54b above), or they are not morphologically defective for tense or mood. The licensing of IMP in the complementizer area is presumed not to be an issue if negation can satisfy this requirement (Zanuttini 1997: 7). Many languages have prohibitives with special morphology in the negative element, which, following the same reasoning based on dedicated forms, may be presumed to also bear an IMP feature (but see 2.6.2).

The above analyses have described much cross-linguistic variation in Romance, where dedicated forms tend to require surrogates (52–53), and Germanic, where they tend to be negated (Dutch (56), Polish (57) cf. Zeijlstra 2006: 405–06, exs. 1–2).

(56)   a. *Jij   slaapt   niet.*
           you   sleep   NEG
           'You don't sleep.'
       b. *Slaap!*
           sleep
           'Sleep!'
       c. *Slaap   niet!*
           sleep   NEG
           'Don't sleep!'

(57)   a. *(Ty)   nie   pracujesz.*
           you.2SG   NEG   work.2SG
           'You don't work.'
       b. *Pracuj!*
           work.2SG.IMP
           'Work!'
       c. *Nie   pracuj!*
           NEG   work.2SG.IMP
           'Don't work!'

Various theoretical revisions have been proposed centered around a common mechanism of movement blocking and failed licensing of IMP, in the complementizer or in the true imperative form. By way of illustration, Rivero and Terzi (1995) propose that in Germanic IMP sits in a lower structural position (IP or inflection phrase) where negation cannot block verb movement, while in Romance IMP sits higher than negation (CP) and blocks movement (see Isac and Jakab 2004 on Balkan languages).

All of these analyses share a common view that the negative imperative puzzle is a syntactic phenomenon (Han 2001 is a (partially) semantic view).

Differences in implementation notwithstanding, the theoretical apparatus deployed has evolved into a near consensus: the failure to meet specific licensing requirements. If a final decision on implementation cannot be achieved yet, it is because none of the above options is exempt from empirical lacunas, or from theoretical scrutiny due to the ad hoc set-up of the problematic licensing environments (see van der Wurff 2007b: 57–65 for an appraisal).

2.6.2   New typological data on the negation of imperative clauses

New typological data provides fresh perspectives on the negative imperative puzzle. It relegates surrogation to a less prominent role than was earlier assumed. Surrogation is the least frequent option exercised in the negation of imperatives. According to van der Auwera and Lejeune (2005b) and van der Auwera (2010), the strategies to negate imperative clauses can be reduced to three: prohibitives (auxiliary, particle, affix, lexicalization (Lat. *vŏlo/nōlo* 'to wish'/'not to wish')), negation of the imperative verb, or surrogation. Among these, surrogation is the least frequent (58).

(58)   a. Prohibitive: 327 languages
         b. Negation of the imperative: 113 languages
         c. Surrogation: 55 languages

The last of these (58c) is presented as an areal feature of Western Europe and Western and Central Australia.

There are two new cross-linguistic generalizations relevant to the study of the negation of imperative clauses, which undercut the proposed relation between dedicated imperative verb forms and the need for a special proviso for the negation of the imperative clause on the basis of licensing conditions. The role of a dedicated or true imperative is key in the majority of the above analyses: it is taken as a morphological reflex of IMP. Van der Auwera and Lejeune (2005b) and van der Auwera (2010) report that prohibitive constructions are used to negate not only true imperative forms, but also non-dedicated forms, and in similar proportions: 131 of 236 dedicated forms have prohibitives, and 28 of 78 non-dedicated forms have prohibitives, too.[35] This generalization casts doubt on the correlation between dedicated imperative forms and the impossibility of negating this form ordinarily. If dedication is a morphological reflex of IMP in the verb, licensing IMP does not automatically call for a different strategy for negation. Earlier generative analyses pay careful attention to this variable. They focus on predicting under what conditions true imperatives can be negated. This is termed the negative imperative puzzle. However, it is unexpected that verb forms without IMP would also require special provisos for their negation. This would constitute a second puzzle not yet analyzed (59b).

(59) a. *The true negative imperative puzzle*:
         Dedicated imperative verb forms may not be negated.
      b. *The non-dedicated negative imperative puzzle*:
         Non-dedicated imperative verb forms may not be negated.

The second generalization concerns surrogation in prohibitives. Considering data from the same surveys, 183 of 327 imperative forms that require a prohibitive for their negation are still able to retain the original imperative form.[36] That is, the negation of the imperative may still be different (by the addition of auxiliaries, particles or affixes), but not the imperative verb form itself. This second generalization further disassociates true imperative forms from the negation of imperatives, be that via surrogation, prohibitives or both. In effect, the true negative imperative puzzle is reproduced within prohibitives, where surrogation may also take place.

(59) c. *The true negative imperative puzzle in prohibitives*:
         Dedicated imperative verb forms may be retained in prohibitives.

We do not know at this point whether non-dedicated forms in prohibitives can also keep the same form. If they did, this would give rise to a puzzle parallel to (59c) for non-dedicated forms. These additional puzzles become so if a syntactic solution is needed for split paradigms and a connection is hypothesized with dedicated imperative verb forms.

While the defective approach to imperative verb forms is not affected by these two generalizations, other generalizations that we covered earlier are. Imperatives have tense morphology in many languages, which undermines the proposal by Zanuttini (1996). Although they tend to be interpreted as politeness markers (see Aikhenvald 2010: 142–45), mood-related projections are also proposed for imperatives on account of Balkan languages (Terzi and Rivero 1995; Isac and Jakab 2004; Hill 2010). This also undermines the proposal by Zanuttini (1997), Zanuttini and Portner (2003). If evidentiality is a type of mood (Cinque 1999), there is additional evidence that imperative clauses have mood projections.

It is important to bear in mind that the approaches just mentioned – defective verb forms – are predicated on the theoretical assumption that the negative imperative puzzle responds to syntactic licensing constraints: in this particular case, failure to license the sentential projection selected by clausal negation. This is why imperative verb forms were initially conceived as defective for

tense or mood. If there is no cause for syntax to be responsible for split paradigms, the basis for this theoretical assumption also goes away.

If the affirmative–negative paradigm split does not follow from the syntax
preventing dedicated imperative forms under certain syntactic configurations,
the question remains of what causes said morphological split. The next section
identifies sources of language change that lead to split paradigms, which stand
as alternatives to a syntactic approach.

2.6.3   *Sources for split affirmative–negative paradigms*

Diachronic developments in morphology explain why some prohibitives feature different negative markers. New negative markers arise from strengtheners
via Jespersen's cycle (van der Auwera 2010). The original strengthener may
be reanalyzed as negation (French *pas*, originally 'step'), or be phonologically
reduced with the original negation (Latin *ne oinum* 'one'), *non*; Dutch *niet*,
'not+something'). Consequently, a different negator in imperatives need not
be the morphological reflex of IMP. It is also noteworthy that special negators
themselves need not be dedicated and can be used elsewhere in the language
(e.g., subjunctive clauses: Zeijlstra 2006).

An important aspect to consider in this regard is that prohibitives render the
need for a matrix negative unnecessary, presumably for politeness (cf. van der
Auwera 2010). Some prohibitives are derived from predicative constructions,
from verbs meaning 'stop,' 'abstain,' 'see (to it that),' or a combination of negation and a verb in an auxiliary function, such as 'be unwilling.' The following
sentences illustrate some of these prohibitive constructions: an 'auxiliary' verb
unique to imperatives (60a; Zulu), a prohibitive marker derived from a combination of negation and a (modal) verb, as in the example from Afrikaans (60b; van
der Auwera 2010: 6, ex. 11b; 10, ex. 22a); verbs with negation lexically built in
(e.g., 'not want' or 'be unwilling to': Mandarin Chinese (60c) cf. Chen-Main
2005: 5, ex. 5; Latin (60d) cf. Allen and Greenough 1983: sec. 285, 450, ex. 1).

(60)   a. *musa   uku-ngen-a!*
           PROH.AUX   INF-come-INF
           'Don't come in!'
        b. *moeni   dit   vir   hom   gee   nie!*
           PROH   this   for   him   give   NEG
           'Don't give it to him'
        c. *bu2yao4   dong4!*
           buyao   move
           'Do not move!' / 'Stop moving!'
        d. *noli   putare*
           be.unwilling   suppose.INF
           'do not suppose!' (be unwilling to suppose)

Since the original imperative verb becomes a complement to the prohibitive auxiliary, this can lead to additional differentiation between the affirmative, a root form, and the negative, a dependent form (e.g., an infinitive in (60a,d). This is a major source of paradigmatic splits. Prohibitives are the most frequent form of negated imperatives, and predicative constructions with or without negation built in constitute the bulk of these.

A third source for split paradigms is syntactic, but in the reverse role from what it would be expected to play in the analyses of the negative imperative puzzle. Instead of preventing the negation of particular dedicated (and non-dedicated) forms, it creates environments for certain phonological operations to apply, leading to the introduction of asymmetric paradigms. Basque is a compelling case.

As we saw earlier, Basque imperatives can be infinitives, which may lose their infinitival mark (61), analogously to the loss of thematic vowels in Romance (62).

(61)   *Etor(ri)!*
         come-INF
         'Come!'

(62)   a. *Sal-i-r*
            come.out-THV-INF
            'To come out'
         b. *¡Sal!*
            Come.out.VROOT
            'Come out!'

When expressed with auxiliaries, the affirmative imperative undergoes substantial phonological reduction. For instance, the affirmative imperative below (63a) can be pronounced as *eizu!* or *izu!* (verb + auxiliary) – alternative forms that emerge in informal written registers.

(63)   a. *Egin   ezazu!*
            do.INF   AUX.2SG(E).3SG(A)
            'Do it!'
         a'. *Izu!, Eizu!*

Phonological reduction seems the norm. Other examples include *emadazu* 'give it to me' (cf. *eman iezadazu*), *ikustazu* 'see (it)' (cf. *ikus ezazu*) and countless others.

Negated imperatives (63b), by contrast, have a different word order where the auxiliary is fronted and negation cliticizes on it. Negation and the auxiliary blend in this case as *etzazu* (dissimilation of *ezez* with loss of medial *e* and further dissimilation of *ezz* – the first *z* turns into *t*).

(63)   b. *Ez   ezazu   egin!*
           NEG AUX.2SG(E).3SG(A)   do.INF
           'Don't do it!'
        b'. *Etzazu egin!*

The same phenomenon of phonological reduction applies to hortatives when construed with an overt auxiliary, but crucially not with subjunctives, which have an overt complementizer. The affirmative in (64a) can be reduced to *utzi-dazu* [*let* + aux], whereas the negative (64b) cannot. Negation cliticizes to the auxiliary: *etzadazu*. NB: it may appear that in some examples the verb moves to the position of the auxiliary and picks up its inflection, but synthetic verb forms in Basque are radically different from these and plenty of other forms would not be amenable to this analysis.

(64)   a. *Utz-i   iezadazu   egi-ten!*
           Let-INF   AUX.2PL(E).3SG(A)1SG(D)   do-IMPF
           'Let me do it!'
        a'. *Utzidazu egiten!*
        b. *Ez   iezadazu   egi-ten   utz-i!*
           NEG   AUX.2PL(E).3SG(A)1SG(D)   do-IMPF   let-INF
           'Don't let me do it'.
        b'. *Etzadazu egiten utzi!*

The phonological changes in negative imperatives resemble those in D&I (e.g., *ez zara* [NEG be.2SG] > *etzara* 'you are not'). In contrast to affirmative imperative verb forms, affirmative verbs and auxiliaries in D&I do not undergo phonological reduction (unlike, say, *dizque* [(they.)say.that] 'non-direct evidence' in Latin American Spanish, with finite forms of *ser* '(individual level) be', *haber* 'have' and *estar* '(stage level) be': Kany 1944). This phenomenon is specific to the syntactic configuration of affirmative imperative-hortative clauses in Basque (vs. negated imperatives and affirmative and negated hortatives with subjunctives and explicit complementizers).

If we put aside that French Basque dialects may require surrogates with infinitives and that certain synthetic imperative forms cannot be negated (Hualde and Ortiz de Urbina 2003), from the perspective of the orthographic conventions in force today, Basque would be classified as a language that can negate imperative verbs directly. At some point, writing conventions may catch up with the actual pronunciation of these forms in the spoken language.

All in all, different syntactic configurations seem to lead to different domains for phonological reduction to apply, with the corollary that the affirmative and negative imperative forms can diverge over time – both morphologically and syntactically (synthetic vs. analytical). The syntax can thus feed a paradigmatic change in the morphology. Earlier generative analyses, by contrast, assume that syntactic configurations prevent the licensing of certain paradigmatic forms.[37]

2.6.4   *An alternative morphological account*

Earlier we introduced a generalization concerning negation. Under negation imperatives have fewer grammatical categories, or their values are partly or fully neutralized (Aikhenvald 2010). Coupled with the above set of generalizations, the negative imperative puzzle can be reconceived as a loss of markedness. The verb form itself may not be dedicated under negation. This alternative account makes concrete cross-linguistic predictions and is easily testable.

The morphological account of surrogation can be assessed against the markedness hierarchy of van der Auwera et al. and Aikhenvald. If surrogation is a morphological phenomenon, it will respect this hierarchy. If syntactic, it need not do so. The burden of proof thus lies in finding languages where "true" hortatives can be negated but "true" imperatives cannot. This pattern would reverse the established markedness hierarchy, and a syntactic approach would be necessary to account for the counterexamples. But if languages happen to conform to this hierarchy, the negative imperative puzzle could be reinterpreted as a small part of the third generalization – in itself, part of a broader generalization about markedness under negation (Aikhenvald and Dixon 1998).

If we peruse familiar paradigms considered under the above analyses, focusing on Romance, where surrogation is the norm, the markedness hierarchy is respected. Typically, hortatives are not dedicated and can be negated, while imperatives are dedicated and resist negation: Catalan, Italian (Zanuttini 1997), Mallorquin, Romanian (Diaconescu 1999; Maiden 2006; Hill 2007, 2010), Spanish (Rivero 1994). French imperatives are not dedicated (van der Auwera et al. 2004).

A full example of the compliance with the markedness hierarchy for second person imperatives and third person hortatives is given below for Mallorquin (Romance (65–66) cf. Mónica Marcos-Llinás, p.c.). In the affirmative, imperative verbs have dedicated forms (65a,b), while hortatives feature subjunctives (66a,b). Under negation, imperatives resort to subjunctives as surrogate forms (65a′, b′), while subjunctives can be negated ordinarily (66a′,b′).

(65)   a. *¡Fes-ho!*
            do.IMP.2SG-3SG.ACC.MASC
            'Do it!'

a'. *¡No   ho   facis!*
    NEG   3SG.ACC.MASC   do.SUBJ.2SG
    'Don't do it!'

b. *¡Feis-ho!*
    do.IMP.2SG-3SG.ACC.MASC
    'Do it!' (plural addressee)

b'. *¡No   ho   faceu!*
    NEG   3SG.ACC.MASC   do.SUBJ.2PL
    'Don't do it!' (plural addressee)

(66) a. *¡Que   ho   faci!*
    COMP   3SG.ACC.MASC   do.SUBJ.3SG
    'Let him/her do it!'

a'. *¡Que   no   ho   faci!*
    COMP   NEG   3SG.ACC.MASC   do.SUBJ.3SG
    'Don't let him/her do it!'

b. *¡Que   ho   faceu!*
    COMP   3SG.ACC.MASC   do.SUBJ.3PL
    'Let them do it!'

b'. *¡Que   no   ho   faceu!*
    COMP   NEG   3SG.ACC.MASC   do.SUBJ.3SG
    'Don't let them do it!'

The Romance family is a representative area of surrogation. Within generative linguistics, and with particular reference to this phenomenon, its prominence lies in that fact that the scholarship dedicated to solving the negative imperative puzzle has focused on this family. To our knowledge, Australian languages have not been considered. Since Romance appears to respect the markedness hierarchy, the burden of proof for now lies in future syntactic analyses to find reversals in markedness. Future research on the other geographical area of surrogation, the languages of Western and Central Australia, and additional languages that need to resort to surrogation, will likely determine whether a syntactic approach is viable. The list of 55 languages can be found at this address: http://wals.info/feature/71A. Unfortunately, there seems to be no information available at this point about the negation of hortatives in this resource. But even in the event that a few exceptions were found, a syntactic approach to surrogation would have to be overhauled, since the analyses would have to be emancipated from the idea of so-called true imperative forms – the underlying basis common to all syntactic analyses.

2.7   Conclusion

Far from introducing further complexities in the analysis of the imperative clause, the typological evidence demonstrates uniformity and cohesiveness in the imperative type across languages. The revised empirical base presents the imperative clause and imperative verb forms not as a collection of random facts and language-specific quandaries, but rather as a uniform set of grammatical properties, morphosyntactic and semantic, which are clearly identifiable from one language to the next. From a theoretical standpoint, this represents a sharp turn from a majority of exceptionalist analyses, predicated on the received empirical base, to analyses that must seek the inclusion of the imperative clause as part of core grammar.

It seems fair to remark, in hindsight, that research on the negation of imperative clauses in generative grammar may have been "hugging the computational-syntactic ground too closely," while the logic of negative incompatibility, as a conceptual necessity, was casually overlooked (see Chapter 4.2.6.1 for an LPH assessment and references therein).

The next chapter lays the foundations for an inclusive analysis of the imperative clause within Minimalism based on the representation of a syntax–pragmatics interface.

3 *Foundations for an analysis of the imperative clause*

3.0   Chapter overview

The first part of this chapter introduces the philosophy of the minimalist program and justifies the relevance of the study of imperatives for the development of syntactic theory. In light of the recurrent morphosyntactic and semantic characteristics of the imperative type (see Chapter 2), it is fitting to pursue an analysis within a philosophy that entertains an innatist view of grammar. This is the aim of the minimalist program for linguistic theory (Chomsky 1995–2008). It's worth underscoring that "minimalism" is not a *theory* of language but a *program* for linguistic research.[1] Minimalism is not unlike the philosopher's Ockham's razor principle (or the Latin *lex parsimoniae*): when considering competing hypotheses, the principle selects the one that eliminates questionable explanations, makes fewest assumptions (economy) with shorter derivations (parsimony) beyond virtual conceptual and empirical necessity. With respect to imperative clauses, conceptual and empirical necessity concerns an account of the unique properties introduced in Chapter 1 (1.1.1) within a conceptual perspective of syntax.

The second part argues for the need to represent indexicality in the syntax beyond the imperative clause. In Chapter 4, we propose a predicate-argument relation between syntax and the context of utterance as a means to capture the universal restriction that the subject of imperatives be the addressee and other unique properties of the imperative clause. To this end, it becomes necessary to consider an extension of syntactic theory to include what Speas and Tenny (2003; see also Baker 2008; Giorgi 2010) have referred to as a syntax–pragmatics interface. Since our subject of study is the imperative clause, we are mostly concerned with the representation of indexicality in the syntax, but our review of earlier work will show that indexicality may be only part of several "pragmatic" notions to be encoded (such as point of view or perspective in logophoricity). This chapter thus lays the foundations for a minimalist analysis of the imperative clause based on a syntax–pragmatics interface.

The current chapter opens with a brief overview and discussion of the minimalist program (3.1). One of the guiding principles of minimalism is the strong minimalist thesis (SMT), a reductionist heuristic that seeks to eliminate complexity and isolationism in linguistic analysis. The study of imperatives is timely and relevant for the development of the minimalist program, including an assessment of SMT (3.1.1). The unique characteristics of the imperative clause (Chapter 1) constitute a direct challenge for the viability of SMT. Two important developments allow approaching the imperative clause from a minimalist perspective, nonetheless. The first (3.1.2) is a *revised empirical base* (cf. Chapter 2), which sets the imperative clause as a core grammatical phenomenon on a par with D&I. The revised empirical base grants structural and morphological complexity to the imperative clause and imperative verb forms. Because imperatives can be deemed structurally closer to D&I, this reduces the need for exceptional provisos in the syntactic analysis of imperatives.

The second development is theoretical, namely novel proposals to represent a syntax–pragmatics interface (3.2). In philosophy of language, following Kaplan (1977/89), the context of utterance consists of the speaker, addressee, time, place and world of the utterance, a set of indexical (or directly referential) elements. Speas and Tenny (2003), Bianchi (2003) and Sigurðsson (2004) propose to represent said context in the left periphery of syntactic structure. Sigurðsson proposes a compositional representation of indexical elements, namely Logophoric Agent (speaker), Logophoric Patient (addressee), Time of the event and Location of the event. In keeping with the SMT, Sigurðsson proposes that all clauses feature a context of utterance or a reported context. On the other hand, Bianchi proposes that (root) finite clauses feature a Logophoric Centre with a similar set of elements, but restricts the presence of a reported context to a subset of dependent clauses. In contrast to Sigurðsson and Bianchi, Speas and Tenny propose a verbal representation of the context. We present Speas and Tenny's proposal after the discussion of logophoricity and conjunct-disjunct systems (3.3) to explain more clearly the role of a third pragmatic argument in their theory that relates to the notion of point of view.

The next section (3.3) expands on a subset of the diverse phenomena adduced as supporting arguments for representing the context: indexical shift (Schlenker 1999, 2003), logophoricity (Hagège 1974; Clements 1975) and conjunct-disjunct person-marking systems (Hale 1980; DeLancey 1986, 1992). Indexical shift shows that, under propositional attitude verbs, indexical elements can be interpreted relative to a context of utterance or a reported context. In turn, logophoricity demonstrates that a certain class of pronouns can only be interpreted in a reported context. These phenomena illustrate structure-sensitive interpretation and/or syntactic distribution of indexicals and, as a result, constitute empirical grounds for the syntactic representation of the utterance/reported context.

Speas and Tenny's (2003) representation of the context (3.4) focuses on the pragmatic roles *speaker, hearer* and *seat of knowledge*. They propose that the projection Force Phrase (Rizzi 1997) or Speech Act Mood Phrase (Cinque 1999) is verb-like, introducing the *speaker* as its subject, a complement clause as its object and the *hearer* as its dative. This is reminiscent of the performative hypothesis (Ross 1970), which proposes underlying deep syntactic structure representations that type the sentence (e.g., "[I order you to] go!"). Speas and Tenny utilize the representation of the context to derive basic sentence types by the different type of complements Speech Act Mood Phrase selects. They also include a certain passive operation (dative shift, Larson 1988) that determines whether the speaker or the hearer controls the reference of the third pragmatic argument. The combination of these two parameters yields basic sentence types in their system. We provide a discussion of Speas and Tenny's proposal.

This chapter ends with a summary (3.5).

3.1   The minimalist program

The linguistic expressions are the optimal representation of the interface conditions, where 'optimality' is determined by the economy conditions of UG [universal grammar]. Let us take these assumptions to be part of the minimalist program (Chomsky 1995: 171; see pp. 168–71).

(a)   "Languages are based on simple principles that interact to form often intricate structures and ... the language faculty is non-redundant, in that particular phenomena are not 'overdetermined' by principles of language." (p. 169)

(b)   "The language is embedded in performance systems that enable its expressions to be used for articulating, interpreting, referring, inquiring, reflecting and other actions." (p. 169)

(c)   "The performance systems appear to fall into two general types: articulatory-perception and conceptual-intentional. If so, a linguistic expression contains instructions for each of these systems. Two of the linguistic levels, then, are the *interface levels* A-P and C-I providing the instructions for the articulatory-perceptual and conceptual-intentional systems, respectively." (p. 169)

(d)   "Each language determines a set of pairs drawn from the A-P and C-I levels." (p. 169)

Imperatives across languages share syntactic, morphological and semantic properties that are both homogeneous and consistent. Thus the imperative class of linguistic expressions (cf. (d) above) is a well-defined type. The universal character of the imperative clause makes it a suitable target for analysis under an innatist view. Accordingly, the revised empirical base invites new theoretical perspectives to the analysis of the imperative clause. These coordinates provide a new orientation that curtails earlier exceptionalist or isolationist accounts in that the unique characteristics of the imperative clause were treated as unrelated to grammatical properties.

The theoretical tool we have chosen to analyze the syntax of imperatives is hosted within the school of generative linguistics. It is the minimalist program for linguistic theory (Chomsky 1995–2008). As in Government and Binding Theory, the minimalist program is predicated on an innatist view (initially inspired by a (Cartesian) philosophical idea and now by the "Evo Devo revolution" in biology (Chomsky 2010) and the biolinguistic enterprise (Di Sciullo and Boeckx 2011).

For children to learn a language presumably requires extensive trial-and-error experience and feedback. Yet most linguistic guesses that children make during the acquisition process are right and parental or caregiver feedback is limited. When provided, feedback may be ignored at an early age. In spite of salient surface differences across languages, substantive language universals continue to be found that bring world languages closer together. Thus the inherited goal of minimalism is to characterize the core grammar underlying the faculty of language and the parameters that govern cross-linguistic variation. Language is conceived as a highly constrained computational system that forms linguistic expressions to be interpreted by the articulatory-perceptual (AP) system and the conceptual-intentional (CI) system.

Minimalism (see above) is articulated on two fundamental ideas. First, minimalism is a reductionist research program that seeks to trim down the theoretical complexity of earlier models, with a greater emphasis on economy and simplicity. It is important to note that said emphasis is also found in the previous four decades of earlier generative work (see Freidin and Lasnik 2011 for enlightening parallelisms), but in minimalism economy and simplicity take a central role. Second, minimalism is concerned with how the language faculty interacts with and integrates within the cognitive system (Faculty of Language Broad (FLB)) and what is unique to the faculty of language (Faculty of Language Narrow (FLN); recursion cf. Hauser, Chomsky and Fitch 2002, 2010). Language is viewed as an optimal or perfect solution to pair sound and meaning. This way language is seen to respond in its design to external requirements to interface with these interpretive systems.

As a heuristic for an integrated cognitive theory of language, minimalism asks to what extent received lines of research can be reinterpreted not as manifesting strictly linguistic phenomena but as reflecting instead interface requirements that language must meet. It also posits the related question of which aspects of grammar are linguistics proper and which are shared with the overall cognitive architecture of the brain. Both of these questions are as relevant as they are abstract and difficult to address within current linguistic methodology. The first is directly relevant to the study of the imperative clause, where the dividing line between core grammar and the pragmatic interface is blurred in the requirement that the grammatical subject of the imperative verb be the addressee. Hence, research into the imperative clause is research into the frontiers between core grammar and the interfaces.

With regard to the first question, the degree to which new and received lines of research in linguistics are amenable to minimalist reanalysis is a matter that has inspired much debate (see the collection of papers in Hornstein, Nunes and Grohmann 2005; Sauerland and Gärtner 2007; and specially Boeckx 2011 for a timely overview and discussion of the minimalist program). There are areas where the minimalist program has improved or developed earlier lines of inquiry, or where it has contributed novel ideas. Some of these areas include predicate-argument structure and thematic relations – the little v hypothesis (Harley 2011); the plausible reduction of referential dependencies – binding and control – to movement or agreement (Drummond, Kush and Hornstein 2011); greater parallelism between syntax and semantics – merge and functional application (Ramchand 2011); and the plausible decomposition of clause formation into cycles to meet memory limitations (Uriagereka 2011).[2]

Methodologically speaking, and still with reference to the first question, in minimalism the boundaries at the interface are fuzzy. There may be a built-in bias toward delaying or ostracizing the analysis of more challenging data, particularly when grammatical principles seem insufficient or yield inconsistent results. In this respect, Drummond, Kush and Hornstein (2011) reflect on their methodological decision to pursue an analysis of referential dependencies as a syntactic phenomenon instead of delegating it to the interfaces:[3]

> There was a second motivation behind the early resistance against banishing construal to the interface hinterlands. It stems from our present epistemological position with respect to our understanding of the properties of grammar versus those of the interfaces. We understand the first far better than we do the second. As such, treating construal as consequences of interface operations functions to weaken our theoretical obligations. All things being equal, grammatical proposals are easier to evaluate, develop and understand than those based on interface principles and properties that we have barely

begun to develop. Methodologically, then, treating phenomena in terms of the grammar – especially those that have grammatical fingerprints all over them – is the right way to go. (p. 398)

The second question presents an ambitious and difficult task. For argument's sake, consider the study of Earth's oceans. Oceanographers describe the cresting of waves as a speed differential. The water at the bottom slows down as it approaches the coast, while the water on the surface maintains its speed. This provides a satisfactory explanation of this natural phenomenon. We can adopt a more ambitious perspective on wave cresting and ask why bodies of water move in the first place, and why they do so in certain time intervals and predictable directions. Part of the answer to this question lies in the gravitational force that the moon exerts on our planet and in the temperature changes caused by the geological activity of the planet. It is doubtful that oceanographers could deduce the existence of gravitational fields and geological activity from wave cresting. This does not deny the fact that, ultimately, wave cresting is a response to these factors. Once these facts are discovered, connections can be drawn and dependency relations established. Under the new minimalist emphasis, linguists are called upon to consider the broader implications of their research for neuroscience, but this for now we must do relying on traditional linguistic methods or converging with other closely related human science for scientific validation of the field.

The question of the role of language in the human sciences is intimately related to the emergence of language in our species and the role it may have played in its evolution. In the biolinguistic enterprise the emergence of language is presumed to have come about as a genetic change ("rewiring of the brain," Chomsky 2010: 59) or adaptation (Pinker and Jackendoff 2005). Language is considered by Chomsky to be a perfect solution (or compromise) to interface with preexisting cognitive systems (Hauser, Chomsky and Fitch 2002; see the collection of papers in Larson, Déprez and Yamakido 2010; Di Sciullo and Boeckx 2011). Under these diverging hypotheses of the biological origin of language there is a necessarily speculative disagreement over its origin as a single catastrophic mutation vs. adaptive co-evolution of language and the brain (Deacon 1997; Dessalles 2007, 2010).[4]

The minimalist program has greatly succeeded in reducing theoretical overheads. As Freidin and Lasnik (2011: 4) put it: "as a guide for research on linguistic theory the MP [minimalist program] continues to have an important heuristic and therapeutic effect on hypothesis formation in linguistic analyses (fn. 10: And, in particular, by prohibiting analyses that merely mirror the complexity of the data.)" The debate between what belongs to the interfaces and what to the core grammar has in some respects taken an unexpected turn. Rather than attributing more and more linguistic properties to external pressures, more and more linguists claim for syntactic structure a wealth of pragmatic information about the interpretation of utterances (i.e., the cartographic approach of Rizzi 1997; Cinque 1999 and subsequent work; see 3.2). Along with other colleagues who propose this alternative view, our own account of imperative syntax claims the indexical properties of the context of utterance as a syntactic domain (Chapter 4). While under minimalism syntax has become simpler, its scope has grown considerably compared to Government and Binding Theory, with the addition of new, empirically warranted projections, and the reanalysis of some interface properties as rooted in syntactic structure.

3.1.1   *Toward a minimalist analysis of the imperative clause*

As a test case, the syntax of imperatives has a substantial theoretical value in the assessment of the SMT (Chomsky 2008), a guiding principle in the interpretation of minimalism as a reductionist methodological heuristic. The syntax of imperatives presents a challenging case to this tenet of the minimalist program. The imperative clause displays a number of unique properties that undermine a generalized structure-building process. As noted, unlike D&I, an imperative can rarely function as a dependent clause outside certain well-identified cases (2.4.1). This introduces an asymmetry with respect to other clause types, in that D&I clauses can function as a complement to a verb.

A representative example of the revisionist pressure of the SMT is the formation of verbs or auxiliaries by head movement. Head movement is, from a minimalist perspective, under suspicion as a potential articulatory phenomenon. If the creation of inflected verbs is syntactic, the merge operation needs to be enriched with internal merge, leading to two distinct operations: external merge and internal merge. This incurs a higher computational complexity in the basic structure-building mechanism. In its theoretical appeal, a single merge operation simplifies the computational system. It could also afford the aforementioned parallelism with the semantic operation of functional application. On the other hand, phonology, too, has been argued to possess displacement operations (metathesis, local dislocation: Harris and Halle 2005). A computational asymmetry could potentially be introduced one way or another.

Other unique characteristics of imperative clauses include reduced or nonexistent tense, person and number paradigms, compared to D&I in the same language. Perhaps the most conspicuous of these characteristics is the relevance of context in syntactic structure; namely, the requirement that the grammatical subject of the imperative clause be the addressee. As an amalgam of diverging morphosyntactic characteristics, imperative clauses should fall outside the study of core grammar. To consider imperative clauses taxes the SMT with a host of accommodating assumptions, specifically tailored to the integration of this unique sentence type. This is illustrated, for example, in Jensen (2004a) and Zanuttini's (2008) syntactic approach to the second person restriction in the subject of imperatives. These analyses share with our own the intuition that the imperative clause must be amenable to principled syntactic analysis. But they introduce a projection exclusive to imperatives – Zanuttini's JussiveP, and additional functionality of Tense that is only required in the imperative clause – Jensen. Both accounts constitute a departure from the SMT perspective.

3.1.2   *The SMT and the revised empirical base*
In spite of their divergent properties, it seems inescapable that imperatives need to be integrated within UG. As vindicated in the previous chapter, the available surveys on sentence types (Sadock and Zwicky 1985; König and Siemund 2007) present the imperative clause as part of a triad of core sentence types, alongside D&I. The recent surveys on imperatives (Xrakovskij 2001; van der Auwera and Lejeune 2005a, 2005b; van der Auwera 2010; van der Auwera et al. 2004; Aikhenvald 2010) attest to the uniform syntactic, morphological and semantic characteristics of imperative clauses, most of them being universal or near universal. The revised empirical base reinstates morphological complexity to the imperative clause and imperative verb forms (2.3), which brings this type closer to D&I. These regular and recurring grammatical properties, coupled with the prominent role that is attributed to imperatives in the acquisition of propositional language by children (Salustri and Hyams 2006; Aikhenvald 2010 and references therein), suggest treating imperatives as a product of core grammar. From an evolutionary perspective, too, as noted at the end of our introductory chapter, the imperative type could arguably have been a stepping-stone into propositional language. Imperatives then add to a set of research inquiries, like case theory or head movement, which, pending ongoing research and insights arising from it, appear to be neither readily amenable to minimalist reanalysis/reduction, nor imposed from above – the interfaces; yet they are necessary and integral to any innatist theory of language.

While the revised empirical base is an important step towards a unified treatment of basic sentence types, there remains a defining characteristic of imperative clauses that appears to be non-grammatical. Imperatives are to be understood as unique clauses in that they meet at least one external condition: the requirement that the subject be the addressee. After all, in this area imperatives introduce a unique asymmetry compared to other known clause types.[5] From a minimalist perspective, this may be interpreted as syntax requiring access to the CI interface. Otherwise, it is not clear how linguistic research on imperatives could proceed from here. It would be a return to the concession that certain syntactic properties of the imperative clause are irreducible.

Novel theoretical developments also provide fresh perspectives for the examination and interpretation of the revised empirical base. Three recent proposals advocate a syntax–pragmatics interface. We introduce two of these proposals next. Representing the context of utterance in the syntax will enable us to pursue a novel syntactic account of the imperative clause (Chapter 4), one where its indexical and morphological properties follow not from specific deficiencies or unique characteristics, the predominant view in the earlier literature (van der Wurff 2007b), but from general properties of grammar. This analysis will be compliant with the SMT.

3.2   Encoding the context of utterance in syntax

For Kaplan (1977/89), the context of utterance consists of the speaker, addressee, time, place and world of the utterance, a set of indexical (or directly referential) elements.[6] Indexicals (e.g., *I*, *you*, *here*, *now*) play a prominent role in the study of reference. Indexicals must be anchored to refer to the context of utterance.[7] Definite expressions, by contrast, cannot usually refer to first and second person. Only under extraordinary circumstances can definite expressions refer to first and second person (see 3.3).

Speas and Tenny (2003), Bianchi (2003) and Sigurðsson (2004) advance new theoretical proposals to represent indexicality in syntax to various degrees. Sigurðsson and Bianchi entertain a full representation, while Speas and Tenny focus on the pragmatic roles of *speaker*, *hearer* and *seat of knowledge*. These proposals continue a trend that incorporates in the syntax projections related to pragmatic aspects about the interpretation of language. This trend is most apparent in the cartographic approach (Cinque 1999 and subsequent work), which includes, among others, projections related to information structure, such as new and old information (topic and focus, Rizzi 1997), and the speaker's source of information (evidentiality, Speas 2004). Importantly, this set of projections also includes Force (Rizzi 1997) or Speech Act Mood (Cinque 1999).

The four authors adopt the view that indexical information should be encoded in clause structure, a novel move in contemporary mainstream syntax (see, however, Rizzi 2004).

(3)   "Features of the speech act event are not outside clausal structure as usually assumed. They are crucially syntactic, I claim, and we must revise our ideas accordingly. There has been a strong trend in linguistics since the 1970s to escape this conclusion." (Sigurðsson 2004: 10)

b.   "The pragmatic force of a sentence and the pragmatic roles of discourse participants have traditionally been considered to be peripheral to the syntactic component of Grammar ... the idea that syntax encodes extensive pragmatic information was rejected as being too unconstrained in the 1970s ... We will argue that basic syntactic principles constrain projections of pragmatic force as well as the inventory of grammatically relevant pragmatic roles." (Speas and Tenny 2003: 1)"The proposal we will make differs from the traditional view in the philosophy of language, in which the asymmetric structure of the sentence is opaque to the principles that determine the pragmatics of the sentence." (Speas and Tenny 2003: 3)

c.   "(3) The syntactic property of finiteness encodes the logophoric anchoring of the clause.
        ...
        "(4) Every clause is anchored to a Logophoric Centre: a speech or mental event, with its own participants and temporal coordinates, which constitutes the centre of deixis." (Bianchi 2003: 3)[8]

It is noteworthy that around the same period Chomsky comments in a footnote on the possibility of reinstating a version of Ross's performative hypothesis. The comment is motivated by the Spell-Out of phases, in particular, by the Spell-Out of root clauses or CPs: "This requirement could reduce to Spell-Out of sister of the head if we adopt some variant of Ross's phonologically empty performative analysis (Nissenbaum, personal communication)" (Chomsky 2004: 108, fn. 17 on p. 125).

We begin by discussing Sigurðsson's and Bianchi's proposals. Sigurðsson and Bianchi developed their proposals aware of each other's work (Sigurðsson 2004: 1; acknowledgements). Both propose that person features are interpreted in relation to a context of utterance, parallel to the interpretation of tense being dependent on speech time (Reichenbach 1947). Sigurðsson and Bianchi develop a full representation of the context as a syntactic domain. They approach finiteness from a syntactico-pragmatic perspective. Presentation and discussion of their proposals will take the rest of this section.

3.2.1   Sigurðsson (2004)

We begin by discussing Sigurðsson's proposal. For Sigurðsson, the context of utterance does not include, strictly speaking, the speaker or the addressee of the speech act itself, but rather the "active vs. passive participants of speech ...

the local LOGOPHORIC AGENT VS. LOGOPHORIC PATIENT" (p. 9). Sigurðsson offers a declarative and direct speech as evidence that the constant meaning of first and second person pronouns is logophoric (1: ex. 10, p. 9).[9]

(1)   a. **I** love **you**.
          1SG = the speaker = LOGOPHORIC AGENT (& also the 'loving one')
          2SG = the addressee = LOGOPHORIC PATIENT (& also the 'loved one')
        b. John said to me: '**I** love **you**.'
          1SG = John = LOGOPHORIC AGENT (& also the 'loving one')
          2SG = the speaker = LOGOPHORIC PATIENT (& also the 'loved one')

Sigurðsson notes in a footnote (16, p. 9) that *speaker* and *addressee* can still be preserved as technical terms if enriched with labels such as "primary" vs. "secondary" or "basic" vs. "derived."

Sigurðsson proposes to conceive logophoricity as a feature analogous to theta-features (argument roles in predicate-argument relations; agent, theme) and phi-features (person, number and gender). He further assumes that phi-features are interpreted with respect to theta-features and that logophoric features are, in turn, interpreted against phi-features.

In addition to the logophoric agent (Λ_A) and patient (Λ_P) roles, Sigurðsson proposes that there are also projections headed by speech time (S_T) and speech location (S_L). Above all these, ForceP would close off clause structure (see the bracketed representation in (2): p. 29, ex. 52).[10]

(2) $[_{CP}$ Force ... Λ_A ... Λ_P ... S_T ... S_L **[IP ...** Pers ... T ... **[vP ...** θ ... E_T ...]]]

A partial explanation of (2) is given:

> I make the minimal assumption that [the syntactic speech event] contains
> the time and location of speech, S_T, S_L respectively, and the inherent speech
> participants, that is, the logophoric agent and patient, Λ_A and Λ_P. By distin-
> guishing between Speech Time, S_T, and Speech Location, S_L, I am taking
> an anti-localist view of temporal deixis. In addition, I assume that S_L is the
> Fin feature of Rizzi (1997) and Platzack and Rosengren (1998), i.e., the
> 'high' EPP feature that is matched by +/- SPEECH LOCAL (+/-S_L) elem-
> ents, canonically +S_L subjects or –S_L expletives, whereas S_T is matched by
> T(ense), attracting it in V1/V2 environments. (p. 11)

According to Sigurðsson, the formation of expletives appears to be systematically based on speech distant location (English *there*) or speech distal argument (French *il*) rather than speech distal time (see discussion of Icelandic *Það*
'there, it'; pp. 15–17). If typologically confirmed, this would be a compelling
argument to separate speech time from speech location, and to establish a relative ordering between these two projections.

As supporting evidence, Sigurðsson additionally discusses logophoricity (see n.8), indexical shift, long-distance anaphora, the person case constraint, and double access readings. In order to expedite the narrative and avoid redundancy, we define a proper subset of these and other phenomena in the next section, where we illustrate them with examples, and discuss their relevance as supporting arguments. The three papers converge to a degree on the argumentation and phenomena adduced. We now proceed to provide a concise discussion of Sigurðsson's proposal.

3.2.1.1 Discussion

Sigurðsson's contribution is a preliminary investigation into the representation of the context of utterance in the syntax that appeals to minimalist goals.[11] His proposed theory adheres to the SMT since the structure generalizes to all root and subordinate clauses. This way, he helps bring attention to the paradigmatic shift necessary to pursue further investigation of indexical phenomena in the syntax. His article brings forward diverse supporting arguments, which seem to make the case for such a shift.

With particular reference to the proposed syntactic representation, it is intuitively appealing that the logophoric agent occupies a higher position than the logophoric patient, but it is not obvious why the opposite order could not hold. The global and local speech act participants seem to be thematic roles, but they do not participate in a predicate-argument relation. The local speech act participants may be construed as arguments to propositional attitude verbs in some dependent clauses (e.g., speech predicates in logophoric clauses). A more verbal representation of the context of utterance, like the one offered by Speas and Tenny (3.4), or our own LPH (Chapter 4) would complement Sigurðsson's proposal by providing a predicate.

Sigurðsson provides a plausible ordering of logophoric agent > logophoric patient > speech time > speech location on account of said pattern in the formation of expletive pronouns and the assumption that speech act participants sit higher in structure. Further probing into relative orderings could be effected by examining the positional restrictions of (inflected) vocatives (Hill 2007) relative to pleonastic pronouns. A priori, the more peripheral position of vocatives relative to expletives (for example, "John, there is extra paper in the storage room") would serve as preliminary confirmatory evidence of Sigurðsson's claim.

Although Sigurðsson makes an argument to separate speech time from speech location, it is important to note that the deictic center of these elements can be the speaker, the addressee or both. In Catalan (Romance), for example, a speech location element such as "here" can be interpreted as 'next to addressee', that is, 'here (relative to the addressee)' (Klee and Lynch 2009). Since this use is possible over the phone, the addressee need not be physically present in the speech location. Furthermore, there are special cases where the location and time of the speech event are displaced (as in recorded messages: "I am not here right now," Recanati 2004). In such cases it is the temporal location of the addressee that serves as a reference point, while the spatial location refers to the position that the speaker occupied in space at the time of the recording. Future work building on Sigurðsson's proposal needs to take into account that the interpretation of speech time and speech location can be relative to the time and/or location of the addressee. This would be, in essence, an extension of Sigurðsson's compositional approach to deixis.[12]

3.2.2   Bianchi (2003)

We now transition to a succinct overview of Bianchi's proposal. On her part, Bianchi specifically relates her proposal to "finiteness," understood as the ability (i) to license a referentially independent subject and (ii) to have an absolute tense interpretation anchored to speech time (pp. 1–2). Bianchi proposes an alternative theory of the licensing of independently referential subjects based not on nominative case licensing, which, she argues, is not sensitive to finiteness, but to person licensing, which apparently is (see pp. 4–8 for details).

Bianchi coins the term "Logophoric Centre" for what we are referring to as context of utterance.[13] She defines the Logophoric Centre[14] as follows (3–4, Bianchi 2003: 11, exs. 26–27):

(3)   A Logophoric Centre is a speech or mental event which comprises
        (i) an obligatory animate participant (Speaker/Source)
        (ii) an optional Addressee (for speech events)
        (iii) a temporal coordinate
        (iv) possibly spatial coordinates (for physical events)
        and is associated with a Cognitive State of the participant(s) in which the proposition expressed by the clause must be integrated.

(4)   The external Logophoric Centre (eLC) is the external speech event.
        Finite clauses encode the eLC in [+finite] Fin^0, which is an anchor for
        (i) person agreement
        (ii) absolute and absolute/relative tense (in the sense of Comrie 1985a)

As parallel data, Bianchi offers the case of logophoric pronouns and indexical shift. She goes on to analyze certain cases of obligatory control (following Borer 1989; Landau 2000) as also requiring a logophoric center represented in dependent clauses, which are deemed to be [–finite]. Logophoric centers are thus postulated for finite (indicative) clauses, and certain control clauses.

We illustrate Bianchi's supporting phenomena with examples in the next section (3.3). What Bianchi means by "cognitive state" or "source" may be brought under the umbrella of point of view, which is discussed further in later sections: logophoric pronouns (3.3.2), conjunct-disjunct systems (3.3.3) and Speas and Tenny's proposal (3.4).

3.2.2.1   Discussion
Bianchi's contribution also aims to steer syntactic research in the direction of indexical phenomena. While her article does not cover nearly as many different phenomena as Sigurðsson's, Bianchi provides very detailed argumentation for the necessary conceptual relationship between licensing independently refer-ential subjects and independent tense, and the logophoric center. This depth of argumentation will eventually need to be developed for the various phenom-ena that these four authors touch upon as supportive arguments. We follow Bianchi's lead and concentrate on three such phenomena in the current chapter and dedicate a chapter to the discussion of Basque allocutives. Additionally, Bianchi's approach to representing the context of utterance is more focused on the prominence of the speaker or sentient entity whose point of view is reported. She banks on taxonomies of logophoricity (Hyman and Comrie 1981; Sells 1987; Culy 1994), which focus more on the source/subject than the addressee, the latter being comparatively less attested (Culy 1997). A more extensive look at supporting phenomena, poignantly inflected/verbal vocatives (Hill 2007), Basque allocutive agreement (Chapter 5), and imperative clauses, warrants inclusion of the addressee in Bianchi's logophoric center.[15]

3.3   Supporting phenomena for representing indexicality in syntax

This section illustrates and discusses three indexical phenomena: indexical shift (3.3.1), logophoricity (3.3.2) and conjunct-disjunct person-marking systems (3.3.3). For their elucidation, these phenomena seem to require the syntactic representation of a reported context of utterance under propositional attitude verbs and/or a context of utterance in root clauses. For convenience, we refer to the root context of utterance as *utterance context* and to the reported context of utterance as *reported context*.

The above-mentioned phenomena belong to a more extensive set of data that suggests that indexical elements constitute part of syntactic structure.[16] Additional supporting arguments, which we will not discuss due to space limitations, include long-distance anaphora, evidential and evaluative adverbs, epithets, free indirect discourse, switch-reference systems, the person case constraint and indexical verbs. The reader is referred to Speas and Tenny (2003), Bianchi (2003), Sigurðsson (2004) and references therein. If we are correct in analyzing the imperative clause as a predicate-argument relation with the utterance context, the imperative clause is arguably the most significant of these phenomena by virtue of being a universal clause type. Taken together, the above-mentioned phenomena suggest that postulation of a syntax–pragmatics interface is a conceptual necessity and is thus in keeping with the SMT. With particular reference to imperatives, the representation of a syntax–pragmatics interface opens up new theoretical possibilities, previously unexplored, in a syntactic account of the imperative type.

It has been called to our attention that most of these structural domains impose de se readings, or self-ascription, in the relevant pragmatic contexts (see Chierchia 1989; Anand 2006, 2009). As an example of unintended self-ascription, consider the following example from Chierchia. Pavarotti is watching a concert of himself on television. He is impressed with the performance, but fails to realize that he himself is the performer. For a definite description to refer to a first person requires absence of knowledge that such definite description actually refers to the self. In Italian, the sentence equivalent to the English "Pavarotti believes that he/the man on TV is a genius" is compatible with a pragmatic context of self-ascription (de se) or with an unintended reference to self (de re). As it turns out, a number of structural domains are sensitive to this distinction in that they impose de se readings. For example, in Italian the sentence "Pavarotti believes him[self] to be a genius," with a non-finite dependent clause, must be interpreted as self-ascription. This suggests that de se is syntactically encoded.

A most intriguing fact is that the trail of de-se-only structural domains runs rather parallel to the supporting arguments for the representation of the utterance/reported context in syntax (see Anand 2006, 2009). Tenny (2006: 265) comments that in time a syntactic articulation of de-se-only environments may be possible in relation to syntactic projections that conform to the context of utterance, in particular Speech Act Mood Phrase (which introduces the speaker; Speas and Tenny 2003, 3.4).

3.3.1   Indexical shift

This section opens with a succinct background to the expected behavior of indexical elements in syntax, and the emergence of data from less-studied languages where the evaluation of indexicals can shift from the utterance context to a reported context. After defining the phenomenon of indexical shift, close attention is paid to cross-linguistic variation in its manifestation, for it is supportive of a compositional approach to the syntax of indexicality (à la Sigurðsson 2004).

3.3.1.1 Indexicals

Earlier we mentioned that Kaplan (1979) introduced the context of utterance as a means to capture the directly referential nature of first and second person pronouns and temporal and locative pronouns. At the time Kaplan made his proposals all available data pointed to indexical pronouns as indifferent to the syntactic configuration in which they occurred. He thus placed the mechanism of direct reference after syntax:

> The problem is that on my analysis, the mechanism of direct reference operates *before* the familiar semantical notions of truth and denotation come into play ... The mechanisms of direct reference certainly are not *post*semantical. But equally surely they are not syntactical. (Kaplan 1989: 575–76; abridged from Bianchi 2010: 2; emphasis in the original)

Indeed, regardless of the position of the indexical pronoun, the context of interpretation is, invariably, the utterance context. For example, consider the interpretation of "I" in a root declarative clause (5a), a relative clause (5b), an adjunct clause (5c), and in indirect discourse (5d). In all instances, "I" means the "speaker of the utterance context."[17]

(5)   a. I am visiting with my parents this summer.
         b. The former employee that I saw at IBM was Mary.
         c. When I left, Mary was still working.
         d. Mary said that I am too easy with my daughter.

There appears to be only one exception. In direct discourse (5e), "I" means "speaker of the reported context"; in this particular case, "Mary."[18]

(5)   e. Mary$_i$ said: "I$_i$ am too easy with my daughter."

Hence, outside direct discourse, all indexicals must be interpreted relative to the context of utterance (cf. 5a–d).

Kaplan (1979) postulates that there is no operator in natural language that can overwrite the context indexes. This hypothetical operator is dubbed the monster operator. Over time, new data has started to emerge from languages whose indexical pronouns can be interpreted in a reported context. The syntactic domain where this is possible is rather restricted. It occurs primarily in indirect discourse, in the complement clause of (a subset of) propositional attitude predicates, in particular languages.

3.3.1.2 Monsters

Schlenker (1999, 2003) proposes a revision of the mechanisms of direct reference – a plea for monsters – in response to new data from Slave (Athabaskan), Navajo (Athabaskan) and Amharic (Semitic, Afro-Asiatic) that demonstrates that indexical shift is possible. For Schlenker there exists a natural language operator that can overwrite the utterance context with values from a local context. For example, consider the following sentence in Navajo, which illustrates what Speas calls a "direct discourse complement" (6: p. 2; ex. 1), building on earlier work by Schauber (1979) and Willie (1989).

(6)   *Jáan   chidí   naháḻnii'*   *ní.*
       J   car   3SGO.PERF.1SGS.buy   3.say
       'John$_i$ says he$_i$ bought a car.'
       (Lit: 'John says I bought a car')

The sentence in (7) is ambiguous between a direct and indirect discourse reading. This is so because first person can refer to the "speaker of the utterance context"; or it can *shift* and refer to Jáan instead, the "speaker of the reported context." Accordingly, it is important to diagnose whether "shifted" indirect discourse has grammatical dependencies with the main clause, to make sure we have not confused it with direct discourse.

Speas (1999) provides a battery of diagnostics that distinguish between direct and indirect discourse in English (pp. 4–5), and applies these to the Navajo direct discourse complement (henceforth DDC). Although not all tests identify DDC as indirect discourse (e.g., there is a person shift characteristic of direct discourse cf. the literal gloss in 7), most other tests indicate that DDC represents indirect discourse. Among these, a compelling argument is found in that DDC does not constitute an island for extraction. For instance, DDC can participate in question formation (7: p.6, ex. 8a).

(7)   *Háadilá$_i$ Kii Mary [t$_i$]   díníḻnish   yilní*
       where at   K M   2SGS.work   3SGIO.3SGS.say
       'Where did Kii tell Mary to work?'
       (LIT: Where did Kii say to Mary you work)

Another important argument is that indexical shift is partial in Navajo. According to Speas, not all indexicals are interpreted in the reported context. Some indexicals, such as demonstratives (8a: p.6, ex. 10), or temporal adverbs (8b: p.7, ex. 11) are interpreted relative to the speaker of the utterance context – his or her position in space and time, rather than the position in space and time of the speaker of the reported context. In this respect, the interpretation of "that" and "tomorrow" in the examples below mirrors that of Basque, English,

Italian or Spanish, while the interpretation of the first person pronoun remains in the reported context.

(8)   a. *Kii nléí*   *tsin yítséél ní*
               K   that.yonder tree chop   say
               'Kii says he chopped the tree over there.'
               (Lit: Kii says I chopped that tree over there)
    b. *Kii yiskáago   Kinḹání góó   deeshá ní*
               K   tomorrow Flagstaff to   go   say
               'Kii says he is going to Flagstaff tomorrow.'
               (Lit: Kii says I am going to Flagstaff tomorrow)

Although indexical shift originally appeared to be a low frequency phenomenon, the number of languages that shift indexicals has increased considerably. To mention a few, these include Donno So (Niger-Congo, Culy 1994), Zazaki (Indo-European, Anand and Nevins 2004), Nez Perce (Plateau Penutian, Deal 2008), Uyghur (Turkic, Shklovsky and Sudo in press; Sudo in press), and Indo-Aryan and Dravidian languages more generally (Sigurðsson 2004: 21, fn.40 via a p.c. from K. V. Subbarao). Indexical shift has also been reported in sign language (Quer 2005 on Catalan sign language). While it is yet to be determined the degree to which indexical shift is available in the world's languages, judging from the lineage of the above-mentioned languages, it is not a marginal characteristic. Indexical shift is geographically widespread.[19]

In these languages the diagnostics also demonstrate that what appears to be direct discourse on the surface is in effect shifted indirect discourse. For Zazaki, Anand and Nevins find grammatical dependencies (2004: 22–3), such as embedding of the shifted clause into relative clauses and licensing of negative polarity words ("anyone") in the shifted clause by matrix negation. For Uyghur, Shklovsky and Sudo (in press) and Sudo (in press) provide diagnostics such as question formation, collective reporting of speech acts, and licensing of negative polarity words (see Sudo in press: 11–12).

Under a compositional approach to the syntactic representation of the utterance/reported context, where each indexical appears in an independent projection (Speas and Tenny 2003; Sigurðsson 2004; LPH, see Chapter 4), isolated, partial or complete shifts can be addressed. It is important to pay close attention to cross-linguistic variation in the manifestation of indexical shift. As it turns out, one, multiple or all indexicals can shift their context of evaluation.[20]

3.3.1.3 Variation in indexical shift

Indexical shift is a unitary phenomenon in two respects. First, the interpretation of indexicals is ambiguous relative to the context in which the pronouns are interpreted (utterance vs. reported). Secondly, the syntactic domain is the (finite) complement clause of (some) propositional attitude verbs in the relevant languages. Beyond these two factors, there are at least four parameters that articulate cross-linguistic variation in the manifestation of indexical shift.

The first parameter of variation concerns what propositional attitude predicates allow context shift. These range from speech predicates, to psychological predicates, to verbs of direct perception. In Zazaki, for instance, only *vano* 'say' allows context shift, while in Uyghur finite complements of attitude verbs obligatorily shift. Shklovsky and Sudo provide abundant examples: *dä-* 'say, tell,' *sözla-* 'speak, talk,' *maxtan-* 'brag,' *quayil qil-* 'persuade, convince,' *aghrin-* 'complain,' *wäda qal-* promise; *bil-* 'believe, know,' *oyla-* 'think,' *ansir-* 'worry,' *ümid qil* 'hope,' *xejal qil-* 'dream about'; *angla-* 'hear,' *oqu-* 'read,', etc. Thus, in Zazaki, context shift manifests as an idiosyncratic lexical property of a prototypical speech predicate, while in Uyghur it shows up as a class property of propositional attitude verbs.

A second parameter is the extent to which indexical words shift – from first person only, to second person, and temporal and locative pronouns. Anand and Nevins state, "All indexical expressions in Zazaki are in principle shiftable" (2004: 2). By contrast, in Navajo (cf. 9) temporal and locative indexicals do not shift under the same speech predicate. Subclasses of propositional attitude verbs differ in whether they shift only first person pronouns or also second person ones. It appears that speech predicates may be able to shift both first and second person, while other subclasses may only shift first person (Navajo, Slave, Uyghur, cf. Anand and Nevins, Shklovsky and Sudo). Hence, the degree of shift may be, at least in part, a lexical property. Further research is necessary to establish the representativeness of these preliminary generalizations.

A third parameter is whether indexicals shift as a block or not. In contrast to the Navajo example, where only first and second person shift (cf. 9), in Zazaki all indexicals must refer to the same context. Anand and Nevins refer to this property as the "shift-together constraint" (10: p. 4, ex. 13) and claim that the same constraint applies to Slave (Rice 1986). In the example below, the abbreviation AUTH(c*) means speaker of the utterance context and ADDR(c*) means the addressee of the context of utterance. By "I" and "you" in the glosses Anand and Nevins mean the speaker and addressee of the reported context, respectively. Thus, the first non-literal gloss in (9) represents "shifted" indirect discourse, the second "non-shifted" indirect discourse. The third and fourth non-literal glosses represent unattested interpretations that mix the utterance context with the reported context. Note that these were possible in Navajo.[21]

(9)   *Vizeri*   *Rojda Bill-ra va*   *kE*   ***Ez to-ra miradissa***
      Yesterday   Rojda Bill-to said   that   I you-to angry.be-PRES
      'Yesterday Rojda said to Bill, "I am angry at you."
      'Yesterday Rojda said to Bill, "AUTH(c*) is angry at ADDR(c*)."
      '*Yesterday Rojda said to Bill, "AUTH(c*) am angry at you."
      '*Yesterday Rojda said to Bill, "I am angry at ADDR(c*)."

A fourth parameter is the particular syntactic domain in the complement clause where indexicals must shift. For Uyghur, Shklovsky and Sudo propose that the monster operator sits relatively low in the complement clause in light of correlations between case assignment, syntactic position and interpretation (shifted, non-shifted). This particular property of Uyghur is unique, but the data Shklovsky and Sudo present seems robust.

Some of the approaches to indexical shift have understandably banked on lexical differences. Schlenker (2003) proposes a lexical underspecification approach where indexicals have either bound or free context variables. English indexicals are specified for the context of utterance, while Amharic indexicals are underspecified, and thus can shift (i.e., be interpreted relative to either context). The implementation of Schlenker's idea builds on the representation of a root and embedded context in the syntax,[22] which is featurally compatible with particular lexical entries. By contrast, Anand and Nevins argue that Schlenker's account cannot predict the "shift-together constraint" and present an alternative analysis where the locus of variation is the presence or absence of context-shifting operators in the lexical entries of the relevant languages. The proposed operators shift all indexicals (OP$_V$ Zazaki *vano*) or only a subset of them (OP$_{AUTH}$ for Slave *hadi* 'he says,' which shifts first person only).

The relevance of indexical shift for the current discussion is that it presents the possibility of viewing indexicality as syntactically encoded in some languages in the complement clause of propositional attitude verbs. This, in turn, suggests that the utterance context may be represented in the syntax. The same indexicals can refer to one context, or the other, in the observance of language-specific interpretative constraints (Schlenker, Anand and Nevins, Shklovsky and Sudo).

3.3.1.4   What dependent clauses feature a reported context?

An important question remains concerning what dependent clauses would require a reported context. Bianchi (2003) proposes to represent a logophoric center in finite (indicative) clauses and a subset of non-finite dependent clauses (e.g., a subset of control clauses). Sigurðsson proposes to generalize the syntactic representation of the context of utterance to subordinate clauses as well:[23]

> Subordinate clauses have a secondary, anaphoric speech event, with speech features (S_T, S_L, Λ_A, Λ_P, ...) that inherit their values from preceding elements, that is, either from the silent elements of the overall matrix speech event or from overt elements in a preceding clause. (Sigurðsson 2004: 21; ex. 31)

This move is a point of departure to enable a syntactic approach to indexical phenomena in dependent clauses and it is compliant with the SMT. But it does not shed light on why precisely in certain subordinate clauses some or all indexicals can or must accept ordinary arguments as antecedents, such as arguments to propositional attitude verbs. While decidedly not the most desirable solution, it may turn out that only a subset of dependent clauses exhibit a reported context (with Bianchi). In this line, working on logophoricity and long-distance anaphora, and adopting Discourse Representation Theory (Kamp 1981), Sells concludes that the discourse representation structures (DRS) for the verbs in question should be augmented:

> I think that work of this sort makes it quite clear that predicates of propositional attitude and consciousness, for example as represented in DRSs, should have more structure in their arguments than merely the propositional content of those arguments. (1987: 467)

We return to the important question of whether the reported context could be generalized to all dependent clauses in subsequent sections. Indexical shift warrants representation of the reported context for propositional attitude verbs.

3.3.1.5 Summary
New data shows that indexicals can be interpreted locally under propositional attitude verbs. Language variation in indexical shift is supportive of a compositional representation of the context (à la Speas and Tenny 2003; Sigurðsson 2004; LPH cf. Chapter 4). The distribution of indexical shift suggests that only a subset of dependent clauses may encode indexicality in the syntax (Bianchi 2003).

Next we discuss logophoricity, a second indexical phenomenon where propositional attitude verbs define a syntactic domain with atypical indexical properties.

3.3.2 *Logophoricity*
Logophoricity provides further evidence for the existence of a reported context in that certain African languages feature a special class of indirect

discourse pronouns that are not licensed in root contexts. The phenomenon is well characterized by a combination of grammatical hierarchies that describe its manifestation across the relevant languages (Hyman and Comrie 1981; Culy 1994; Huang 2003). At the same time, the particular distribution of the pronouns suggests that it may not be possible to generalize a reported context to all subordinate clauses. An important debate that concerns the analysis of logophoricity is whether it expresses point of view as a primary or secondary meaning (Sells 1987 vs. Culy 1997). This debate also concerns the representation of the context of utterance in the syntax, as its proposed projections have been related to the expression of point of view (Speas and Tenny 2003). This subsection concludes with a comparison between indexical shift and logophoricity.

3.3.2.1 Reported speech pronouns in African languages
In the 1970s the study of African languages revealed the use of a special class of pronouns. Their antecedent must be the person whose speech, feelings or perspective is reported (Hagège 1974; Clements 1975). In addition to the pronominal system, which crucially constitutes a different paradigm in the language, logophoricity can manifest via inflection in the verb (Hyman and Comrie 1981; Curnow 2002a; Bond 2006) or by means of special complementizers (Sells 1987), often derived from the verb "say."

For example, in Mundang (Niger-Congo) the logophoric pronouns are $zĺ$, $ázĺ$ (strong form), and *Min* (possessive); they refer to singular antecedents only. The following are examples with speech predicates (10: Sells 1987: 446, ex. 1). An example with a psychological predicate is given for Tuburi (Niger-Congo) in (11: p.447, ex. 5).

(10)   a. *a   fa   mo   ?I   zĺ ne̞*
          Pro   say   you   see   Log Q
          'He$_i$ asked if you saw him$_i$.'
        b. *a ri 3I lwafan sa:*
          Pro say Log find thing beauty
          'He$_i$ said that he$_i$ had found something beautiful.'

(11)   *hI:nI d3O   ne   ga   St   Hi?tflgI*
          fear make   him   Comp   Log   fall illness
          'He was afraid of falling ill.'

Syntactically, these pronouns appear in dependent clauses under propositional attitude verbs – speech predicates, psychological predicates, and verbs of direct perception, contingent on the language. In his survey of 32 languages, Culy (1994) derives an implicational hierarchy (12) of verbs that license logophoric morphology in their complements. Huang (2003: 65, ex. 31) provides a revised implicational hierarchy in (13).

(12)   Speech > Thought > Knowledge > Direct perception

(13)   A revised implicational universal for logocentric predicates
        Speech predicates > epistemic predicates > knowledge predicates > psychological predicates > unmarked directional predicates

The most typical logophoric clause will be selected by a speech predicate, predominantly the verb *say*. If a language allows the rightmost type of predicate in the hierarchy, it is predicted to allow all of the predicate types to its left.

These grammatical hierarchies add to earlier ones that have been proposed to characterize the distribution of logophoric pronouns/verbal morphology. These include grammatical function, person and number (14: Hyman and Comrie 1981: 33), and thematic role (15: Huang 2003: 64, ex. 30).

(14)   a. Subject > Non-subject
        b. Third > Second > First
        c. Singular > Plural

(15)   Agent > Experiencer > Benefactor > Others

According to these grammatical hierarchies, the most likely logophoric pronoun will be specified for third person singular and it will refer to an agentive subject in the main clause of a speech predicate.

An important observation to make, which stems from the contemplation of these hierarchies, is that, regardless of logophoricity being a somewhat atypical areal phenomenon, it conforms to multiple implicational hierarchies (cf. 13–16) that apply elsewhere in the grammar of the world's languages (e.g., the Accessibility Hierarchy, Keenan and Comrie 1977; markedness in person and number). Furthermore, two other indexical phenomena share the same syntactic domain with logophoricity. Indexical shift and the concomitant logophoric use of conjunct-disjunct morphology, which will be discussed next, are also restricted to propositional attitude predicates. Even if logophoricity seems geographically isolated, its manifestation shows a strong connection to grammatical phenomena in other languages.[24]

3.3.2.2   What clauses allow logophoric pronouns?
If indexical shift supported a compositional approach to the syntactic representation of the context, logophoricity suggests that only select clauses may represent a reported context. In effect, exceptions to logophoric environments (i.e., outside propositional attitude verbs) introduce an additional complication

to generalizing a reported context in dependent clauses (cf. Sigurðsson 2004: 21; ex.31, quoted above). There is variation in whether relative clauses allow logophoric pronouns. Mundang, for example, does not accept logophoric pronouns in relative clauses. By contrast, in Tuburi, logophoric pronouns are possible in relative clauses that modify a constituent inside the complement clause of a propositional attitude verb, or in relative clauses that modify a constituent in the main clause of a propositional attitude verb (see Sells 1987: 446–47 and references therein). Other exceptional cases where logophoric pronouns (Ewe, Clements 1975) and long-distance anaphora (Icelandic, Sigurðsson 1986[1990]) are licensed include purposive clauses (quoted in Sells 1987: 475).

These exceptions point to an alternative theory where only certain dependent clauses provide the environment to license indexical shift and logophoricity – alternatively, binding conditions or locality may be at issue. Unfortunately, this alternative theory is a departure from the SMT in that it introduces asymmetries across dependent clauses and, it would appear, across languages, too. It is difficult to envision how the exceptional distribution of logophoric elements could be captured in a syntactic theory that encodes indexicality without postulating asymmetric structures. Much work is yet to be done if the phenomena in question are to be successfully integrated under the umbrella of syntactically represented reported contexts.

In spite of the above-noted exceptions, Sells (1987), Culy (1994) and Curnow (2002a) agree that the complement clause of propositional attitude verbs is the main or exclusive domain of occurrence. Here "complement clause" is to be read in its broad sense. One or more logophoric pronouns can occur in multiple clauses referring back to (typically) the subject of the propositional attitude verb – and, less often, the addressee (Banda Linda (Niger-Congo), Donno So (Niger-Congo), Ewe (Niger-Congo); see Culy 1997: 849–50 and references therein). As noted, logophoric pronouns may also occur in relative clauses modifying a constituent in the matrix clause or in the complement clause.

3.3.2.3 The meaning of logophoric pronouns

An area of contention regarding the analysis of logophoricity concerns whether it expresses point of view as its primary meaning (Sells 1987 and references therein vs. Culy 1994, 1997). It is a relevant point to elucidate whether logophoric pronouns indicate indirect discourse and thus reflect a reported context, or if, alternatively, logophoric pronouns are an independent mechanism to express point of view.

Using Discourse Representation Theory (Kamp 1981), Sells (1987) develops a pragmatic account of logophoricity and long-distance anaphora. Logophoricity is seen not as a primitive notion, but is reduced instead to three semantic notions: *source*, *self* and *pivot* (building on similar observations by Kuno 1973; Clements 1975; Banfield 1982; Sigurðsson 1986[1990], among others).

> I propose that there is no unified notion of logophoricity per se and that logophoric phenomena are instead a result of the interaction of these more primitive notions: the source of the report, the person with respect to whose consciousness (or "self") the report is made, and the person from whose point of view the report is made. (p. 445)

> These roles define different discourse environments, depending on the specification of each – namely, whether each role is predicated of a sentence-internal referent, or of the external speaker. (p. 456)

Sells justifies the need for pragmatic roles such as evaluative adverbs and epithets in the discussion of point-of-view phenomena (Banfield 1982). The relevance of source, self and pivot is further justified in accounting for cross-linguistic differences in the licensing of logophoric pronouns and long-distance anaphora in languages such as Ewe, Japanese and Icelandic. In consideration of cross-linguistic data, Sells arrives at the following implicational hierarchy for said pragmatic roles (16).

(16)   Source > self > pivot

In contrast to Sells, Culy (1997) proposes that logophoricity and long-distance anaphora serve a primary syntactic purpose, the interpretation of point of view being secondary.

> Both types [long-distance anaphora, logophoric pronouns] have a primary use (clausal co-reference and indirect discourse marking respectively), with a common secondary use (point of view). (p. 846)

Culy makes the case that logophoric pronouns of various types find their counterparts in non-logophoric pronouns across languages. Furthermore, Culy notes that multiple logophoric pronouns can occur in a single clause. On the assumption that logophoric pronouns must express point of view, the occurrence of multiple pronouns contradicts Banfield's (1982) generalization that there can be only one point of view per clause.

Instead, Culy views point of view as pragmatically inferred when a logophoric pronoun or an ordinary pronoun is unexpected in a particular syntactic domain, and in this respect, Culy argues, logophoric pronouns run parallel to equally unexpected "unlicensed" uses of anaphora.

> Logophoric pronouns are indirect discourse forms that represent point of view only when they are not licensed by a predicate. (p. 856)

> In cases where a logophoric pronoun indicates the point of view of the internal protagonist, the use of a personal pronoun indicates a point of view other than that of the internal protagonist. (p. 856)
> If we take the personal pronouns to be the unmarked case, then we can say that a marked form (logophoric pronoun, reflexive) is used to indicate a marked situation (the point of view expressed is not that of the narrator). (p. 857)

Culy refers the reader to Huang's (1991, 1996) Neo-Gricean pragmatic theory of anaphora for an exploration of this idea (p. 858, n.17).

If logophoricity is to be taken as an argument for the representation of a reported context, it is important to try to provide a resolution to these divergent analyses. In what follows we draw some parallels with the epistemic interpretations of evidentiality and their grammaticalization, which may serve to reconcile the indirect discourse/point-of-view analysis.

The recruitment of "indirect discourse pronouns" to express point of view can be seen in the larger context of grammaticalization (Hopper and Traugott 1993). The study of evidentiality, with its focus on elucidating primary (evidential) vs. secondary (epistemic) meaning (Aikhenvald 2004), presents an interesting parallel to the grammaticalization of point of view. Aikhenvald refers to certain meanings acquired by evidential markers as "epistemic extensions" of core evidential meaning. For example, the Basque reportative particle *omen* is used to convey that the information is second-hand, third-hand or hearsay. *Omen* can also be used to indicate a lower level of certainty, to cast doubt on the information or the source, or to displace personal responsibility from the veracity of the information reported (Alcázar 2011). Accordingly, we may say that these epistemic uses represent the speaker's point of view on evidence, a secondary or pragmatic layer of meaning, which arises from salient conversational implicatures in the use of evidential morphology (similarly to Culy 1997).

The first of these pragmatic implicatures of *omen* has arguably semanticized and no longer requires reported evidence. In this use, *omen* now represents the speaker's certainty. When these implicatures semanticize in evidentiality, they yield a point-of-view meaning that is non-evidential. For example, languages with complex evidential systems tend to use direct evidence markers as certainty markers that do not require direct evidence (Aikhenvald 2004). It is plausible that logophoric pronouns serve as a means to encode point of view in indirect discourse (as Sells 1987 and references therein argue), in addition to the "unlicensed" contexts of Culy (1997), where logophoric pronouns cannot indicate indirect discourse. This is not tantamount to saying that logophoric pronouns do not serve a primary role to mark indirect discourse (*pace* Culy

1997), much like evidential morphology retains its function in spite of developing epistemic extensions (Aikhenvald 2004).[25]

From a syntactic perspective, the question to be asked is whether it is coincidental that point of view, broadly construed, arises in the indexical phenomena that serve as supporting arguments for the representation of the context of utterance and the reported context. For Speas and Tenny (2003), this relationship is not coincidental. But we will defer discussion of this issue till Section 3.4.

3.3.2.4   Comparison between indexical shift and logophoricity
It is fitting to attempt to compare indexical shift with logophoricity. Their different geographical distribution patterns notwithstanding, their syntactic distribution is parallel.[26] Thus it is tempting to view indexical shift as a case of lexical ambiguity in indirect discourse (à la Schlenker 2003) and logophoricity as a case of lexical specificity in the same context: indexicals syntactically restricted to indirect discourse. Yet there appear to be multiple differences beyond this preliminary treatment. First, we are not aware of logophoric temporal or locative pronouns equivalent to shifted interpretations of these indexicals (e.g., Zazaki; Anand and Nevins 2004). Secondly, addressee logophoric pronouns are comparatively infrequent (see Culy 1994, 1997). By contrast, being able to shift second person pronouns seems common enough to invite preliminary lexical classification into predicates that can shift first person only or both first and second person (Shklovsky and Sudo, in press). Then there is the question of the person specification of the logophoric pronoun/verbal morphology. Third person logophoric pronouns are indexical in that they typically refer to the speaker of the reported context. Second person logophoric pronouns are indexical in that they typically refer to the addressee of the reported context. Yet first person logophoric pronouns are rarely, if ever, to be found. For Huang, who adopts the view that logophoric pronouns express point of view, this gap is to be expected.

> It follows, therefore, that the fact that first-person logophoric markers are very rare, if not non-existent, in natural languages, is hardly surprising, given that logophoric markings are one of the (most common) devices the current, external speaker (which is encoded usually in terms of a first-person pronoun) utilizes in reflecting the perspective of anyone else (usually an internal protagonist) but him or herself. (2003: 62).

It is not clear why a first person should be absent if logophoric verbal morphology can be first person (Hyman and Comrie 1981; Curnow 2002b) – or if indexical shift can apply to first person pronouns.

3.3.2.5 Summary

Some African languages display reported speech pronouns in what seems to be an areal feature. The distribution of logophoric pronouns is mostly restricted to complements of propositional attitude verbs. The meaning of logophoric pronouns has been argued to encode point of view and/or indirect discourse marking. While one phenomenon may not be reduced to the other, indexical shift and logophoricity suggest that the context of utterance and the reported context can be represented in the syntax and that morphology can refer to either the utterance context only (the familiar case: Basque, English, Italian, Spanish), the reported context only (logophoricity) or both (indexical shift).

The next phenomenon that we will discuss is conjunct-disjunct systems: person morphology that varies its interpretation depending on the type of speech act (declarative, interrogative) or the type of clause (complement of propositional attitude verbs).

3.3.3 Conjunct-disjunct person-marking systems

Conjunct-disjunct systems double as logophoric marking under propositional attitude verbs and person marking in root clauses, with puzzling asymmetries in the interpretation of person relative to the speech act (Hale 1980). Like indexical shift, conjunct-disjunct marking constitutes evidence for a reported context and an utterance context. This section begins by defining the term and reviewing its history. The meaning of conjunct-disjunct systems is interpreted to signal "epistemic authority" (Hargreaves 1990, 1991, 2005), which is similar to Speas and Tenny's (2003) pragmatic role of "seat of knowledge." The current section concludes with a brief comparison of conjunct-disjunct systems with logophoricity and indexical shift.

3.3.3.1 Person interpretation relative to the speech act

The main distinctive characteristic of a conjunct-disjunct system lies in a shift in the interpretation of person morphemes. The following examples from Northern Akhvakh (Nakh-Daghestanian) serve to illustrate this change in the interpretation of person (Creissels 2008: 1; exs. 1–2). The perfective markers of the past tense *–ada* and *–ari* also indicate person, as follows. In a declarative clause, *–ada* encodes first person (17a), while *–ari* is used for second and third person (17b). By contrast, in an interrogative, *–ada* is interpreted as second person (18a), while *–ari* takes on the values of first person and third person (18b).

(17)   a. *de-de*   *kaʁa*   *qwar-ada.*
         1SG-ERG   paper   write-PFV.ASS.INV
         'I wrote a letter.'

   b. *me-de / hu-s̲w-e / hu-λ̲-e*
      2SG-ERG / DEM-OM-ERG / DEM-OF-ERG
      kaʁa   qwar-ari
      paper   write-PFV
      'You / he / she wrote a letter.'

(18) a. *me-de   čŭda   kaʁa   qwar-ada?*
         2SG-ERG   when   paper   write-PFVASSINV
         'When did you write a letter?'
      b. *de-de /   hu-s̲w-e /   hu-λ̲-e*
         1SG-ERG /   DEM-OM-ERG / DEM-OF-ERG
         čŭda   kaʁa   qwar-ari?
         when   paper   write-PFV
         'When did I / he / she write a letter?'

Conjunct-disjunct systems tend to observe restrictions in the type of predicate for which they can indicate person, as the following definition that we take from Curnow (2002a: 614) shows. The quote also identifies what is meant by the terms *conjunct* and *disjunct*, the history of which we elaborate on next.

> A language contains a conjunct/disjunct system if, given an agentive, intentional, volitional context (or a relatively neutral context with a verb that is most commonly interpreted as an intentional, volitional action performed by an agentive subject), statements containing a first person are distinct from those that do not contain first person reference, while questions containing second person are distinct from those that do not contain second person reference. The marking used to distinguish first person in statements and second person in questions is the "conjunct"; the other form is the "disjunct."

3.3.3.2   On the history of the term
The term conjunct-disjunct itself is rather opaque (for an overview of available terms see Curnow 2002a: 612–13). According to Creissels (2008: 3), the specific term conjunct-disjunct becomes predominant after Hale's (1980) work on Kathmandu Newari. The term initially applies to a system that encodes same/disjoint subject reference across the subject of a speech predicate and the subject of its complement clause. The morphological difference lies in person agreement on the verb. In its original intended use, *conjunct* marking refers to same-subject reference (19a, logophoric) when the dependent verb is volitive or agentive, while *disjunct* names disjoint subject reference (19b: Creissels 2008: 3, ex. 3). The conjunct-disjunct system is independent of person in the complement clause.

(19) a. *wǫ: lā   na-e   dhakạ: dhạl-a.*
         he.ERG   meat   eat-CONJ   COMP   say-PST.DISJ
         'He_i said that he_i will eat meat.'

b. *wǫ:*   *lā*   *na-i*   *dhakạ:*   *dhạl-a.*
   he.ERG   meat   eat-DISJ   COMP   say-PST.DISJ
   'He_i said that he_j will eat meat.'

Hale (1980: 97) considers logophoricity jointly with the person-marking asymmetry between declaratives (1 vs. 2/3) and polar/wh-interrogatives (2 vs. 1/3), shown above for Akhvakh (18, 19). Hale analyzes the person-marking asymmetry as resulting from abstract performative verbs, thus drawing an analogy between the logophoric use of the "quotative frame" and the use in root clauses. Later work generalizes both phenomena as "speaker" or "assertor" marking in root declarative and interrogative clauses and in the complement clause of propositional attitude verbs.

3.3.3.3   Logophoric uses

If Curnow did not include the logophoric use of conjunct-disjunct systems in his definition above, it is because the language under study, Awa Pit (Barbacoan), does not employ conjunct person marking for logophoricity. As Curnow observes, the relevant complement clauses of speech predicates are non-finite. The duality of conjunct-disjunct systems as encompassing a person asymmetry and a logophoric use seems to be the norm. The same-subject vs. different-subject system, for which languages can deploy multiple devices (Bond 2006), is specifically identified as a logophoric system.

> In [Newari and Tsafiki], the conjunct/disjunct system operates in some subordinate clauses on the basis of logophoricity. That is, in essence, conjunct is used in a subordinate clause of speech or thought when the subordinate verb has the same subject as the matrix clause, while disjunct indicates noncoreference between a subordinate and a matrix clause (Dickinson 1999; Hale 1980). (Curnow 2002a: 616)

The relevance of conjunct-disjunct systems for the representation of the reported context is evident in their logophoric use. As a person marker in root clauses, conjunct-disjunct morphology refers to the speaker or the addressee of the utterance context. Overall, then, conjunct-disjunct morphologies are interpreted relative to the utterance context or to the reported context. In this particular facet, they share this property with indexical pronouns in indexical shift, which can also be interpreted relative to either domain.

3.3.3.4   On the meaning of conjunct-disjunct systems

While logophoricity can be generally characterized as indirect discourse pronouns (recruited to express point of view), and indexical shift as an ambiguity in the domain of evaluation of an indexical expression, it is not immediately obvious how to interpret conjunct-disjunct systems beyond their logophoric use. What does the asymmetry in the interpretation of person signify? If it responds to syntactic encoding of the context of utterance, why does it shift its interpretation from a declarative to an interrogative?

Hargreaves (1990, 1991, 2005) proposes that what conjunct-disjunct systems express is "epistemic authority."[27] In a declarative, the speaker of the utterance is responsible for the contents of the statement. By contrast, in an interrogative, it is the addressee that is presumed to possess the relevant knowledge. Hargreaves's idea is strengthened in the declarative pattern typically exhibited by rhetorical questions or test questions (where information is not sought or the answer is known) and in involuntary actions/mirative contexts (e.g., see Hale 1980: 99 on Newari). In a reported context, the epistemic authority can be construed as the "source" of such context.

3.3.3.5 General comparison: indexical shift, logophoricity, conjunct-disjunct

We conclude with a brief comparison of conjunct-disjunct systems with logophoricity and indexical shift. All three phenomena find a common syntactic domain in the complement of propositional attitude verbs. In their logophoric use, conjunct-disjunct systems relate to logophoricity. Although their manifestation is not necessarily pronominal, logophoric languages can also resort to verbal inflection (Hyman and Comrie 1981; Curnow 2002b; Bond 2006). Conjunct-disjunct systems and indexical shift share that they can be interpreted relative to the utterance context and a reported context. But the interpretation of conjunct-disjunct systems in root clauses presents a shift from first person to second person that is not attested in indexical shift.

3.3.3.6 Summary

Some languages present person morphology whose interpretation is contingent on the speech act. The same markers are interpreted as logophoric under propositional attitude verbs. In root clauses, the meaning of conjunct-disjunct morphology relates to the epistemic authority of the clause.

For Speas and Tenny (2003), the person asymmetry in conjunct-disjunct systems is the morphological reflex of a syntactic operation. To discuss this idea in detail, we now turn to a discussion of their proposal.

3.4   Speas and Tenny (2003)

Speas and Tenny (2003) propose to represent part of the context of utterance in the syntax, specifically what they call the pragmatic roles *speaker* and *hearer*, and a third role, *seat of knowledge*, which can be equated with Hargreaves's "epistemic authority" after the discussion of conjunct-disjunct

systems. In addition to encoding part of the context, Speas and Tenny's proposal aims to represent a broad notion of point of view via the identity of the
third pragmatic role. The seat of knowledge is a pronominal element that is
syntactically controlled by its closest c-commanding antecedent. The closest
antecedent is ordinarily the speaker, unless the hearer is promoted structurally in a passive-like operation analogous to "dative shift" (Larson 1988).
Furthermore, Speas and Tenny extend their proposal to typify basic clause
types syntactically. This is done by means of two parameters: the type of
complement a force projection with verbal features selects and whether in
that verbal projection the hearer argument has been promoted to control the
seat of knowledge.

In what follows, we introduce Speas and Tenny's proposed theory, illustrate it with tree diagrams and point to the most supportive argumentation
they adduce. Next we provide a discussion of their theory. This section ends
with a brief technical discussion of some of the assumptions that Speas and
Tenny make.

3.4.1   *Representing the context as Speech Act Mood Phrase*

Speas and Tenny enrich the syntax with projections that mediate the syntax-
pragmatics interface. This includes a revision of the role of Force Phrase (Rizzi
1997) or Speech Act Mood Phrase (Cinque 1999), the projection that encodes
the force of the utterance. Following Cinque, Speas and Tenny adopt the name
Speech Act Mood Phrase. For Speas and Tenny, this projection is split into two
levels in a way reminiscent of transitive or ditransitive verbs, as shown in the
technical discussion at the end of this section. According to the authors, the
Speech Act Mood Phrase contains three arguments: the SPEAKER, the HEARER
and the UTTERANCE CONTENT. These arguments are placed in structural positions
analogous to those of the subject, indirect object and object, respectively. The
tree diagram below illustrates the structure of Speech Act Mood Phrase or sap
for short (20 cf. Speas and Tenny: 6, ex. 9).

(20)

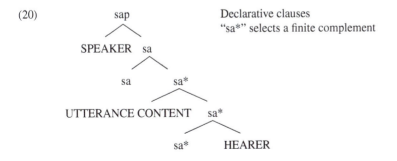

Declarative clauses
"sa*" selects a finite complement

Speas and Tenny refer to the argumenthood analogy just mentioned and elaborate on the identity of the thematic argument UTTERANCE CONTENT:

> We may think of the SPEAKER as the agent of the speech act, the UTTERANCE CONTENT as the theme and the HEARER as its goal. (p. 6)
>
> We use the term UTTERANCE CONTENT as a vague cover term for the role assigned to the (rest of the) sentence. Sometimes the content is a proposition, but sometimes, as in a command or a quote, it is not (p. 22, fn. 9)

The representation of sap is extended to all root clauses and at least some dependent clauses (e.g., complements of propositional attitude predicates).

In enriching Speech Act Mood Phrase with verbal features, Speas and Tenny put forward the possibility of viewing speech acts as verbal types. This move is reminiscent of the performative hypothesis (Ross 1970, PH). The PH assumes deep structures that type the sentence, as in (21). In effect, Ross argues that the imperative meaning of the bare verb clause (21a) is derived from its deep structure representation (p. 224, fn. 13).

(21)   a. (I order you to) go!
        b. (I say to you that) John is here.
        c. (I ask you whether) Is John here?

The performative verb and its arguments were presumed not to be realized because they were targeted by a performative deletion rule. Speas and Tenny reinstate the view that root clauses are, in effect, complement clauses to a higher predicate.[28]

Although reminiscent of the PH, Speas and Tenny approach the syntactic typing of grammaticalized speech acts in a novel way. The PH typed the sentence by means of the semantic import of the abstract predicate. Speas and Tenny do not consider the head of Speech Act Mood Phrase a verb proper, but verb-like. Instead Speas and Tenny propose that grammaticalized speech acts derive in the syntax from two parameters. The first is the type of clausal complement that the UTTERANCE CONTENT is (finite or non-finite). The second is more complex. It concerns a third pragmatic argument, the SEAT OF KNOWLEDGE, and a passive-like operation that structurally promotes the HEARER to a position where it controls the reference of said argument. To elucidate their clause-typing proposal, we need to elaborate on this third pragmatic argument first and the position it occupies in clause structure.

In addition to SPEAKER and HEARER, Speas and Tenny (p. 11) propose to represent a third pragmatic role that represents point of view, broadly construed.

> Reference to some notion of *point of view* can be found in discussions of a variety of grammatical phenomena, including long-distance binding, logophoric pronouns, psychological predicates, and switch reference. These are all constructions in which the grammatical form depends in some way on the *sentient individual* whose *point of view* is reflected in the sentence.

This includes the above-mentioned notion of "epistemic authority" that the third pragmatic role refers to. Speas and Tenny employ the SEAT OF KNOWLEDGE as part of the mechanics of one of two parameters to typify basic clause types.

The location of the SEAT OF KNOWLEDGE is at the top of the clausal complement UTTERANCE CONTENT. The latter is comprised, in its higher segment of clause structure, of the projections Evaluation Phrase and Evidence Phrase. Speas and Tenny speculate that these two projections could be two layers of the same projection. They name the combined projection Sentience Phrase. Their tree diagram reflects this alternative analysis (22: p. 17, ex. 34).

(22)   UTTERANCE CONTENT (its upper structural layers)

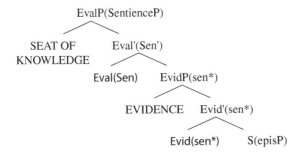

As seen in (22), Evaluation Phrase has a subject position for the pragmatic role SEAT OF KNOWLEDGE, "or sentient 'mind,' who can evaluate, or process, or comment on the truth of a proposition" (p. 16).

Speas and Tenny believe that the SEAT OF KNOWLEDGE is crucially involved in the grammaticalization of speech acts. The SPEAKER is the SEAT OF KNOWLEDGE in a declarative clause, while in a question it is the HEARER. This is equivalent to Hargreaves's proposal (1990, 1991, 2005) regarding conjunct-disjunct systems. Speas and Tenny additionally extend the idea to the imperative and certain subjunctive clauses as well, where HEARER and SPEAKER are the SEAT OF KNOWLEDGE, respectively.

The SEAT OF KNOWLEDGE, Speas and Tenny further argue, can stand in a relation of control from the SPEAKER or the HEARER. This is determined in their system by the closest c-commanding antecedent. Ordinarily, this will be the SPEAKER by default, unless the HEARER is promoted to the object position, in which case this will be the closest c-commanding antecedent. This is an operation analogous to dative shift (Larson 1988; e.g., "John gave the book to Mary" > "John gave Mary the book").

In an ambitious move, Speas and Tenny enrich their proposal by providing structural permutations on the tree diagram in (20), which represents the structure of a declarative clause, to account for different types of grammaticalized speech acts. The promotion of the indirect object to the object position is offered as the structure of interrogative clauses (23: p.7, ex. 10), which take a finite complement for UTTERANCE CONTENT, and imperative[29] clauses (also 23: p. 7, ex. 11), which take a non-finite one according to Speas and Tenny.

(23)

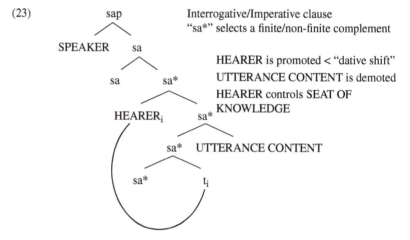

Interrogative/Imperative clause
"sa*" selects a finite/non-finite complement

HEARER is promoted < "dative shift"
UTTERANCE CONTENT is demoted
HEARER controls SEAT OF KNOWLEDGE

Speas and Tenny argue that conjunct-disjunct systems and certain Japanese psych predicates provide evidence for the promotion of the hearer in questions.

In addition, Speas and Tenny propose two declarative-like structures: the quotative and the subjunctive. The quotative (24: p. 8, ex. 13) is the structural counterpart to a declarative clause. For quotatives, Speas and Tenny assume that the speaker is replaced by an expletive because the speaker is not reporting his or her own thoughts (following a p.c. from Anna Maria Di Sciullo).

(24)

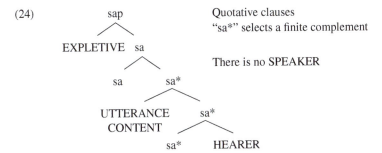

Quotative clauses
"sa*" selects a finite complement

There is no SPEAKER

The clausal complement of a subjunctive clause (25: pp. 7–8, ex. 12) is seen as non-finite (like imperatives).

(25)

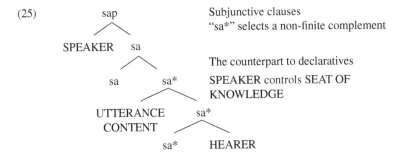

Subjunctive clauses
"sa*" selects a non-finite complement

The counterpart to declaratives

SPEAKER controls SEAT OF KNOWLEDGE

Speas and Tenny justify their typology, arguing that, like predicate-argument relations in the lexicon, the speech acts that grammaticalize in world languages are also highly restricted. In their proposal, the speech acts grammaticalized in the syntax are five: the declarative, interrogative, imperative, subjunctive and quotative clause. They argue that this stands in sharp contrast to recognized taxonomies of speech acts in philosophy of language:

> the striking fact is that although there seem to be anywhere from 5 to 37 distinct types of illocutionary act [cf. Searle 1979: promises, declarations, warnings, forgivings…], no language grammaticizes more than those [five] discussed above.

3.4.2   Discussion

We now turn to a discussion of Speas and Tenny's proposal. Like Bianchi (2003) and Sigurðsson (2004), Speas and Tenny's contribution demonstrates that indexical phenomena can be approached from a syntactic perspective. Their proposal is ambitious in that it attempts to articulate point of view and derive basic clause types. The incorporation of a third pragmatic role, the

SEAT OF KNOWLEDGE, is grounded in general pragmatic/semantic conditions on the interpretation of indexical phenomena (logophoricity, epithets, evidential adverbs), and its proposed control relation in conjunct-disjunct systems. But the syntactic typing of grammaticalized speech acts does not seem to follow from the proposed binary classification (see below). Compared to Bianchi and Sigurðsson, the main advantage of Speas and Tenny's proposal may lie in its partial return to the conceptual bases of Ross's (1970) PH.[30] The introduction of a predicate allows for a generalized analysis of the SPEAKER and HEARER as verbal arguments with thematic roles. The two-layered structure, following the little vP hypothesis and the assignment of roles, proceeds parallel to ordinary predicate-argument relations and is thus compliant with the SMT (see also the reference to the proposal of Canac-Marquis below). Speas and Tenny do not provide room in their proposal for other indexicals like the time and location of the speech event. Said indexicals seem to be part of the syntactic representation as they enter interpretive relations with the speaker and hearer arguments. Speas and Tenny offer the most extensive set of supporting phenomena for the representation of the context, but the breadth of scope leaves room for only limited discussion or comparison. Overall, Speas and Tenny effectively persuade the syntactic community to reconsider indexical phenomena as possibly amenable to principled syntactic analysis and demonstrate that the representation of the context can be utilized to articulate point of view.

Both Speas and Tenny's proposal and the PH seek a resolution to the syntactic encoding of speech acts in syntax. In this regard, the PH appealed to the lexical meaning of the performative verb ("state," "ask," "order"). Although Speas and Tenny have a verbal element heading sap, they do not resort to its semantics to typify sentences. Instead Speas and Tenny derive grammaticalized speech acts by means of binary features: whether the UTTERANCE CONTENT argument is a finite or non-finite clause; and whether a process of dative shift has occurred – with its attendant change in the argument that controls the reference of the SEAT OF KNOWLEDGE (from SPEAKER to HEARER). As noted, part of the latter binary parameter has robust initial support in conjunct-disjunct systems. But the proposed binary classification does not ultimately contribute to a clear division among the three basic sentence types. Let's begin by considering complications that arise when we consider the SEAT OF KNOWLEDGE as a partial discriminator between clause types.

It is important to observe that the SEAT OF KNOWLEDGE can be the SPEAKER or the HEARER for the same grammaticalized speech act. In conjunct-disjunct systems, genuine questions are marked with the conjunct, while rhetorical questions or test questions are marked with the disjunct. This is congruent with the logic of the supporting data. The HEARER is the SEAT OF KNOWLEDGE or epistemic authority in genuine questions, while the SPEAKER is the SEAT OF KNOWLEDGE in questions that require no answer or where the SPEAKER already knows the answer. The second parameter employed by Speas and Tenny is finiteness. Typologically, it is not clear that a non-finite analysis of the imperative clause is warranted (Chapter 2: 2.3). Hence, this second parameter, too, may turn out to be non-discriminatory.

An apparent conflict in Speas and Tenny's proposal lies in the duplicity of a "silent" verb encoding the force of the utterance (the verb is the head of Speech Act Mood Phrase), and not resorting to this same predicate as a means to typify the sentence. Yet, faced with the non-discriminatory results of finiteness and the control relation of the SEAT OF KNOWLEDGE, a return to the conceptual bases of the PH seems warranted. The PH has been paraded as a paradigmatic example of *teoria non-grata* (see, among others, the general sentiment reported in van der Wurff 2007b and Speas and Tenny's attempt to disassociate their proposal from the PH in their appendix). In hindsight, the PH may come to be seen in a better light as foreshadowing facets of the cartographic approach in its development of pragmatically related projections in syntax. After several decades, the conceptual bases of the PH return as a point of departure for the representation of the context in syntax and the syntactic typing of basic speech acts.

Even if the complications of these two binary parameters could be worked out, the typology afforded by the two syntactic parameters does not seem to be fully realized. Recall that there appear to be only three universal types: the declarative, interrogative and imperative. The introduction of quotatives and subjunctives as core types is not supported by the two available surveys on sentence types (Sadock and Zwicky 1985; König and Siemund 2007). Despite Speas and Tenny's emphasis on the limited number of grammaticalized speech acts, it is important to note that our cross-linguistic knowledge in this area is quite limited. There might well be a variety of minor grammaticalized speech acts on a language-particular basis. Some of these potential types are recognizable in familiar languages; for example, exclamatives, imprecatives, threats, promises, challenges, evidentials, narrative styles (free indirect discourse).

There are additional reasons not to consider the subjunctive and the quotative as basic clause types. Treating the quotative as a grammaticalized speech act, separately from other evidential values (various forms of direct evidence and inference), is at variance with established classifications in this area of research (Willett 1988; Plungian 2001; Aikhenvald 2004). In none of these classifications are quotatives treated as a separate or overlapping category (vs. mirativity: unexpected or surprising information cf. DeLancey 1997, 2001; or intersubjectivity: information shared (or not) between speaker and addressee, cf. Nuyts 2001). Even in languages where evidentiality is an incipient grammatical category, such as Romance and Germanic, the interpretations of these forms fall into the classifications based on grammatical systems (Squartini 2007a, 2007b, 2008; but see Aikhenvald 2004). Since Speas and Tenny follow Lyons (1977) in taking mood morphology as compelling evidence for their proposed set of grammaticalized speech acts, based on declarative, interrogative, imperative and subjunctive mood, ignoring similar alignments in the evidential literature is contradictory to their thesis. Furthermore, the quotative aligns with evidential morphology and syncretized manifestations across languages rather than mood morphology.

For the subjunctive, its classification as a basic clause type is difficult to maintain. Judging from their examples, and pending further clarification, by "subjunctive" Speas and Tenny seem to mean 'root subjunctive' clauses. Of the five examples given for illustration, two include Latin hortatives – in the third person plural and first person singular (p. 4, exs. 4ab), one exclamative in English (p. 4, ex. 5b) and two examples from English and Latin that are difficult to characterize (p 4, exs. 4c, 5a). There is reason to classify hortatives as a type of imperative clause (2.4.2). Returning to the given examples, and regarding the exclamative type, this appears not to be a universal type, according to Sadock and Zwicky (1985), but a rather frequent minor type, which is based on declaratives or interrogatives (2.5.3).

How Speas and Tenny's theory can be extended to represent minor sentence types is beyond the scope of their paper and our discussion. If we follow Sadock and Zwicky's insight, it appears that the three core types give rise to additional types: declaratives > evidential declaratives, exclamatives; interrogatives > exclamatives; imperatives > imprecatives. The core of Speas and Tenny's proposal can serve as a syntactic basis to pursue this insight.

In the remainder of this section, we review three important technical assumptions regarding the tree diagrams shown above. Discussing them here allows us to expedite the narrative.

3.4.3   *Two-level representations*

Speas and Tenny adopt two widely embraced ideas in their proposed syntactic representation (20). The first is that there exist combinatorial principles that restrict the set of possible lexical items or conceptual structures (with Hale and Keyser 1998, 1999). Lexical items can be atoms (e.g., nouns) or three types of structural relations: (i) head-complement (unaccusative verbs, or thematic intransitive verbs, e.g., *arrive* (26c)); (ii) head-specifier (unergative verbs, or agentive intransitive verbs, e.g., *work* (26a)); and (iii) head-external argument (transitive or ditransitive verbs, e.g., *break* (26b)).

The second assumption is that verb–argument relations can be split into a two-level representation: Larsonian "shells" (Larson 1988), an idea adopted and developed by Hale and Keyser, and Chomsky (1995). In "VP shells" (Larson 1988), a base verbal projection introduces the object, while another on top of it introduces the subject (26), at least in the case of transitive predicates.[31]

(26)   a. $[NP_1 \ V_1]$ a′. John worked
       b. $[NP_1 \ V_1 \ [V_2 \ NP_2]]$ b′. John broke the window
       c. $[NP_2 \ [V_2 \ \cancel{NP_2}]]$ c′. John arrived

As noted, Speas and Tenny view speech acts as ditransitive structures selecting a subject, an indirect object and a complement clause.

Speas and Tenny, then, follow Canac-Marquis (2003) in generalizing that syntactic structures are also constrained by combinatorial principles (e.g., Hale and Keyser) and that the maximum layers that a head projects is two. For Canac-Marquis, the higher layer results from head movement to check features. Once its features have been checked, the head will not move again, and thus will not project additional levels of structure (although it can merge with a higher head that will project its own base phrase layer). For Speas and Tenny, the end result is that the most complex projection allowed for a head in syntax is a transitive or ditransitive shell (two layers), if and when the head moves to check features.

Having elucidated these important technical aspects of Speas and Tenny's tree diagrams, we conclude this chapter with a summary.

3.5   Summary

This chapter has introduced alternative architecture for encoding indexicals in syntax, presumably adhering to the minimalist research program for linguistic theory (Chomsky 1995), a hypothesis historically predicated on the philosophical idea of innatism, assuming in some quarters a biolinguistic perspective (Larson et al. 2010; Di Sciullo and Boeckx 2011). The imperative clause is a substantive argument for the human faculty of language in view of its universal uniqueness as a speech act and near universal clause type. At the same time, the imperative clause is a moving target for the reductionist heuristic of the SMT. It appears to have resisted principled syntactic analysis with direct ties to general principles of clause structure. The revised empirical base, we have argued, restores morphosyntactic complexity to the imperative clause and brings it closer to D&I. An outstanding issue for a grammatical analysis lies in its context/indexical access: speaker intentionality, speaker time, speaker–addressee irreflexivity and asymmetry, negative incompatibility, as well as its role as a complex predicate (see Chapter 4) of varying deontic force along with morpho-lexical content. Common wisdom recognizes the subject of the imperative clause as second person while third and first person are also acknowledged. Since Ross's (1970) much-criticized PH, attempts to derive a computational complexity of clause types have been abandoned. The enterprise will be recast in Chapter 4 as a "light" performative hypothesis (LPH), with its attendant implications for resolving the unique morphosyntactic characteristics of the imperative (1.1.1), which the proposals reviewed in this chapter fail to address.

In this chapter, we have reviewed recent proposals that seek to represent the context of utterance in the syntax. The supporting evidence suggests that certain indexical phenomena cannot be elucidated without recourse to representing an utterance context and a reported context across root clauses and certain dependent clauses. The representation of this context, it has been suggested, must be compositional: indexical shift can be partial, logophoricity extends to the speaker and the addressee of the reported context only, and conjunct-disjunct systems target the epistemic authority via the speaker or the addressee. For Speas and Tenny, the force projection is verb-like and introduces the speaker and addressee as its arguments. This is congruent with an important domain in the manifestation of the reported context: propositional attitude verbs, whose explicit arguments typically serve as antecedents to logophoric elements or allow for an ambiguous interpretation of indexicals. Furthermore, the classification of sentence types cannot be successfully addressed via Speas and Tenny's proposed parameters of finiteness and dative advancement. This reattempt to typify basic speech acts in syntax brings us back decades later to the conceptual bases of Ross's (1970) Performative Hypothesis and its predecessors (Austin 1962; Katz and Postal 1964) in a minimalist thesis in a phase theory of syntax (Chomsky 2008, 2010; Berwick and Chomsky 2011), which we will approach in Chapter 4.

4 *The syntax of imperative clauses: a performative hypothesis*

4.1 Functional v

We propose that the syntax of imperative clauses[1] is uniquely characterized by encoding a "light"[2] (functional) verb v, which mediates the thematic role dynamics between the Speaker of an imperative expression and its Addressee at the context–syntax interface. The Addressee thematic role is assigned to the grammatical subject argument of the (lexical) verb V.[3] Under this scenario, the contextual meaning of an imperative clause is characterized as a "prescription" (Xrakovskij 2001), informally [Speaker$_i$ "prescribes" at time t$_i$ [Addressee to *DO P*]]. The formalization and theoretical consequences of this context-unified hypothesis of the imperative clause under minimalist assumptions will be developed in the course of this chapter. Although intuitively foundational in the history of ideas in generative grammar (Katz and Postal 1964), the proposal is partially revisionist in its claim of virtual (conceptual) necessity in encoding indexical properties of context for an adequate description of the syntax of imperative clauses.

The proposal is identified as a "light" (functional) performative hypothesis (LPH), in contrast with the original (lexical) performative hypothesis (PH).[4] LPH constitutes a reassessment, both in category and computation, beyond the initial framework and empirical bases of PH developed in generative grammar (Ross 1970; cf. Sadock 1969, 1974). The conceptual bases are set apart as follows.

4.1.1 Antecedents of the performative hypothesis

In Ross's PH the "performative" element was, arguably, assumed to be a lexical head V within a representational deep structure (DS) syntactic framework (Chomsky 1965). In LPH, in contrast, the "performative" is crucially recast as a functional (auxiliary-like) verbal category v within a minimally conceived bi-phasal derivational system driven by the operation Merge and Agree. Two dependency-related phases are assumed CP(vP).[5] CP encodes the functional

F phase interfacing with vP, the lexical content phase, in the spirit if not the letter of Chomsky (2001, 2008). Conceptually, we propose that imperative clauses are syntactically homologous to an expression *F(p)* with the compositional interpretation of a complex predicate [v[V]], in correlation with previous thinking (Megerdoomian 2008; Pantcheva 2009). If substantiated, LPH is a closer approximation to the philosophy of language speech act hypothesis (Austin 1962; Searle 1969, 1979).

In this chapter we flesh out LPH at the (function (content)) interface for the syntax of imperative clauses. Recent prevailing theoretical studies approaching a similar function-to-content issue have proposed dedicated syntactic projections, such as Rivero and Terzi's (1995) Mood Phrase, Modal Phrase (Poletto and Zanuttini 2003), Jussive Phrase (Zanuttini 2008: 10). The latter is a novel syntactic projection dedicated to capturing the thematic property (Addressee) of the grammatical subject of core imperatives. In Jensen (2004b) the person restriction in the realization of the Addressee is attributed to an exceptional tense phrase (TP) modality [$T_{Imp}°$, 2φ], where 2φ is interpreted as the *intended agent*. Intuitively closer to LPH, Koopman (2001) proposes an abstract analysis for Maasai imperatives, positing a silent causative-like verb with semantics similar to the English verb *get*.

Our proposal follows a recent surge of empirical and analytical interest in imperatives. There is a comprehensive volume of studies on imperative clauses in generative grammar with an extended introduction by the editor (van der Wurff 2007b). The contributors account for a wide range of independent proposals, and recognize a mix of syntactic and context properties, with particular attention to the inherent specification of the addressee. Unprecedented in scope and depth, Kaufmann (2012) develops a challenging context-to-semantics position on the meaning of imperatives. Aikhenvald's (2010) empirical account of canonical imperatives and command strategies across societies and cultures of the world enriches the primary database at hand. Yet, in spite of renewed research interest and challenging analyses of prominent properties of imperative clauses in typologically different languages, a unified understanding of the ontology of the imperative as a speech act remains a desideratum; namely, (a) what is an imperative expression? and (b) what is the necessary and sufficient form of a syntactic model that accounts for the imperative clauses humans use and don't use in speech? For LPH answers to these question are its central empirical and theoretical goal.

We argue for an LPH within the conceptual assumptions and descriptive adequacy that may be expected in accordance with a minimalist program (Chomsky 1995, 2008). With particular reference to imperative clauses, LPH claims the following. A core function of the imperative speech act, namely the illocutionary/imperative force (IF) of the sentence type, is encoded in the functional phase $[_{CP} [_c IF]]$. The syntactic effect of IF in CP is to license[6] the choice of a directive light verb head in the lower phase $[_{vP} [v]]$. Accordingly, in the content phase the vP's external argument e^i in the Spec of $[_{vP} e^i [v]]$ is assigned the theme role of the Speaker, hence deriving the deontic-thematic inter-phase syntax of the imperative clause.

Along the same functional chain, v probes/selects a complement content phase vP, whose external argument e^j in Spec of $[_{vP} e^j [v]]$ is assigned the thematic role of Addressee, in virtue of its indexical binding relation with the Speaker argument: $[_{vP} e^i [v [_{vP} e^j [v]]]]$. Under LPH interface derivation, the Addressee is also the syntactic subject of the imperative clause type, as expected. We return to the Speaker^i>Addressee^j thematic relation central to a unified understanding of the imperative clause type, in 4.1.3.

As briefly introduced, LPH makes a number of predictions that will be argued for in the course of the chapter. Among them we briefly present the following.

4.1.2   Imperatives as root clauses
The proposed (function (content)) syntactic interface restricts imperative expressions to matrix clauses,[7] a strong empirical claim on which LPH firmly stands (Alcázar and Saltarelli 2008b, 2012).[8] This locality prediction follows from the central postulate of a licensing relation between the functional property IF and the light verb v: $[_{CP}[_c IF [_{vP}[_v v]]]]$. As a direct consequence, LPH aligns with Austin's intuitions and Ross's (PH) claims about "indirect discourse imperatives" (IDI) *I/*you order *I/you to go!* as a bona fide [Speaker [Person1] >Addressee [Person2]] condition on imperative expressions: $[_{CP} [_c IF [_{vP} I [_v order [_{VP} [_v ~~order~~ [_{vP} you to go]]]]]]]$.

In IDI, the lexical head V merges with v forming a complex predicate with the sentential force of IF inherited from the functional phase CP, including the [Person1>2] restriction. Thus, under minimalist phase-theoretic assumptions, functional LPH makes it possible to recapture PH intuitions about IDI by more narrowly identifying the performative as a complex predicate $[v[V]]$ of functional force and lexical content. In the course of this chapter, moreover, we attempt to show that LPH offers a competitive approach to the study of the semantics–syntax interface of the imperative clause.

4.1.2.1   Imperative temporality
Preliminary considerations on the distribution of tense oppositions in imperative clauses can be gathered from their syntactic compatibility with temporal adverbs. If the imperative clause types in (1) are interpreted as directive

expressions, then any imperative hypothesis must constrain temporality to "future orientation" (cf. Kaufmann 2012: 93) in order to comply with descriptive adequacy in the syntactic computation of imperative clauses (1).

(1)   a. Buy a Fiat now/ tomorrow/*yesterday!
       b. I order you to buy a Fiat now/tomorrow/*yesterday!
       c. You should buy a Fiat now/tomorrow/*yesterday!

Under LPH, restrictions on imperative temporality follow as a corollary of the performative nature of the expression: [Speaker$_i$ "prescribes" at time t$_i$ [Addressee to *DO P*]]. Namely, the restricted tense opposition in the syntax of imperative clauses (1) is accounted for by encoding the role of the Speaker in the functional phase (CP). Under Speaker's time orientation, present and future but not *past imperative events are licensed at the (function (content)) interface, in accordance with a descriptive account of the *agrammatical past time adverbials (1).

Nevertheless, it has been claimed that "imperatives about the past do exist in languages other than English" (cf. van der Wurff 2007a: 45). We will return to discuss putative cases of past imperative clauses later (4.5).

4.1.3   *Speaker^i>Addressee$^{*i/j}$ relation*

The central tenet in an LPH account of directive expressions externalized as imperative clauses is the general definition of the hierarchical dyadic pair relation: [Speaker^i>Addressee$^{*i/j}$]. Informally the restriction claims that from a speech act perspective of imperatives "an actant does not act upon her/himself." The directive Speaker>Addressee relation is formally defined by the principles of referential irreflexivity (2a) and structural asymmetry (2b) (Reichenbach 1947: 118–19).[9]

(2)   Anti-reflexivity:
       a. irreflexive
       b. asymmetric

The anti-reflexivity principle uniquely defines canonical imperative clauses as well as the imperative–hortative system. Formally, referential irreflexivity (2a) reasonably excludes self-ascription, thus providing a logical contextual account for the otherwise unexplained paradigm of (2a) grammaticality: "protect *myself/yourself/*him/*herself!" Asymmetry (2b) defines the implicational identity of the Addressee, referentially disjoint from the Speaker, hence shedding some light on the ontology of indexical v grammatical categories (cf. 4.2.4).[10]

4.1.3.1   Thematic relations: from context to content

Under anti-reflexivity assumptions (2), in LPH the contextual (CP) Speaker>Addressee thematic relation is construed in the content phase (vP) as a syntactic dependency effect, which is mediated by a closed class of "light" performative verbs v. Thus LPH encodes sentential force [$_{CP}$IF] operator-like parameters of the imperative speech act not as abstract argument heads but as thematic θ-role dependencies.

4.1.3.2   On person and person values

One descriptive advantage of encoding the [Speaker>Addressee] relation as a CP-licensing of predicate-argument function in the root-phase vP is the def-inition of Person values. Under LPH, Person 1>2 are derived as a plausible by-product of the [Speaker>Addressee] via general principles (4.1.3 (2a,b)). Attendant implications beyond imperatives follow. Along this line of reasoning, Person values fall into two sets: P1>2 vs. P3. Empirical evidence from gram-maticalization tends to support a bipartite morphosyntactic behavior beyond imperatives. The variation in the selection of functional auxiliaries BE(P1,2)/ HAVE(P3) in Abruzzan dialects is one such type of indexical grammatical-ization. This phenomenon would remain a curious fact of language, except under a morphosyntactic hypothesis encoding the relation Speaker>Addressee, such as LPH. In keeping with tradition, we will be informally using mor-phological Person 1>2 in alternation with the thematic Speaker>Addressee relation.

4.1.3.3   Deictics in philosophy and in linguistics

The LPH interface scenario opens an analytical path for a parallel/unified account of *context of utterance* in the philosophy of language (Kaplan 1977, 1989; Schlenker 2003) and linguistics (Bianchi 2003; Baker 2008; Giorgi 2010), which suggest a convergence. Other parameters of indexicality appear to fall under the same (function(content)) phase-theoretic hypothesis when we consider a minimalist account of the parallel behavior of impera-tive sentences with demonstratives and time/space adverbials, such as "come/*came now/*yesterday! Give/*gave me that book there/*here near you/*me!"[11]

4.1.4   Imperatives as functional expressions: CP(vP)

It should be made explicit that under LPH an imperative expression is inter-preted compositionally as a complex predicate, where a CP functional property of the head IF probes/merges with a dependent vP phase, concretely its lexical content. The *F(p)* compositional nature of imperatives becomes more patently plausible when we consider that the lexical (semantic) properties of most verbs like *eat, sleep, go*, etc. do not contain, in an obvious way, imperative features. Yet *eat!, sleep!, go!* are bona fide imperative expressions and clauses. In contrast, lexical verbs like *demand, order, expect* can be argued to have properties of imperatives. Nevertheless, they do not readily stand alone as commands as one might expect: **demand!, *order!*. Even when they do in indirect discourse (*I/*You demand (order, expect) that you leave!*) their imperative use is restricted to first person (the Speaker).

4.1.4.1 Functional expressions F(p) and complex predicates [v[V]]
These apparently recalcitrant facts about imperative expressions and derived clauses, which would require exceptional statements under strictly lexical theories of imperatives, follow directly as a consequence of an LPH that states that imperatives encode IF as a functionally derived complex predicate of imperative expressions: *F(p)* (Searle 1979: 1). In this respect, LPH, if substantiated, unifies elements of the philosophy of language from Austin and Searle's speech acts at their interface with syntax. In another respect, LPH stands on a syntactic category asymmetry between functional and lexical verbs: [v[V]] (cf. Saltarelli and Alcázar 2010 on Apulian aspectual "light" verbs). The functional/lexical nature of "light" v vs. V is at the syntactic edge between function (CP) and (vP) as recent studies on "semi-lexical" categories tend to suggest (Corver and van Riemsdijk 2001).

4.1.5 The performative hypothesis revisited
In contrast with LPH, the original PH's viability within the conception of the theory of grammar of the 1960s was, in hindsight, handicapped by the choice of a lexical head (V) rather than a functional head (v) as the category for the performative verb. We retrace the original descriptive goal and critical thinking that led to the rise and fall of PH, and consequently to the abandonment of the topic without a viable alternative hypothesis of imperative clauses. Informally, an earlier pre-sentential operator-like I(mperative) remained unexplored (Katz and Postal 1964).

Under a minimalist research program and a derivational Merge-driven computational system, new empirical evidence on the grammaticalization of imperatives and other clause types will be adduced to justify LPH as a step toward a unified theory of imperatives and their place in the architecture of clause types. Ultimately, we hope to contribute to an understanding of the other ineffable speech act question: what can one DO and NOT DO with words? (in deference to J. L. Austin).

4.1.6   *Essential structure of the "light" performative hypothesis (LPH)*

On the assumption of foundational tenets discussed in the preceding section (4.1), this chapter is structured as follows. Section 4.2 introduces LPH as an integral component of a general theory of imperative expressions, which aims at comprehensive empirical coverage within a strong minimalist research thesis (SMT) for the theory of language (Chomsky 2008). In terms of empirical coverage, beyond canonical imperatives (*go!*) lies an extended (hortative) set of imperative expressions where the Addressee and the Performer may be referentially disjoint (*let them go!*) or overlap in reference (Speaker-inclusive exhortations, *let's go!*).[12] In LPH analysis said imperatives present a causative vP which heads the prescription selected by the light verb [Speaker *prescribes* [Addressee to *cause* [Performer to *DO P*]]]. For syntactic implementation, a comprehensive account of imperative sentences requires access to the full argument structure parallel to the speech act (Speaker-Addressee-Performer).

Toward this goal, Section 4.2.3 states the functional formula for the meaning of the imperative expression as a "prescription" from Speaker to an Addressee. Section 4.2.4 introduces the role of Performer of the imperative expression in the interplay between the Speaker, the Addressee and a third party. Under this scenario an LPH unified analysis of canonical and extended (hortatives) clauses is addressed and illustrated, along with prohibitions (4.2.6).

Section 4.3 argues for the functional nature of syntactic v as it concerns the description of imperative clauses in relation to context. Independent computational arguments are presented for justifying a prescriptive v in the lower left periphery of the content phase (vP) as the natural syntactic interface locality for encoding indexical properties, in critical contrast with alternative mainstream proposals, along with analytic imperatives (IDI) (4.3.4), allocutive (Addressee) agreement in Basque (4.3.5), thematic role and Person values (4.3.6).

Section 4.4 expounds on empirical evidence for the grammaticalization of the Speaker, Addressee and Performer. Special attention is given to the subject of imperatives (4.4.1), imperatives in vocative expressions (4.4.4), third person imperatives (4.4.5), and exhortations in Spanish (4.4.6).

Section 4.5 revisits imperative temporality in view of retrospective (4.5.3) and conditional (4.5.4) imperatives. Cross-linguistic evidence for the proposed prescriptive "light" verb v is presented in section (4.6). A summary and conclusions follow in section (4.7).

4.2   A "light" performative hypothesis (LPH)

In this section, LPH is developed in direct comparison with other mainstream proposals for encoding indexical properties of the imperative clause in the syntactic framework of generative grammar. A challenging theoretical position is Zanuttini's (2008) Jussive Phrase.

4.2.1   Encoding the Addressee

Recognizing the central role of the Addressee as the "grammatical subject" of the imperative verb clause, a dedicated functional projection is proposed: the Jussive Phrase (JP, Zanuttini 2008: 197(3)):

(3) $[_{JP}$ Op $[_{Jussive} [_{XP}$ Subject$_i [_{X^0} [_{VP} t_i [_v [_{VP} [...]]]]]]]]$

Accordingly, the syntactic representation of an imperative clause is characterized by a higher Jussive Phrase (JP), which projects as its external argument a Jussive operator (OP) arguably binding the variable Subject$_i$ at the (Speaker$_i$'s) time t_i assigning the role to the Addressee. Computationally, the main verb V^0 (in VP) Head-moves to or Merges with X^0 to Jussive^0, hence syntactically defining its subject as the Addressee. In order to implement this thesis of imperative clauses, it was deemed necessary to assume that UG contains a principle or (semantic) interface condition along the lines of (4).

(4)   UG contains a principle requiring imperative subjects to refer to, or quantify over, an addressee, a group of addressees, or a group containing the addressee(s). (cf. Mauck et al. 2005)

(4) opens a necessary path toward the unification of research at the semantics–syntax interface, arguably in the direction suggested by prevailing studies of the left periphery of syntax (Rizzi 1997, 2004; Cinque 1999, 2002, 2004).

4.2.2   About the Speaker

While encoding the Addressee (4.2.1) is on the right path toward syntactic visibility of context in syntax, it falls short of a general account of the contextual properties of imperative clauses, without considering its bound relation to the Speaker. Alternatively, one may assume a wider perspective. Namely, it seems reasonable to deduce that the "Addressee" hypothesis expressed in (4) does not stand alone as a principle of thematic roles. In a speech act scenario, the requirement of an Addressee follows as a conceptual consequence of a hierarchically binding "Addressor," namely the intentional Speaker$_i$ at the time t_i of the utterance.

As advanced above (4.1), such a view of basic sentence types is arguably implied under what has been known as the (original) "performative hypothesis"

(Ross 1970: 123). Regarding the syntactic approach to the analysis of reduced (small-sized) clause types (i.e., bare verb imperative), it can be presumed that the original PH was inspired by the consideration of context in the philosophy of language of the period (Austin 1962: 32; Searle 1969). For discussion see Sadock (1974), Levinson (1983: Ch. 5), and Xrakovskij (2001), among others, for critical assessments, along with a definition of the meaning and the computation of imperative and other major clause types.

4.2.3   On the functional meaning of imperatives

With particular reference to imperative sentences, Ross's (1970: 223 referencing Austin 1962: 32) PH proposed that an utterance like "go!" contains a performative main (lexical) verb V, as it would, explicitly, in IDI "I order you to go!" While consistent with the intuition from which PH may have arisen, our LPH claims, in contrast, that such an understanding of Austin's (1962) "performative" is a functional (overt/covert, auxiliary-like) v, rather than a lexical head V.[13] Concretely, it is proposed that imperative utterances are more precisely interpreted as "prescriptions" encoding the (indexical) parameters of the speech act, such as participant roles, temporality and locality. Its syntactic computation, we have been proposing, involves the functional phase CP in composition with the (lexical) content phase vP. A preliminary assessment of imperatives as "prescriptions" in LPH is outlined in (5). See 4.3.3.1 for a phase-theoretic account.

(5)   LPH-based theory of imperative expressions
    a. [A$_i$ t$_i$ "prescribes" [B$_j$ to *DO P*]]   *Go!*
    b. [A "prescribes" [B to "cause" [A/*B/C to *DO P*]] *Let me/*myself go*
                                           *Let *you/yourself go*
                                           *Let him/*himself... go!*
    (i)   The imperative is a "prescription": a linguistic expression $F(p)$ derived in association with the functional properties vP common to the feature class of explicit imperative predicates such as *demand*, *request*, *prohibit*, in composition with a lexical content predicate V.[14]
    (ii) Participant argument roles:
          Speaker A$_i$ (= prescriptor) at time t$_i$
          Addressee B (= recipient/intended goal of the prescription)
          Performer C (= performer of *P*)
    (iii) The prescribed expression *DO P*

An imperative clause type, conceived as a "prescription" (cf. Xrakovskij 2001), is defined in LPH by the class property (sentential force) of performative verbs (5b.i) uttered by Speaker$_i$ A at time t$_i$ to an intended Addressee B$_j$ (5b.ii) in the speech act$_i$. In this respect, it is a common view that only the

Table 4.1 *Arguments and roles*[a]

Type	Speaker	Addressee	Performer	Imperative sentence
1	A	B	B	*Go!*
2	A	B	C	*Let him/her/them go!*
3	A	B	A	*Let me go!*
4	A	B	A+B	*Let... go!* (incl. of the S)
5	A	B	A+C–B	*Let... go!* (excl. of the S)

[a] Absent from this parametric table are apparent gaps in the paradigm, such as self-exhortations which do not comply with the hierarchical Speaker>Addressee referential disjunction in canonical imperatives (Speaker$_i$>Addressee$_{*i/j}$; cf. 4.1.2). Evidence in analytic (IDI) and canonical imperative: "I want you to protect *myself/*himself!", "protect *myself/*himself!" Co-reference in extended imperatives between the Addressee and the Performer (Speaker A, Addressee B, Performer B) does not violate the Speaker>Addressee relation.

Addressee B can be the realized or interpreted grammatical subject of the prescribed expression (5a): "I demand that you/*I go!", "go!"

4.2.4   About the Performer

An extended paradigm, however, referentially disjoins the Performer C from the Addressee B (5b.ii): "let him/me/*you go!" This suggests a more comprehensive parametric syntactic theory of the imperative types which would account for (5a) as well as (5b).

Under LPH, imperative sentences involve the argument structure and role distribution parameters shown in Table 4.1.[15] Considering the identity of the Performer argument, imperative expressions naturally divide into canonical or extended types (hortative). In the first, the Performer must be co-referential with the Addressee (type 1). In the latter, there is no such requirement, giving rise to multiple but patterned possibilities. For example, the Performer may be disjoint from both the Speaker and Addressee (type 2). It may be co-referential with the Speaker only (type 3), with both Speaker and Addressee (type 4: inclusive exhortation), or with the Speaker and a third party that is not identified as the Addressee (type 5).

4.2.5   Canonical and extended (hortative) imperatives

A rich literature on imperatives and commands in use across the world's languages (Aikhenvald 2010) distinguishes different strategies: exhortatives or hortatives, imperatives directed to first person inclusive Addressees; Immediate Imperative ("do immediately"); Canonical Imperative directed to second person Addressees; and Non-Canonical imperatives directed to non-second person Addressees. In contrast, typological research draws together one

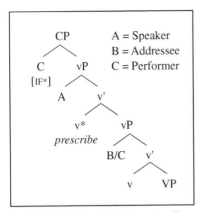

Figure 4.1a *Canonical imperatives*[16]

unified general type: the imperative–hortative system (van der Auwera et al. 2008: Ch. 72).

In this chapter we use the terms *canonical* imperatives (*go!*) and *extended* (hortative) imperatives (*let … go!*). Under LPH assumptions, both types are formally a unitary syntactic type (4.2.3 (5a,b)). Strictly speaking, canonical imperatives have an Addressee that is also a Performer (Figure 4.1a), whereas in extended imperatives the Addressee may also be a Causer (Figure 4.1b).

The computational difference between canonical and extended imperatives, LPH claims, is rooted and derived in the syntax (as illustrated above).[17] Extended imperatives contain a "causative" v^{c}P selecting the prescription vP. The "causative" syntactically disjoins the Addressee from the Performer.

4.2.6 Imperatives and prohibitions

It is generally recognized that the imperative verb paradigm tends to be incompatible with negation and that this incompatibility is resolved in many languages with a different morphological paradigm (subjunctive in Spanish (6b), infinitive in Italian, gerund in Marsican). In some cases, such as Gallo-Romance varieties like Piemontese, the Neg particle is postposed (arguably cliticized) to the imperative form of the verb.[18] Latin, among other languages, selects a distinct morpheme: *nōn*, *nē*-Imp.

4.2.6.1 Negative incompatibility

The issue of negative incompatibility has been attributed to the intentional conceptual nature of the imperative speech act, hence as "an instrument of the Speaker" (Reichenbach 1947: 336).[19] What is negated is the content *f(~p)*, not the imperative function *~f(p)*. The logical validity of imperative has been (and

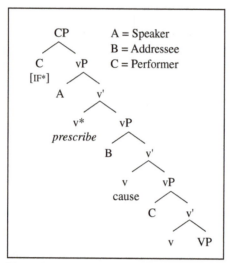

Figure 4.1b *Extended imperatives*

continues to be) the subject of debate since Frege. There is, however, some agreement that imperatives are neither true nor false, as hinted by Austin speaking of commands (Austin 1962, Lecture I). Under LPH, imperative clauses are more like "prescriptions" (Xrakovskij 2001), not strictly "statements."

If so, then it might be suggested that there is a logical and conceptual reason for the fact that negative imperative verbs (i.e., "true" negative imperatives (TNI, cf. Zeijlstra 2006)) are uncommon in a minority of languages.[20] Under this assumption we can expect that different syntactic strategies would be employed to express directives: (Speaker$_i$ at Speaker$_i$/Utterance time t$_i$ Orders (Addressee$_j$ (NOT (to DO something)).

4.2.6.2 Grammaticalizing prohibitions
The grammaticalization of prohibitions comes in different forms, for example, through lexicalization in "allow/prohibit," "go/stop," "accept/refuse," "confirm/deny." It's more evident as lexicalization through Neg-incorporation, as in the Latin antonyms *vŏlo* 'I am willing' vs. *nōlo* 'I am unwilling.' In many languages, dedicated negative particles exist for prohibition, such as, again, in Latin *nē* Neg-commands, and *nōn* for Neg-statements. In sum, in prohibitive expressions the Neg particle may be dedicated (Vietnamese, Zulu, Latin), or it may license/select different moods (Spanish, Italian, Marsican) or appear morphosyntactically construed with the root or an auxiliary v or a main V verb (English or Gallo-Romance) (cf. van der Auwera et al. 2005a).

In view of empirical and computational considerations, LPH derives imperatives and prohibitions under the same operation Head-Move or Merge (6a,b for
Spanish). The discussion of logical validity confirms the indexical meaning of
the imperative clause as {Speaker uttering a "prescription" to an Addressee}.
Hence, like statements, the prescription itself can be compositionally negated.
Structurally, Neg may be merged higher than the prescription, but lower that
the function C. Neg may value illocutionary force (if dedicated) or may form
a complex predicate with the "prescriptive" verb. Neg may select Speaker/
Event-oriented mood.

(6)   a. Imperative   b. Prohibition

```
            CP                                    CP
          /    \                                /    \
        C       vP                            C       vP
      ¡habla!  /  \                          ¡no!    /  \
      ¡hable!  A   v'                                A    v'
                  / \                                    /  \
                 v   vP                                 v    vP
               habla  / \                               no   /  \
               hable B   VP                                  B    VP
                          |                                      /    \
                          V                                    Neg    VP
                          |                                    no     / \
                      habla  IND                                     V
                      hable  SUBJ                                    |
                                                                  *habla
                                                                   hable
```

Summarizing, the imperative–prohibition system under LPH shares the
same thematic relation A>B and sentential force C. The indexical and deontic
(IF) properties of v are C licensed. Accordingly, v projects the external argument with the discourse role of Speaker and selects a vP (the "prescription")
whose external argument is assigned the discourse role of Addressee in accordance with the defining irreflexive relation A>B of imperative expression
(4.1.3).

Accordingly, an imperative expression $f(p)$ is indexically equivalent to a prohibition $f(\sim p)$, except for the functional value f with scope over the prescription. Structurally, Negation (Neg) is arguably a predicate. In the illustrations
in (6) the verb *¡habla/hable!* values the force of imperative clauses, while the
negative particle alone (+subjunctive) *¡no (+hable)!* values prohibitive features in the above illustrated examples.

4.2.7   Revisiting person restrictions: disjoint Addressee/Performer

Recall (4.1.3.2) on deriving Person1>2 values from the defining irreflexive
principle of thematic relation in imperative expressions (4.1.3).

Under LPH assumptions, the Performer role is not intended as a new thematic relation (beyond the Speaker>Addressee) or part of our theory's ontological commitment. Whatever theta role the Performer argument bears, it will be determined by the lexical content with which it is construed. Consider, for example, the theme in "go!" or the agent in "finish your soup!" and similarly in "make them go!" or "make them finish their soup!" In these cases the intended Performer is also a Causee/Causer). The Performer role thus serves a narrative function in our discussion, theta role assignment being determined, as a theorem, by the verb.

Moreover, there is a distributional reason for disassociating the role of the Addressee from that of the Performer under LPH. Namely, the Person1>2 restriction is required for the Speaker>Addressee only. The Performer is exempt from Person restrictions, as observed in the following directives expressions consistently with anti-reflexivity (4.1.3):

(7)   a. I/*you want you to leave! or leave!
       b. I/*you want you to let me/him leave! or let me/him/*you leave!

It can be argued, in hindsight, that the original (Ross 1970) PH was an intuitively and empirically legitimate hypothesis. Its failed justification (cf. Sadock 1974) can be attributed to (i) the absence of a formal disambiguation between functional v and lexical V, (ii) a minimalist "derivational" (vs. "representational") computational mechanism, and (iii) the cardinal speech act principle of irreflexivity (4.1.3). The latter principle will be assumed here as a core property of speech act dynamics. It endows LPH with access to the context of utterance with improved understanding of those imperative clauses that we find in human speech ("protect yourself!") and those we don't find ("protect *myself").

4.3   The functional nature of little v (in vP)

Conceptually, the Speaker>Addressee dependency relation is intended as a (sentential) context dependency, explicitly derived in imperative syntax via prescriptive v. We present arguments that justify the need for such a syntactic head v in the "higher/left periphery" of the lower/content phase vP. The focus will be on the functional nature of prescriptive v, its phase syntax and its intended deontic effects.

Assume with Chomsky (2008) that v is the set of functional choices in the vP phase (F clause type: imperatives, interrogatives, declaratives) each licensed as a choice from the higher functional phase $[_{CP}IF]$. In accordance with an SMT, said F/choices may be identified as abstract deontic properties (4.2.3 (5.b.i)) grammaticalized as a dedicated set of functional ("light") verbs as morphosyntactic particles or inflectional paradigms.

4.3.1   Deriving imperatives

Hence, in LPH syntactic computation of imperative clauses, a "prescriptive" v is a choice of v in the lower vP phase. vP is licensed by IF in the higher functional phase CP, postulating the properties of the speech act sketched in (4.2.3 (5)). In phase-theoretic terms for canonical imperatives (4.2.5, Fig. 4.1a) IF is a functional probe merging with a content vP. As a consequence, the inherited features of v project an external argument (denoting the Speaker). Moreover, v selects a complement vP, whose subject stands in a local binding relation with the Speaker, hence denoting the Addressee. Thus, under LPH, the Speaker>Addressee relation is ultimately derived as a syntactic dependency theorem, conceivably along with Person (/Number) restrictions. Thus, if substantiated, LPH pre-empts the need for special statements like (4), dedicated syntactic projections/restrictions, Jussive Phrase (Zanuttini 2008), or TP modality [T_{imp} 2φ] (Jensen 2004b).

4.3.2   Encoding Speaker and Addressee: the wider perspective

In this subsection we critically digress to defend encoding properties of the context in the narrower theory of syntax. Beyond imperative clauses, the basic assumptions of LPH optimally extend to parallel empirical grounds of interest identified in the philosophy of language as context of utterance, such as indexical elements: a set of properties of linguistic expressions that, for their interpretation, require access to the Speaker <Person1SG>, the Addressee <Person2>, as well as aspects of time <now> and place <here> and modality (cf. Kaplan 1989; von Stechow 2002; Schlenker 2003; Anand and Nevins 2004; Kaufmann 2012). Other challenging hypotheses about the semantics–syntax interface have recently been proposed arguing for the encoding of Speaker, Addressee and other indexicals in syntax, which is likely to result in an expanded architecture of the functional phase CP.

4.3.2.1   Speaker and Addressee as null arguments

Responding to crucial empirical evidence on the interpretation and licensing of the person values of pronominals in Amharic (Schlenker 2003), Baker (2008: 125–26 (29–30)) proposes that (i) "all matrix clauses and certain embedded clauses have two special null arguments [NAH hypothesis] generated within the CP projection, one designated S (for speaker) and the other A (for addressee)" and (ii) "in the absence of overriding control relationships, S designates the person who produced the CP and A designates the person who the CP was addressed to."

In Baker's hypothesis (NAH), the Speaker and Addressee are generated within the context CP projection. In addition, they require an independent person licensing condition without direct association to illocutionary force. While recognizing the role of Speaker and Addressee at the semantics–syntax interface, Baker's proposal, in contrast with LPH, is silent about the LPH Speaker>Addressee irreflexive relation (4.1.3), from which Baker's Person Licensing Condition is predicted as a consequence of a more general principle.

On the empirical side, NAH is silent about disambiguation of homophonous imperative/declarative in languages like Italian or Maasai (cf. Koopman 2001), in particular, Italian homophonous *mangiate in fretta(!)* 'hurry up and eat!/you are eating in a hurry)'. Syntactic homophony is a well-known evolutionary result of morphological reanalysis and phonological shift. Beyond intonation and contextual demonstrations, the two types have distinct syntactic threads, including (a) the realization and word order of the overt subject, (b) root vs. embedding status, and (c) negation/prohibition. These, among other issues, require functional context, such as IF, for an adequate syntactic account.

Under LPH computation, the Speaker and Addressee roles are ultimately derived from the argument structure of the content phase vP, crucially dependent on its association with IF: arguably, the illocutionary force of the functional CP context. In general agreement with Baker's null arguments in CP cf. (i) above, LPH derives Speaker>Addressee as A'-bound variables in the content phase (see 4.3.3.1 below).

4.3.2.2   About Speaker's knowledge

It seems legitimate, on reflection, to inquire whether under LPH the sole justification for encoding thematic roles such as Speaker as the intentional initiator of the speech act is a virtual conceptual necessity for an adequate description of the seemingly ineffable syntax of imperative clauses.

We have argued, in this respect, about the strictly "root" nature of the imperative utterance, its Person (1>2=Speaker>Addressee) functional irreflexivity of the intentional directive (4.1.3), and its future-oriented temporality (4.1.2.1). Nevertheless, there is more in utterance grammaticalization that requires access to Speaker for a descriptively adequate computation of syntax.

Most recently, Giorgi (2010) provides independent syntactic arguments for reclaiming the Speaker as an epistemic head in a C-layer of the (extreme) left periphery. The following is proposed. "There is a syntactic position in the leftmost periphery of the clause, and precisely in the Complementizer layer [CP], that encodes the temporal – and presumably spatial as well – coordinates of the speaker" (Giorgi 2010: 7).

Giorgi describes the following garden variety of syntactic evidence: "In Italian the Complementizer can be omitted in subjunctive contexts and can never be dispensed with if the embedded verb is in the indicative mood. The sentence complement to a *believe* predicate in Italian – *credere* – selects for subjunctive and, accordingly admits Complementizer Deletion" (Giorgi 2010: 66–67 (1–2)).

(8)   *Gianni ha detto *(che) è partita*
        Gianni said that she left(IND)

(9)   *Gianni crede (che) sia partita*
        Gianni believes that she left(SUBJ)

Although speakers' intuition appears to be robust on (8) and (9), an explicit lexical subject of the subordinate clause, such as Luisa in (10), degrades acceptability. Remarkably, speakers' judgments improve if the subject of the main verb is first person singular (11).

(10)   #*Gianni crede Luisa abbia telefonato*   (Giorgi's (6) p. 68)
        Gianni believes that Luisa called(SUBJ)

(11)   *Credo Luisa abbia telefonato*   (Giorgi's (7) p. 68)
        (I) believe Luisa called (SUBJ)

Giorgi claims that *credo* in (11) "only specifies the epistemic status of the speaker with respect to the proposition that follows. In these cases *credo* (I believe) has to be treated as an epistemic head, 'disguised' as a verb" (p. 69). The author suggests that the sentence (11) should be analyzed as a monoclausal and not as a bi-clausal (complex) structure.

While it represents a compelling empirical argument for a descriptive account of Italian syntax, the implementation of the syntactic proposal leaves both theoretical and computational questions unexplored, such as the status of the Speaker's coordinates and their interface with the content phase vP. Moreover, if *credo* is not a lexical verb in (11) its syntactic status needs to be assessed. The claim of mono-clausality, although conceptually convincing, leaves unexplored an account of double subjecthood and relative agreement morphology.

Giorgi's empirical discovery is a good fit within the generalized system of LPH which arguably extends to major clause types. Its LPH derivation would be roughly as follows:

(12) $[_{CP}\text{Speaker}_i[_C [_{vP} x_i [_{v'} [_v \text{ credo } [_{vP} \text{ Luisa } [_{v'} [_v \text{ abbia } [_v \text{ telefonato }]]]]]]]]]]$

In (12) *credo* is a "light" verb v (licensed in C) which selects a complement [vP *Luisa abbia telefonato*]. Hence, an LPH account of Giorgi's mono-clausal interpretation of epistemic *credo* complements (11) would syntactically interface as complex predicates: [v[V]]. In this scenario, Speaker$_i$ epistemicity is accessible from the extreme left periphery through the bound variable x_i coordinate in Spec of vP (cf. also 4.3.3.1 below).

4.3.3   Consequences of an expanded functional CP
In sum, both Baker's and Giorgi's proposals expand the predicate-argument building mechanism to the CP functional phase, beyond vP. On general considerations, the expansion has syntactic implications yet to be formally clarified. Encoding indexicals implies a more powerful generative device, and hence is prima facie inconsistent with an SMT minimalism. Moreover, under an extended CP predicate-argument hypothesis, the thematic relation Speaker>Addressee remains indexical (or syntactically underived). In one respect, under SMT assumptions, LPH compares favorably in that it accounts for one aspect of the Speaker$_i$>Addressee$_j$ thematic relation as a general principle of anti-reflexivity (4.1.3), from which the morphosyntax of the concomitant Person1>2 category is derived as an epiphenomenon. In short, relevant aspects of indexical syntax have been recognized (specifically by Baker and Giorgi) along with the prospect that encoding indexicals in syntax is a virtual conceptual necessity.

In the following subsection we sketch an A'-binding CP(vP) interface proposal intended to unify in part recent syntactic consideration on the representation of Speaker and Addressee (Safir 2005; Zanuttini 2008 (see 4.2.1); Baker 2008; Giorgi 2010, among others).

4.3.3.1   Operator-variable binding in imperatives
Recall the informal characterization of the LPH functional meaning of the imperative expression as a "prescription" in canonical imperatives clauses like "go!" See section (4.2.3 (5a), illustrated in (4.2.5 Fig. 4.1a) and repeated below (13a).

(13)   (a) $[A_i t_i \text{ "prescribes" } [B_j \text{ to } DO \text{ } P]]$ *Go!*

Under a CP(vP) phase-theoretic architecture of syntax (13a) is formally represented as (13b):

(13)   (b) $[_{CP} Op_i [_{c'} T_i [_C Op_j [_{vP} x_i [_v [_{vP} y_j [_v [_{VP}]]]]]]]]$

where x_i and y_j are (null pronominal) variable arguments in the Spec of the vP content phase and pairwise bound by the null operators in the functional phase CP, namely Speaker-OP_i −x and Addressee-OP_j−y. Note that the Addressee variable y is in the Spec of the v selected vP, hence is the subject of the imperative verb. Technically, A′-variable binding is assumed under the Bijection Principle:

(13)   (c) Every operator A′-binds exactly one variable and every variable is A′-bound by exactly one operator (Koopman and Sportiche 1982).

In computational terms, LPH, in its functional CP(vP) phase-theoretic framework, provides a necessary and sufficient interface condition for encoding context roles in the syntax of imperatives.

Moreover, if substantiated, LPH's approach toward an understanding of the syntax–semantics interface is in keeping with current syntactic approaches toward the representation of Speaker/Addressee roles.

4.3.4   Analytic imperatives (IDI)

On the empirical side, LPH is also favored in that it invites an account of indirect discourse directives (IDI): *I/*you demand that you leave!* IDIs are often disregarded as outside the realm of imperative clauses. Such imperative expressions fall squarely under imperative as a "prescription" and offer evidence of the full realization and effects of functional binding in the lower (lexical) content phase. Under SMT, the LPH *F*-licensing principle would also win over an I(nternal)-merge analysis of indirect discourse directives *I demand (that) you leave*: $[_{CP}F_{Imp}[_{vP} I_i [_v$ demand $([_{VP} [_v$ ~~demand~~ $[_{vP}$ you$_j$ leave]]]]]], where "I$_i$" is the Speaker of the utterance and "you$_j$" is the Addressee functioning as grammatical subject of the "prescription," in accordance with the irreflexivity principle (4.1.3).

Note, in fact, that IDI can also function as an indirect discourse declarative IDD clause type in reported speech: *John said that [I/you/he demands that you leave]*. Hence the ambiguity in interpretation between IDI and IDD is restricted to the first person, that is, under the condition where the subject of the performative verb "demand" is the same (first person *I*) as the Speaker of the utterance and the Addressee/Performer (second person *you*) is the subject of the "prescription" (i.e., the vP selected by the performative v). Under LPH, then, IDI is not an idiosyncratic homophony requiring a special statement. Rather, an IDI is derived as another instance of the canonical imperative, where the performative v is realized as a complex predicate with the lexical V and the expression is subject to the Speaker>Addressee relation (4.1.3).

4.3.5　Addressee allocutive agreement in Basque

We have been arguing for the desirability of an LPH analysis of imperatives (4.1&2), in which the Addressee of the speech act is functionally licensed as the "subject argument of the imperative clause."

From this general proposal two questions follow:

 (a)　Is the Addressee restricted to imperative clauses (vs. D&I)?
 (b)　Is the Addressee restricted to an argument (vs. adjunct)?

The above questions are prompted by the phenomenon of allocutivity in Basque (for a typological perspective, see Antonov 2012, 2013a, 2013b). In Basque, the verb is inflected by a morpheme alternant (ALLOcutive –*k/–n*) consistent with the gender of the Addressee. Curiously, the phenomenon is not observed in imperatives (question (a)). Neither (question (b)) is the ALLOcutive morpheme associated with an argument of the lexical verb. See Chapter 5 for a thorough presentation of Basque Allocutive Agreement (AA), which is briefly advanced in (14) below.[21]

(14)　　Second person agreement marks that reference the Addressee: *-k, -n*
 a.　*Haurr-ak*　　　*heldu*　　*d-it-u-k*
  Children-ABS.PL　arrived　Ø-PL(A)-AUX.HAVE-2SG.MALE
  'The children arrived' (talking to a man(-*k*))
 a'.　*Haurr-ak*　　　*heldu*　　*d-it-u-n*
  Children-ABS.PL　arrived　Ø-PL(A)-AUX.HAVE-2SG.FEM
  'The children arrived' (talking to a woman(-*n*))

From the perspective of LPH, allocutivity, as evidenced in Basque, raises fundamental issues about the nature of the fuzzy interfaces between indexicality>syntax>morphology.

An understanding of Basque allocutivity as a morphosyntactic phenomenon requires, we claim, decoupling functional "light" v from lexical V categories, thus lending empirical justification to the "little v hypothesis" under a CP(vP) phase-theoretic architecture, with consequences for the syntax–morphology interface.

An account of allocutivity, however, exceeds narrow syntax. The conceptual identity of the Addressee would be vacuous (from a speech act perspective) without formal access to the epistemicity of the Speaker in an irreflexive and asymmetric logical relation (4.1.3). In this respect, we believe that an account of allocutivity makes a compelling case for encoding the Speaker (as well as the Addressee) in syntax, a proposal advocated on independent syntactic evidence (Baker 2008; Giorgi 2010). Moreover, the otherwise puzzling realization of allocutives in Basque declaratives but not in imperatives (cf. question (a) above) brings into direct discussion the central subject of this book and the viability of a performative hypothesis extended to other clause types, reminiscent of Ross (1970).

The analytical question persists: why is allocutivity not realized in imperatives? After all LPH predicts that the Addressee is "the subject of the imperative" (4.2.1), complying with what seems to be a general agreement. This distributional puzzle involves the answer to question (b) above. The Addressee is an argument in imperatives, specifically, the external argument of the "prescription." Under LPH assumptions about Speaker and Addressee, a plausible suggestion follows: the allocutive (i.e., Addressee) is encoded in a CP(vP) phase-theoretic model of LPH. The Addressee identifies a syntactic head: an A'-bound variable y in adjunction to vP. The variable is licensed by an Addressee operator in CP. Under this scenario (see 4.2.1), morphological AA realizes the morpheme –k/–n via Merge and Agree at the syntax–morphology interface in conjunction with Speaker epistemicity at the syntax–indexicality interface.

Under these circumstances, a viable answer to the second question (b, above) is the following. The Addressee is an A'-bound variable in the content phase vP, in Imperative as well as in Allocutive syntax. The difference is in their respective syntactic status: in imperatives the Addressee variable is the external argument (i.e., the Subject) of the "prescription." In contrast, in Allocutives (e.g., declaratives) the variable is an adjunct, specifically in vP adjunction to the proposition. The structural distinction in the locality of the Addressee variable (in imperatives vs. allocutives) offers a higher-order account of its typological realization in the morphosyntax of Basque. Furthermore, under this generative scenario, the grammar gains computational stability and generalization in the derivation of the two clause types: imperatives and declaratives.

The account of allocutive heads as adjuncts (vs. arguments) was originally proposed by Oyharçabal (1993) and more recently employed in Adaskina and Grashchenkov (2009) under distinct hypotheses about the phenomenon and its computational process. A critical assessment of LPH vs. other hypotheses of allocutivity is not pursued further in this chapter.

In the remaining sections of this chapter we provide additional independent empirical evidence in support of LPH, coherent with an SMT minimalist position. In order to be empirically compliant, previous analyses limit coverage to the canonical subtype (4.2.3(5a)) "go!", excluding the other, arguably bona fide, extended imperative type (4.2.3 (5b)) "make him go!" (see Xrakovkij 2001 and van der Wurff 2007b on typological and generative surveys, respectively).

Table 4.2 *Arguments and roles in relation to person and number*

	1		2		3	
	SG	PL	SG	PL	SG	PL
Speaker	✓	*	*	*	*	*
Addressee	*	*	✓	✓	*	*
Performer	✓	✓	?	?	✓	✓

Consider, for example, the studies reflecting on English *let* (Sepännen 1977; Davies 1986; Clark 1993; Potsdam 1998), which would appear to escape the second person constraint. These studies resort to identifying *let* as a modal/ optative auxiliary or inflectional element, hence decoupling the analysis of extended imperatives from that of canonical imperatives. Moreover, in separating categorically these imperative expressions, the crucial distinction between Addressee and Performer roles is missed or not pursued. Neither is the range of person and number values that each role in the imperative sentence can adopt. These issues, we show, can receive a unified treatment under LPH.

4.3.6   *Thematic role and person values*

We return in this subsection to the preliminary discussion of the category Person under LPH (cf. 4.1.3.2) derived as a function of the anti-reflexivity relation Speaker>Addressee in directive speech acts.

Let us cross-reference the thematic relations instantiated by arguments A, B and C that we saw in Table 4.1 with permissible person and number realizations (Table 4.2).

It would seem that, while Speaker and Addressee must abide by specific person values, the Performer is free from person restrictions. The question marks with respect to the second person specification in the Performer can be resolved on the observation that a canonical imperative (*go!*) may be optimally suited to express the type ABB, thus the oddity of second person specification in the Performer outside specific pragmatic contexts.[22]

As previously observed with reference to Figures 4.1a and 4.1b (4.2.5), the Performer must in effect conform to a second person realization in the absence of a causative verb. For clarity, let us reproduce those figures with the permissible person and number realizations listed in Table 4.2 as Figures 4.2a and 4.2b.

What canonical and extended (hortative) imperatives have in common, nonetheless, is that the Addressee must be a second person regardless of

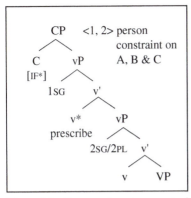

Figure 4.2a *Person values in canonical imperatives*

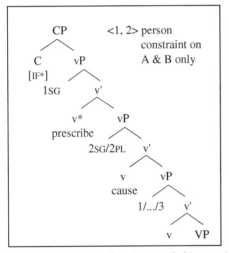

Figure 4.2b *Person values in extended imperatives*

syntactic configuration. It's this shared characteristic that makes it not feasible to elucidate the syntax of imperative clauses without empirical consideration of extended imperatives. Although it must be an integral part of the syntactic account, the presence or absence of the causative verb alone will not suffice. What functional causative v does is absorb (or annul) the second person constraint on the Addressee/Causer, a constraint which exists independently of the causative.

4.3.7   *Speaker>Addressee relation: deontic modality*

As noted, if the Addressee is conferred special status in the imperative clause, so should its "Addressor/Speaker," which thematically binds it. Let us call the relation that must hold of two speech act participants in imperative types a deontic relation or δ-relation. Regardless of how it is formalized, the δ-relation is shorthand for this aspect of the semantics of imperative sentences. The Speaker and Addressee are subject to a <1, 2> person constraint. A last-resort possibility is that the constraint is independently stipulated as an interface condition. The constraint must be met for a given sentence to be uttered or interpreted as an imperative expression.

The LPH again offers the possibility to go one step further: to analyze the δ-relation not as a marked interface condition, but as a corollary of the syntactic computation of the imperative clause. In this alternative view, LPH imperative syntax predicts <1, 2> person constraint via prescriptive v.

Coherently with LPH, the δ-relation, or any hypothesized <1, 2> person constraint, is assessed on a syntactic structure consisting of the Addressee, or "grammatical" subject of the imperative verb, syntactically bound by the Speaker, or "logical" (indexical) subject, which we propose to represent as the external argument of v. In the spirit of the original PH, the Speaker and Addressee are arguments to a lexical verb. In our minimalist LPH revision, the performative is a "light" verb which we refer to as "prescriptive v." Prescriptive v introduces the Speaker in its specifier, and thematically identifies its complement, the "grammatical" subject of the prescription, as the Addressee. The δ-relation is unitarily assessed on canonical imperatives (15a cf. 4.2.2 (5a)) as well as on extended (hortative) imperatives (15b cf. 4.2.2 (5b)).

(15)   a. [A-1p prescribes [B-2p to *DO P*]]
            |_____ δ_____|

        b. [A-1p prescribes [B-2p to cause [A/*B/C to *DO P*]]]
            |_____ δ_____|

Descriptively, we can give an expository list of several salient properties of imperative utterances. Some of these are (i) the unique Speaker>Addressee relation of the imperative expression, (ii) the visibility of the second speech act participant in the predicate-argument structure, (iii) the second person restriction in the realization of the grammatical subject and (iv) the ambivalence of the Performer in the observance of this person restriction (1,2,3). From LPH, we claim, follows an account for these characteristics in a unitary fashion and in compliance with the tenets of the SMT.

4.3.8   *(Function (content)) interface*

The Speaker and Addressee enter a binding relation in imperative clauses owing to the functional chain of syntactic and thematic linking.[23]

(15')   Syntactic and thematic binding

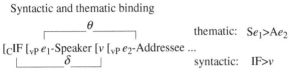

In (15') the δ-features of v are inherited from c-commanding IF. They identify the Speaker>Addressee thematic dependence, along with the morphosyntactic Person $e_1 > e_2$ as a by-product (see 15'). In other words, the visibility of the hearer in the speech act responds to the interaction between prescriptive v and its complement. The arguments of prescriptive v, at the edge of the prescribed vP phase, conform to this selectional requirement. While the requirement is articulated on a Person feature, this is [1>2]. Selectional restrictions on predicate-argument relations may be observed, whether they are shared as an argument by two predicates or not. For example, a predicate such as "read" requires a volitive agent in "x read the newspaper." In "John caused x to suffer an injury," the argument x must satisfy the requirement of Causee and Experiencer.

If the second person constraint is defined via thematic identification, as we have just proposed, we can predict a difference in imperative expressions. The edge of the complement observes a second person constraint. When the edge is v, the Performer must be second person. When the edge is causative v, it is the Causer that must be second person (see Figures 4.3a and b).

4.3.9   *Predicting speaker and addressee realization*

Under present assumptions, the Speaker argument remains phonetically null, while the Addressee argument may be typologically realized. The otherwise pronominal element in [Spec, vP] of the performative v stands in a binding relation to sentential force IF in CP. By contrast, the Addressee, which is syntactically/semantically bound to the Speaker, may be typologically realized. This follows from the LPH: the light performative v selects the prescribed clause as a vP complement clause, with the consequence that its grammatical subject meets the criteria to be a valid Addressee.

4.3.9.1   Deriving the root clause nature of imperative clauses

In this manner, the functional δ-relation characterizing imperative clauses follows directly from general principles of clause structure, voiding a marked

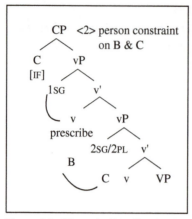

Figure 4.3a *Thematic identification in canonical imperatives*

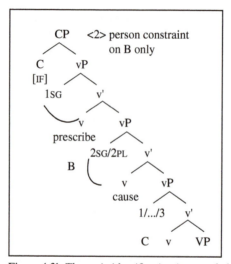

Figure 4.3b *Thematic identification in extended imperatives*

<1,2> person condition. Furthermore, it will be argued that LPH, viewed as a theory of directives, also accounts for the ban on embedding in virtue of the c-command dependence between the functional phase and the content phase ($[_{CP}F\,[_{vP}\,v]]$). This relation licenses the explicit representation of Speaker and Addressee arguments in the content phase. It follows as a consequence of LPH that embedded clauses do not have access to the imperative function.

4.4   Grammaticalization of Speaker, Addressee and Performer

In the next section we examine evidence that Addressee and Performer arguments are represented independently in the syntax of extended (hortative) imperatives.

4.4.1   The subject of imperatives

While it is common wisdom to encode the Addressee (argument B) as the "grammatical" subject of the imperative verb, our preliminary proposal (5) in its argument-role distribution (6) also requires the Speaker (argument A) to be encoded as the indexical subject of the imperative expression, that is, the virtual external argument e^1 of the light performative verb v (5i). Thus, LPH predicts two subject (external argument) positions in imperative sentences (16).

(16)   a. The grammatical subject of the lexical verb V (i.e., B)
        b. The (indexical) subject of the functional light verb v (i.e., A)

In light of the conceptually extended class of subjects of imperatives, empirical motivation warrants attention. Evidence for the grammatical subject (16a) is realized cross-linguistically as first, second and third person. Yet the Addressee can only be second person. On inspection, such evidence would appear to contradict the view that imperatives are delivered by the Speaker (first person) exclusively to the Addressee (second person).

In canonical imperatives, realized evidence for the grammatical subject argument B includes evidence from pronominal clitics in Spanish (17), Italian (17'), Ewe (18) and English (19). The standard overt realization of contrastive subjects is conclusive evidence for positing a grammatical subject argument B in the specifier of the prescribed vP phase [B *DO P*]. Remarkably, the argument receives the role of Addressee from the δ function of the light performative v. Conjointly, B is assigned the role of the "Performer" as the external argument of the prescribed vP phase.

(17)   a. *¡ve-te!*   a'. *¡vete tú!* (contrastive)   Spanish[24]
            go.THV-2SG.REFL
            'go!'
        b. *¡ir-os!*   b'. *¡iros vosotros!* (contrastive)
            go-2PL
            'go!'
        c. *¡que te   vayas!*
            that 2SG.REFL   go.SUBJ.2SG
            'go! (I said)/go! (abrupt, angry command)'

(17')   a. *vai via!, vattene via (tu)!*   Italian
go2Ps away! go-2PS-LOC away
b. *andate via!, andatevene via!*
go2PP away! go2PP-2PP-LOC away!

(18)   a. *yi!*   Ewe
go
'go!'
b. *mi-yi!*
PL-go
'(you all) go!'
(Agbodjo and Litvinov 2001: 397; exs. from table 2)

(19)   go!   English

Beyond morphologically realized evidence it is also possible to ascertain the syntactic presence of the grammatical subject of the imperative lexical verb. For example, by means of binding of pronoun/reflexive (20a,b), control (20c,d,e), traces (20f,g,h), and quantifier float (20i; van der Wurff 2007b: 34, ex. 90; cf. Zwicky 1988; Potsdam 1998).

(20)   a. Do it yourself/*myself/*himself!
b. Make your/*my/*his own drinks!
c. Try PRO to be careful!
d. Watch him PRO to find out!
e. Speak up even if PRO unhappy!
f. Stop T writing!
g. Don't be easy to spot T!
h. Don't be examined T by that doctor!
i. Don't be both talking at the same time!

Extended imperatives are defined as containing a Performer argument that may be referentially disjoint from the Addressee. From the paradigm (6) we derive a referentially disjoint third person Performer argument C (type 2), as well as a first person argument A (type 3), co-referential with the logical subject A of the light performative. In these extended imperatives, evidence similar to (17–19) may reference the Addressee, the Performer, or both on a language-particular basis.

We note that in Spanish and Italian there is evidence for the B argument in the inflection of the causative verbs (*deja-d* 'let'-2PL, *fa-i* 'let'-2SG), which further warrants the necessity for a second person Addressee in the specifier of the causative vP of the prescription (21, 21'). Basque's absolutive third person plural auxiliary markings (22a), in turn, support the Performer as a separate argument, and similarly early Latin's synthetic second and (formulaic) third person imperative forms (23). Alternatively, Basque can resort to the explicit causative strategy, where the auxiliary indicates concord with the Addressee and the

Performer via separate agreement morphemes (22b,c). Ewe and English also resort to explicit causatives. Ewe (24) shows number marking for the complement of the causative, while English *let* and *make* are invariant (25).

(21) a. *¡dej-a-d-le entrar!*   Spanish
          let-THV-2PL.IMP-him   enter
          '(you all) let him enter!'
      b. *¡dej-a-d entrar a Juan!*
          let-V-2PLIMP enter   Juan
          '(you all) let Juan enter!'
      c. *¡dej-a-d-me entrar (a mí)!*
          let-THV-2PL-me enter (me)
          '(you all) let me enter!'

(21′) a. *fallo entrare!*   Italian
          let(Imp)-him enter
          'let him enter!'
      b. *fai entrare Gianni!*
          let(2SGPRESIND) enter Gianni
          'Let Gianni enter!'
      c. *fammi entrare pure a me!*
          let(IMP)-me enter too me
          'Let me come in too!'

(22) a. *hurbil bekizkit!*   Basque
          get.closer   AUX.3.PL.1SG
          'let them get close to me!'
          (Saltarelli 1988: 305–306)
      b. *utzi   iezai-o-zu   joa-ten!*
          let   AUX-3SG-2SG   go-NOM
          'let him go!'
      c. *utzi   ieza-da-zu   joa-ten!*
          let   AUX-1SG-2SG   go-NOM
          'let me go!'

(23) a. *ollīs salūs populī suprēma lēx estō* (Legg. 3.8)   Latin
          'the safety of the people (shall) **be (SGFUTIMP)** their first law.'
      b. *iūsta imperia suntō,*
          '(let there) be (**PLFUTIMP**) lawful authorities,
          eīsque cīvēs modestē pārentō (id. 3.6),
          and (let) the citizens strictly **obey(PLFUTIMP)** them.'
          (Allen and Greenough 1983: 243, sec. 448)

(24)   *ne yi!*   Ewe
          'let them go!'
          (Agbodjo and Litvinov 2001: 397; exs. from table 2)

(25)   (you/you all) make/let them go!   English

4.4.2   *Actual and virtual Addressee*

Note that the Latin examples above are pleas or exhortations that need not be addressed directly in the act but are directed to a virtual audience. Consequently, the syntactic representation of the Addressee may not be warranted in (23). On theoretical grounds, this option might be unappealing in the context of our proposal, since the Performer argument would then violate the δ-relation. Assuming LPH, however, the Performer escapes the δ-relation because it is not an argument to the performative verb. Alternatively, one might assume that there is no specified argument Addressee and that the type instantiated by (23) is formulaic and may escape the δ-relation. This would be clearly an evasive (or too restrictive) research option, since pleas, exhortations and particularly laws have juridical force (the writer/speaker) implying enforcement by some expected/intended body (addressee: authorities, citizens, people).[25]

This type of example begs the question of how to characterize imperative semantics. The LPH's minimal requirement that an imperative expression be a "prescription" satisfies membership for (23). Nevertheless more needs to be said about "predictability." In Basque (4.3.5), men use the second person masculine when talking alone. Surprisingly, women use the second person masculine too, although one might expect the feminine. With particular reference to the empirical question just raised, we would like to advance again Basque allocutive agreement (to be discussed at length in Chapter 5). Basque speakers display allocutive agreement even in soliloquy, where the presumed audience is at best figurative. In eastern dialects, men use the masculine morpheme in soliloquy, but so do women (a woman would apparently use the feminine if "consciously" addressing herself: Segurola 1992 cf. Alberdi 2003). (Note, parenthetically, that LPH excludes imperative self-ascription under irreflexivity (see Section 4.1.3), hence logically weakening the previous conjecture. Consider, in addition, that gender as a lexical category is a binary feature (values +/-) interpreted as marked or unmarked (default), the latter (masculine) being the unmarked gender. Evidence from Spanish adjectival gender agreement in coordination reduction (VP-ellipsis) supports this reasoning (26).

(26)   [[[compré [un abrigo [~~amarillo~~]] y [~~compré~~ [una camisa [amarill**a**]o]s]
        'I bought a yellow suit and ~~(I bought a yellow)~~ shirt'

Under non-indexical assumptions, a possible analysis of Basque might be that the syntax of imperatives in Basque contains a "dummy" (unrealized) syntactic Addressee even if no audience is present. If the Addressee were to be identified as oneself, women would then use the feminine mark. In light of the soliloquy cases, one might propose that categorical imperatives such as (23), which appear not to address a live audience, actually contain a "dummy" or virtual Addressee. The Addressee complies with the second person constraint on the grammatical subject in abstract. Such an account of raw surface structure contributes neither to a descriptively adequate nor to an enlightening understanding of the interface between narrow syntax and its speech act context.

Alternatively, under LPH assumptions (4.3.3.1(13b), 4.3.5) the unexpected allocutive argument is arguably accessible to syntax as an unrealized A'-bound variable guaranteed by the irreflexive principle which sanctions the Speaker>Addressee relation (4.1.3). All the relevant implications of allocutivity for a generalized indexical syntax will be detailed in Chapter 5.

4.4.3   The functional range of imperatives

Extended imperatives, LPH argues, are considered on a par with canonical imperatives in general functional terms, for not only are they both equally subject to the δ-relation (arguments A&B in 4.2.3 and 4.2.4), but they also express a similar range of meanings. Canonical imperatives can be weak exhortations ("well, consider it!") in as much as extended imperatives can be strong directives ("make him pay for it!"). It would be imprecise to presume that there is a semantic alignment in the strength of the prescription with one or the other. Nonetheless, it is common to find paradigms that discriminate between these two polar uses within canonical imperatives or within extended imperatives. For instance, Old English has two paradigms for canonical imperatives. Visser interprets their use as follows (Visser 1966: 798–99, sec. 842).

> It seems obvious that there must have been a semantic difference between utterances with the forms in (b) [list of imperative verbs, form$_1$] and those with the forms in (c) [list of imperative verbs, form$_2$], but it is not easy to find out the exact nature of this difference. In both cases we have to do with a wish to see an action performed by the person spoken to. It seems a fair assumption that in case (b) the wish had more the character of a command, whereas in (c) it was more like a mild exhortation, and advice or a suggestion (to try to) perform a given action [a footnote refers to a similar state of affairs in Gothic]. … After the Old English period the forms (b) and (c) coalesce, and henceforth there is only one form, which, though often called 'imperative', still has retained all the meanings of the original two forms. (p. 799)

Imperative sentences show some parallelisms with causatives in particular. One of the semantic dimensions articulating choices in causative morphemes/strategies is whether the Causer is acting directly or indirectly on the Causee (e.g., John *made* Mary go vs. John *caused* Mary to go). Significantly, another semantic factor is whether the Causee is in a position to *resist* the Causer (Dixon

2000; or, phrased differently, whether the Causer can impose on the Causee). This independent factor could be behind the gradient use of imperative clauses as commands, requests, suggestions or pleas.

There exist further parallels between causatives and imperatives. Indirectness, for one, plays a fundamental role in the canonical/extended distinction. Also, causatives may present two morphemes in sequence, expressing argument relations reminiscent of extended imperatives. The precise observations of Koopman (2001) on Maasai point to the performative itself as a causative element (see 4.2.4). In light of these parallelisms, an SMT approach to the characterization of the performative would seem to be on the right track. The performative presents parallelisms with causative v because the performative itself is a type of v.

Where canonical and extended imperatives differ is in the syntax: whether or not the Performer is restricted to second person. In canonical imperatives, the Performer must be the Addressee (argument B). Consequently, the δ-relation is assessed on the Addressee/Performer. In contrast, in extended imperatives, the Performer (argument C) may be referentially disjoint from the Addressee (argument B). The δ-relation is assessed on the Speaker and Addressee arguments alone, leaving the Performer argument free from person restrictions.

After this informal excursus into the speech act semantics of imperatives, let us reiterate the patterns shown in the examples immediately above. In extended imperatives, realized person and number morphology may represent the Addressee but not the Performer (verbal inflection in 20–21), the Performer but not the Addressee (e.g., 22a, 23), or it may represent both (22b,c). In the latter two cases, a question arises: which of these arguments is the grammatical subject of the imperative sentence, the Addressee or the Performer? Our theory recognizes three subject arguments in extended imperatives, namely the Speaker or "logical" subject, the Addressee or "grammatical" subject of the prescription, and the Performer or "actual executor." Whether realized morphology is visible only for the Addressee or the Performer, is immaterial to the δ-relation. The δ-relation does not apply to the Performer argument, even if this argument appears to be the "grammatical" subject by virtue of agreement morphology (e.g., 22a, 23). Technically, the Performer in:

(27)   a. 'open the door (you/*me,*he)'[26] vs.   (P*1,2,*3)
       b. 'let us (including you), me, him/them, open the door'   (P1,2,3)

escapes the δ-relation constraint on Person by virtue of not being thematically c-commanded by the Speaker. Observe the grammaticality in canonical (a) vs. (b) extended imperatives.

4.4.4 Imperatives in vocative expressions

Studies that rightly attempt to extend the imperative paradigm struggle with extended imperatives. For instance, consider the following examples of extended imperatives in English (28; cf. Zanuttini 2008 from different sources) where the vocative phrase is not the grammatical subject.

(28) a. YOUR soldiers build the bridge, General Lee!
      b. Your guards be the diversion while we sneak in!
      c. Maitre d', someone sit these guests!
      d. Counselors, everyone be packed up and ready to go in half an hour!

Leaving aside a possible (dedicated) Vocative Phrase analysis, in LPH imperatives in (28) are arguably accounted for as examples of extended imperatives of type 2 (Table 4.1 in section 4.2.4). Let us paraphrase (28c), by means of illustration. The speaker demands the Addressee (= maitre d') to have some waiter (unspecified) sit the guests, the waiter being the actual Performer of the command. If no other subject projections are granted, the Performer becomes the grammatical subject of the prescription. To explain this paradox, Potsdam (1998) appeals to a control relationship condition. Here we reproduce in part footnote 23 from Zanuttini's paper:

> Potsdam (1998, 210–11) formulates the control relationship that holds between the addressee and the subject as follows: "The addressee must be in a control relationship over the referent of the imperative subject." "x is in a control relationship with y if x has potential control over y in some domain z (where z may range over social, military, political, economic, discourse or other situations)."

Admittedly, the synthetic form of type 2 imperatives in English conveys that the Addressee is in a position of authority with respect to the Performer, but so is an analytical form with causative *make, have* or *get*. Zanuttini pursues an analysis of type 2 by appealing to certain shifting morphological properties of her proposed Jussive Phrase (JP). JP is a dedicated functional projection with the sole purpose of accounting for imperatives, more narrowly intended to identify the grammatical subject as the Addressee. How does Zanuttini's analysis allow imperatives to accept a vocative and a subject that are referentially disjoint?

> The difference between core imperatives [addressee = grammatical subject] and set B imperatives [addressee ≠ grammatical subject] then must reside not in the presence of the Jussive Phrase [Addressee Phrase], but rather in its ability to pass its person features onto the subject – i.e., in the syntactic relation it holds with the subject. I suggest that the difference between core imperatives and set B imperatives lies in the fact that the Jussive head enters an agree relation with the subject in the former case but not in the latter. (p. 19)

While LPH concurs with Zanuttini that research on imperative sentences should be extended beyond the canonical type, the Jussive Phrase[27] here is visibly at odds with extended imperatives. It identifies the Addressee by entering an agree relation with the grammatical subject, which in (28) is not the actual addressee.

4.4.5   On third person imperatives

The examples in (28) merit a brief digression on the history of English. Old English and Middle English have third person imperative forms, the remains of which still linger in the language in idiomatic forms, albeit morphologically invariant. For example, "suffice it to say" or "enter the cook" (in stage-directions: "have the cook enter now"). Visser (1966: 802, sec. 846) dates the decline of the simple imperative form to the nineteenth and twentieth centuries, although the variant with *let* existed several centuries before. As a time reference, Visser quotes Charles Coote's *Elements of the Grammar of the English Language* (1788). By that time, *let* was the preferred choice.

> In the third person of either number, as well as in the first person plural, of this mode, we generally make use of the auxiliary *let*, rather than adopt the simple form. Thus, we say, *let him gain*, rather than *gain he*, &c.

Our proposed hypothesis (4.2–4) handles cases like (28) straightforwardly as extended imperatives with an underlying causative vP. It is to be expected that the underlying causative be compressed to a morphologically synthetic form (*gain he!*) or made explicit in an analytical form (*let him gain!*).

4.4.6   On exhortations: inclusivity

In the continued search for realized evidence, we will now examine exhortations, which present a rather interesting case. First person inclusive/exclusive imperatives (Table 4.1 in section 4.2.5 types 4 and 5) also show explicit evidence for positing an underlying Performer argument referentially. Accordingly, they bring about the same questions concerning the identity of the grammatical subject of the prescription as imperatives of type 2 and 3 did. With an additional complication: both the Speaker and Addressee may be referentially involved as a joint Performer. As noted, imperatives of type 4 and 5 are intended by the Speaker for the second person Addressee(s), the Speaker including him/herself (29, 30) or not (31, 32) for exhortatory force. Strict self-exhortation is apparently excluded. Both Spanish (29a) and Italian (29b) show anaphoric evidence for a silent argument C. This is realized as first person plural inflection and/or clitics technically in need of pronominal binding by an antecedent. In contrast, English (30a) and Ewe (30b,c) require an additional realized exhortative "light" predicate (*let*, *give*), hence falling (explicitly) into the extended type (5b). As noted, we assume that (29) and (30) share the same underlying structure, causative v being implicit in (29).

(29) a. ¡*vámonos!*   *¡*voyme!*   Spanish
            go.1PL.REFL
            'let's go!'
      b. *andiamocene!* **vadomene!*   Italian
            go.1PL.REFL.LOC
            'let's go!'

(30) a. let's go!   *go   English
      b. *na mi-yi!*   Ewe
            'let's (you.SG&me) go!'
      c. *mi-na mi-yi!*
            'let's (you.PL&me) go!'
            (Agbodjo and Litvinov 2001: 397; exs. from table 2)

Languages resort to various strategies to express the relevant distinction between the exhortation being inclusive or exclusive, and do so in ways reminiscent of types 2 and 3 (e.g., realized evidence of argument B, C or both in verbal morphology). For example, in Spanish, the explicit causative strategy encodes exclusiveness if the inflection is second person (31a) and inclusiveness if the inflection is first person plural (31b). Arguably, the causative agrees either with the Addressee or the Performer. In Basque, inclusive exhortation is construed with first person plural agreement (32a), again referencing the Performer, while exclusive exhortation requires the explicit causative strategy (32b), which references both the Addressee and the Performer independently.

(31) a. ¡*déj-a-nos*   *hacer-lo!*
            let-THV-2PL   do-it
            'let us do it!'
      b. ¡*dej-émonos*   *hacer-lo*   *por esta vez!*
            let-1PL.REFL   do-it   for this time
            'let's (give ourselves permission to) do it just this one time!'

(32) a. *jan*   *dezagun!*
            eat   AUX.1PL.3SG
            'let's eat (it)!'
      b. *utzi*   *iezai-gu-zu*   *ja-ten!*
            let   AUX-1PL-2SG   eat-NOM
            'let us eat!'

Granted the realized evidence for the "grammatical" subject of the prescription (Addressee or B argument) and the executor (Performer or C argument), what independent evidence is there for an additional vP to introduce a "logical" subject (Speaker or argument A) in imperative sentences?

4.5   Imperative temporality revisited

Recall that the incompatibility of imperative clauses with adverbials referring to past events was semantically interpreted as "future orientation" (4.1.2.1; Kaufmann 2012: 93) and syntactically derived as Operator-bound temporality in a dedicated functional projection (Jussive Phrase, 4.2.1; Zanuttini 2008). Under a speech act conceived LPH, the syntactic incompatibility of temporal adverbs (*yesterday) follows from the perceived meaning of the directive speech act as a "prescription" (4.1) formally characterized by encoding the participants' irreflexive relation (4.1.3) as a virtual conceptual necessity.

4.5.1   *French passé composé*
Direct evidence for the restricted temporality of the speech act and interfacing imperative clauses is grammaticalized in Latin, whose imperative morphological verb paradigm is defective in one of the Tense categories: *Past, Present, Future.

This pragmatically and morphologically discernible fact (temporal speaker/ utterance time) about the dynamics of imperatives under speech act assumptions might be questioned by the so-termed *impératif passé* in French: *"aie terminé ce travaille demain à midi"* (Grevisse 1969: sec. 361) 'have this/that assignment finished tomorrow at noon.' In this case, we have a traditional term of a morphological form of the verb called *passé composé* $[aie_{AUX,p2.sg.subj}+terminé_{PP.sg}]$. The term is used both for an event in the indexical past (before speaker utterance time) as well as for the indexical future, in Grevisse's example preceding a future event. As in Person1,2, used as Speaker-1, Addressee-2 (4.1.3.2), access to indexical time (utterance/speaker time) is of the essence in semantic temporal interpretation and syntactic adverbial compatibility (4.1.2.1). In the case of the restricted temporality of the speech act and its syntactic grammaticalization, the clinching empirical argument rests with a descriptively adequate account of temporal adverbs, predicted as a corollary of LPH.

4.5.2   *On "reproachatives" in Dutch*
Questions about the use of the past form of the verb in exclamative clauses referring to the temporal domain of the past have been prominently reported in the literature as "true" imperative expressions (33).

(33)   a. *had iets gegeten!*
       had something eaten
       'you should have eaten something.'(Proeme 1984; cf. van der Wurff
       2007b)
     b. *had je mond maar gehouden!*
       had your mouth PRT holdPP
       'you should have kept your mouth shut!'(Mastop 2005; Kaufmann 2012)

The possible existence of past imperatives in human languages would, of course, undermine LPH predictions. The theory of imperatives we have been proposing necessarily restricts the temporality (4.1.2.1) of the imperative speech act to Present and Future, excluding *Past. After all, "from a conceptual point of view, it is difficult to imagine an imperative that related to an action in the past. How can someone be ordered to do something in the past?" (cf. van der Wurff 2007b: 45).

Commenting on cases reported for Dutch, Kaufmann (2012: 103) argues that "the speech act type [(33b] is not a COMMAND for a past interval in time (whatever that would be), but rather a REPROACH that what was clearly to be known as advisable has not been complied with."

Intuitively, it seems appropriate to assume that humans perceive or interpret a ("true") imperative speech act (I-language) as opposed to other types from a set of epiphenomenal (E-language) clues which other speech acts may share. One case in point may be the prosody of "exclamation!" shared by both imperative COMMAND and REPROACH, suggesting another look at the classification of speech acts.

Along the same reasoning, the occurrence of the unanalyzed [have+PP] syntactic construct would be no guarantee of a past time interval, as seems obvious from English: "have your head checked!" In some languages, however, there may be clues dedicated to imperativity, such as Negative particle in Latin (nē/nōn). Spanish has at least five verbs (*sal-i-r* 'get out,' *ven-i-r* 'come,' *ten-e-r* 'have,' *pon-e-r* 'put,' *hac-e-r* 'do/make' (cf. *¡haz!*)) for which the occurrence of the bare root may unequivocally identify a true imperative

If this turns out to be a substantive empirical case, the context-to-utterance dependency may indeed be subject to the general anti-symmetry principle (4.1.3 (2b)) assumed in LPH.

Formally, then, the speech act status of E-language data is best evaluated against competitive hypotheses of the functional meaning of the imperative (4.2.3). LPH is such a contender, which in this chapter is being tested and evaluated.

4.5.3   On retrospective imperatives in Spanish

Following the "future-oriented" temporality predicted by LPH (4.1.2.1;
Kaufmann 2012: 93), we consider the so-called "retrospective imperative" in
Spanish: *¡haber venido!* [have.$_{INF}$ come.PP] 'You should have come!' (Bosque
1980; also discussed in van der Wurff 2007b: 45–47).

Spanish complex predicates like [$_v$ *haber* [$_V$ *venido*]] are used in clauses
referring to past intervals *(deberías) haber venido* to express reprimand,
reproach, or retrospective advice by the Speaker, which has not been complied
with by the Addressee in the sense of Kaufmann's "reproachative" interpretation (4.5.2 above).

Note that, as in French *passé composé*, a similar Spanish complex syntactic
construct can be interpreted as a speech act uttered at Speaker's time as a directive with a "prescription" to be complied with at a future time t_1 prior to a
more distant future time t_2: *¡(tundra's que) haber terminado el trabajo (antes
de) mañana!* '(you must) have the work done by tomorrow!' A similar fully
generated construction is found in Italian: *dovrai aver finito il lavoro prima di
domani!* 'You must have the work finished by tomorrow!'

In fairness, the difference between these Romance languages might turn out
to respond to an E-language epiphenomenon relating to the ambiguous effect
of the reduced [infinitive[participle]] complex verb, arguably used in Spanish
at the interpretive expense of the I-language modality grammaticalized in
deberías. If this turns out to be the correct comparative Romance analysis,
¡haber venido! may imply "reproach" rather than true imperative "command"
in Kaufmann's sense.[28]

In conclusion, under a theory of imperative clauses accessible to Speaker's
intention, such as LPH, retrospective speech acts like reprimands or reproaches
fall short of the basic I-language scenario of imperatives, namely 'Speaker$_i$
requests [RIM] at time t_i that...' (in the spirit of Katz and Postal 1964).

4.5.4   On conditional imperatives

Conditional utterances in (34, 35) are, on inspection, an issue for a syntactic
theory of imperative clauses, such as LPH, which claims that imperatives in
conditional clauses are matrix (root) clauses (4.1.2).

Intuitively, the expressions in (34a) can be considered distinct speech acts:
namely "directions" rather than "prescriptions." If the claim can be substantiated, directions fall out of the intentional nature of commands and the
Speaker>Addressee deontic relation. Intuitions are even weaker for (35).

In contrast, (34b) has the modality of a directive prescription although it
is used also with the force of a reprimand, thus calling for a closer look at a
semantic approach as modal subordination (Kaufmann 2012: sect. 6.2).

Conditional imperatives face the semantics-to-syntax interface in a quandary between the classical notion of hypotaxis (subordination) or parataxis (coordination or adjunction).

(34) a. If you are traveling on 405N and want to go to UCLA,
   (i) don't take Santa Monica,
   (ii) at the next exit turn right on Wilshire.
   (iii) then at the second light turn left on Westwood.
   b. Speaker addressing a chatting couple
   (i) If you have to talk, leave the theater.
   (ii) leave the theater, if you have to talk.
   (iii) I demand that you leave the theater!
   (iv) *?that you leave I demand!

(35) (i) If you are thirsty, there is beer in the fridge. (Kaufmann 2012: 6.2.1)
   (ii) If you want my advice, get a pro to do it.
   (iii) If you return my book, I'll return yours.
   (iv) Return my book and I'll return yours.

In apparently true cases such as (34b), the crucial question for a syntactic account of conditional imperatives concerns the hierarchical syntactic status of "if X, then Y" constructions. Is the syntactic relation between the protasis (if X) and the apodosis (then Y) one of subordination, coordination or adjunction? In the event that lexical dependency (embedding) could be established, such as [if X [Y]], conditional imperative constructions would violate the fundamental root (matrix) claimed by LPH (4.1.2).

On first approach, the unconstrained order alternation between protasis and apodosis in conditional imperatives (34bi,ii) suggests that "if, then" expressions do not imply subordination. In fact, analytic imperatives (IDI) prohibit the alternation (34biii,iv). Moreover, conditional imperatives may be expressed by coordination as well (35iii,iv). A tentative syntactic account of conditional imperatives suggests that the protasis (if-clause) is an adjunct to the matrix apodosis (then-clause) in the following structure [[if X] then Y], where the if-clause is adjoined to the matrix clause, and hence is consistent with the LPH claim that imperatives are matrix or root clauses.

4.6   Evidence for a "prescriptive" light verb v

In the preceding sections, a "light" performative hypothesis (LPH) of sentence types has been proposed under minimalist assumptions about the form of a clausal syntax which recognizes a higher function phase CP and a lower content phase vP (36a). Imperative clauses, LPH claims, are characterized by a "light" verb v (36b).

(36)   a.   Sentence types are syntactic objects CP(vP), the choice of v licensed by a force element associated with C.

b.   For imperative force (IF), v inherits the functional property δ common to the class of imperative predicates.

In this section, arguments are developed that justify positing a prescriptive light verb in imperative expressions. The arguments focus on (i) clitic climbing in Romance; (ii) causative-like and particle-like verbs in Ibero-Romance; (iii) the relation of this verb to imperative-specific properties (Maasai, Slavic, Mandarin Chinese and English); (iv) prohibitive constructions and their affirmative counterparts; and (v) subject position in negated English imperatives, alongside the distribution of emphatic *do* and *do-support*. For additional evidence, see Alcázar and Saltarelli (2010) on double and triple agreement phenomena in Spanish imperatives (Harris and Halle 2005 vs. Kayne 2008).[29]

4.6.1   Clitic climbing in Romance

The first argument is strictly syntactic. Romance shows that the position of the unstressed clitic pronoun in imperatives may in fact precede or follow the verb. The variable position of pronouns is reminiscent of *clitic climbing*, where a finite verb takes a non-finite complement, under a characterization like Rizzi's "restructuring" or Cinque's mono-clausality (Cinque 2004). The example in (37) illustrates this effect for Spanish, where it's possible to place the direct and/or indirect object clitic pronouns before the finite verb (37a) or following the non-finite form (37b).

(37)   a. *Lo   quiero   ver*
        it   want.1SG   see.INF
        'I want to see it.'

b. *Quiero   ver-lo*
        want.1SG   see.INF-it
        'I want to see it.'

Along these lines, consider the following data for Italian imperatives (Kayne 1992; Portner and Zanuttini 2003). In the affirmative command (38a), the verb arguably moves to C and the pronoun must follow. In the negative command, on the other hand, the pronoun is free to follow the verb (38c) or precede it (38d). In this case, Italian resorts to the infinitive form of the verb, as the imperative (bare) form is not allowed under negation.[30]

(38)   a. *mangia-lo!*
        eat-it
        'eat it!'

b. *lo mangia!*
   it eat
   'eat it!'
c. *non mangiar-lo!*
   NEG eat-it
   'don't eat it!'
d. *non lo mangiare!*   (*for Spanish. Cf. 39d)
   NEG it eat
   'don't eat it!'

For Kayne (1992) the flexibility in the variable position of the pronoun is reminiscent of the original clitic climbing rule (OCC). However, on standard assumptions, there is only one verb in imperative sentences. Kayne proposes a silent auxiliary position in imperatives, to which the clitic pronoun can climb. More recently, Kayne (2008) re-proposes this auxiliary position for a syntactic analysis of double agreement in Spanish imperatives.

A look at other Romance languages like Spanish also suggests that the clitic pronoun may occupy two different positions. In affirmative commands Spanish displays obligatory enclisis (39a). In contrast, the negative command, where the subjunctive mood must be employed, requires the pronoun to precede the verb (39d).

(39)   a. *¡cóme-lo!*
      eat-it
      'eat it!'
    b. *¡lo come!*
      it eat
      'eat it!'
    c. *¡no cómas-lo!*
      NEG eat-it
      'don't eat it!'
    d. *¡no lo comas!*
      NEG it eat
      'don't eat it!'

On the other hand, Spanish often resorts to infinitives in place of imperative verb forms in the spoken language (Gili Gaya 1961). The infinitive can exist under negation and, compared to the subjunctive, the infinitive presents the opposite case: the pronoun must follow (40c).

(40)   a. *¡comer-lo!*
      eat.INF-it
      'eat it!'

    b. **¡lo comer!*
      it eat.INF
      'eat it!'
    c. *¡no comer-lo!*
      NEG eat.INF-it
      'don't eat it!'
    d. **¡no lo comer!*   (Ok for Italian. Cf. 38d)
      NEG it eat.INF
      'don't eat it!'

Rivero and Terzi (1995: 304, fn. 3) also propose an intermediate verbal projection to host the clitic when it precedes the verb. Their footnote is reproduced here in full:

(41)   In MGk [Modern Greek] and Sp [Spanish] Gerunds, and in Sp Infinitives, Neg precedes V, which is followed by clitics, as in Sp (i) below. We assume that here V raises to a position lower than C and Neg (see Kayne (1991) for Romance Infinitives; Rivero (1994a: section 5) for MGk Gerunds). For Rivero, MGk Gerunds raise to the head of a Modal Phrase, and Terzi (1994) relates this V-movement to the licensing of PRO.

    (i) (a) No   leyéndolo.
            NEG read.GER.it
            'Not reading it.'
       (b) Para no   leerlo.
            for NEG read.INF.it
            'Not to read it.'

Following on Kayne's analysis, Portner and Zanuttini (2003) use this auxiliary position as a modal projection that requires licensing by a modal feature (see also Zanuttini 1997). Portner and Zanuttini bring additional evidence for the existence of this projection, as they note that a verb may be expressed in this position: Paduan *sta* 'be'; Tarantino *scé* 'go' (cf. also our work on Apulian aspectual "light" verbs (Saltarelli and Alcázar 2010). These last studies go beyond imperatives, extending LPH to other indexical properties of the speech act, such as time and aspect (TA).

4.6.2 *Double-verb imperatives*

A second empirical argument reclaiming a second functional head v comes from varieties of Latin American Spanish, which show a second verb-like element in imperatives. We begin with Panamanian Spanish. This variety shows a *–ve* particle in familiar forms (42; cf. Lipski 1994). The verb-like ("go") particle is added after the verb root and thematic vowel with the effect that these imperative forms look the same as their counterparts in other varieties, except that they end in *–ve*.

(42) a. *¡oye-ve!*
      hear-go
      'hear!'

   b. *¡anda-ve!*
      walk-go
      'go!' (Lit. 'walk!')

This dedicated particle can be analyzed as an independent verb, since *¡ve!* on its own is the imperative form of the verbs *go* or *see*; thus *¡ve!* = 'go!' or 'see!'. If that were indeed the case, we could be looking at an imperative verb that has incorporated into a higher verbal position, headed by *ve*, which is now reanalyzed as an auxiliary verbal form reminiscent of morphological causatives (cf. Comrie 1985b; Dixon 2000). This is a possible analysis, but is there independent evidence that *–ve* is an incorporated verb?

A variety of Salvadorian Spanish may shed light on this question (43; Santos Avilés, p.c.). When the imperative sentence only contains the verb (43a,b), the data resembles the examples we have seen from Panamanian Spanish (42). However, if there are additional constituents in the sentence, *ve* no longer appears next to the verb. Instead, it appears after the constituent: for instance, a prepositional phrase (43c); an object (43d).

(43) a. *¡escuch-á*   *ve!*
         listen-VOSEO[31] go
         'listen!'

   b. *¡mir-á*   *ve!*
      look-VOSEO   go
      'look!'

   c. *¡and-á*   *a*   *la*   *casa*   *ve!*
      walk-VOSEO   to   the house   go
      'go home!'

   d. *¡sac-á*   *la*   *mano*   *ve!*
      take.out-VOSEO   the   hand   go
      'pull out your hand!'

   e. *¡no*   *jod-ás*   *ve!*
      NEG   joke-VOSEO   go
      'stop kidding!'

In view of the above distribution, Salvadorian *ve* functions as a sentence-final particle. In effect, it functions as a sort of sentence marker, since *ve* is not compatible with declaratives and interrogatives in this dialect, or with reported imperatives (e.g., "Mary demanded that John leave"). In syntactic terms, the position of *ve* may indicate that it moves to a higher projection such as Force Phrase (Rizzi 1997) or Speech Act Mood (Cinque 1999).

Two additional notes about Salvadorian *ve* are the following. First, it is compatible with negation (43e) even if substitution with the subjunctive must take effect. Second, it is used with second and third person forms. Regarding this last point, *ve* is invariant for person. That is to say, polite addresses use a morphological third person form. Still with the thematic role of Addressee, they do not shift *ve* into the third person suppletive subjunctive (*¡vaya!* = 'go!' [polite]; *¡vea!* = 'see!').

In consideration of the Latin American data, and the world's languages more generally, it seems fitting to identify the second (functional) verbal position in imperatives as an F-licensed light verb v. Under LPH, double-verb imperative clauses like *¡oye-ve!* (42a) are derived as follows.

(44)   Deriving double-verb imperatives
      (a) The F-marked *¡oye!* Merges in v; Agree with e^2 Addressee role-2
      (b) <u>a</u> Merges in v, incorporating *-ve*; Agree with e^1 Speaker role-1
      (c) <u>b</u> Merges in F valuing its imperative feature*¡*!
      [$_{CP}$ F *¡oye-ve!* [$_{vP}$ e^1 [$_{v'}$[$_v$ ~~¡oye-ve!~~ [$_{vP}$ e^2 [$_{v'}$ [$_v$ ~~¡oye!~~ [$_{VP}$ [$_V$ ~~¡oye!~~]]]]]]]]]

LPH provides a functionally equivalent derivation for other apparent double-verb imperatives, such as English (45), Latin prohibitions (46a) and Ewe (46b), which could be the spell-out of the performative. The analysis is extendable to prefix imperatives, like Farsi *be-* and postverbal particle *ma*, together with its "point of view" variants Badiotto (Poletto and Zanuttini 2003).

(45)   a. <u>Go</u> book it!
      b. <u>Come</u> look at it!
      c. Please <u>do</u> come in!

(46)   a. *vide ne quid aliud cures* 'see that you attend to nothing else!'
      b. *yi* 'go', *kpo* 'see' (Ewe cf. Agbodjo and Litvinov 2001: 398–99)

4.6.3   *Maasai, Mandarin Chinese and English*

Further support for the stipulation of the light performative vP comes from essential morphosyntactic and semantic properties of imperatives: namely, (i) resistance to negation as well as (ii) embedding and (iii) temporal interpretation. In order to illustrate this connection, we will now draw from scholarly work on Maasai (Koopman 2001), Mandarin Chinese (Chen-Main 2005) and English (Han 2000a, 2001).

4.6.3.1   Homophony in Maasai imperatives

Maasai imperative verb forms consist of a prefix *tV-* and a final suffix *–a/o* (class I verbs; class II does not feature the prefix). The imperative verb forms

(47a) display a rather remarkable property: they can, seemingly, double as past tense (47b; Koopman: 1; ex 1). Barring a possible role of tonal and/or morphological effects, the past declarative (47b) and the imperative clause (47a) are reported to be homophonous. Nevertheless, the forms of past and the imperative taken in isolation seems to be homophonous.

(47)   a. *tá- nàp- à*
           ta- carry- a
           'Carry him/it/them'
    b. *á-   tá- náp- à*
           1SG- ta   carry- a
           'I carried him'

Historical homophony with the aorist (Gronas 2006; Daiber 2008) has been recognized.[32] Koopman claims that Maasai shows a different syntactic distribution when they function as imperatives. Maasai imperatives, like Romance ones (e.g., Zanuttini 1997), disallow negation (48a) and must resort to suppletive subjunctives (48b, Koopman: 4; exs. 8, 11).

(48)   a. **mɨ- ta- nap- a*
           NEG- ta- nap- a
           'Don't carry it'
    b. *m- ɨ-nap*
           NEG- 2SG- carry
           'Don't carry it'

As we have already mentioned, resisting negation is a well-documented phenomenon in imperative clauses. What is surprising is that the past tense form also disallows negation (49a). The repair strategy in this case is different. An impersonal auxiliary combines with a non-past verb form (49b).

(49)   a. **m- a-   ta- nap -a*
           NEG- 1SG-   ta- carry -a
           'I did not carry it'
    b. *ɛ-ʊ   a- náp*
           3SG-NEG-PAST 1SG-carry
           'I did not carry it' ('carry' is a non-past tensed verb)

Maasai shows other grammatical properties which distinguish the derivational history of functional imperatives from past (declaratives). Accordingly, Koopman proposes an analysis where imperative verbs must license imperative force in C. In contrast, if the same verbal form expresses past tense, it does not license imperative force, hence it is a declarative clause and the agreement pronoun precedes the verb (50b; Koopman: 7, exs. 19, 20). In negated subjunctives, on the other hand, the agreement forms also precede V.

(50)   a. *áá – náp*
        I-you-carry
        'I will carry you' (non-past)
        b. *kɨ- tá-náp- a*
        He-you ta-carry-a
        'He carried you' (past)

(51)   *tánàp- á kɨ*
        ta-carry-a you-me
        'Carry me!'

With regard to the meaning of past tense clauses, Koopman notes that they have an inceptive interpretation with stative predicates (52a, 53), instead of the expected simple past tense. For the latter interpretation, Maasai uses a non-past tense instead, which normally combines with an adverbial element with past temporal reference (52b).

(52)   a. *ɛ- tó-rók- a ɛn-kàrɛ*
        3SG- ta- black-a SG.F.-water(nom)
        'The water became black' and not: *the water was black
        b. *ɛ- tó ápà ɛn-kàrɛ*
        3SG black ago SG.F-water
        'the water was black a long time ago'

(53)   a. *á- tó-nyór-à*
        1SG-ta-love-a
        'I fell in love' and not: *I loved
        b. *ɛ- tá- yéw- ò*
        3SG-ta- want- a
        'He has come to want it' and not: *he wanted it

Koopman proposes a performative-like analysis where the imperative form is a participle selected by an abstract (imperative) V. The author identifies V as a causative with a meaning close to English 'get' and Maasai verb forms interpreted as past tenses (52, 53) or imperatives (Koopman: 10; ex. 32; 11; ex. 35).

The Maasai data and Koopman's analysis align with the conceptual assumption of the LPH proposal for imperatives on basic principles. Namely, (i) imperative clauses are licensed by an imperative force in C, tacitly promoting the need for functional/indexical information in an adequate syntax of imperatives; (ii) LPH also agrees on the temporality of imperatives, but goes further, embracing Reichenbach's speech time within an Austinian speech act perspective on the dynamics of language. In contrast, LPH would propose that the "silent" V in Maasai imperatives is not a lexical V but rather a functional "light" v. This is a crucial methodological distinction, lest we resuscitate the specter of PH, with its attendant consequences.

4.6.3.2   Polite imperatives in Mandarin Chinese

Evidence is presented in support of a performative [v[V]] complex predicate for Mandarin Chinese polite imperatives (Chen-Main 2005).

Polite requests make use of *polite verbs* (*yao1qiu2* 'request, demand,' *quan4* 'urge,' *qing3* 'invite,' *ma2fan3* 'bother,' etc.) that flank the imperative verb. As with the other imperative sentence types that Chen-Main identifies, polite commands also respond to the same restrictions of root imperatives (person restrictions, banning of certain aspect/tense markers, exclusive interpretation as sentences bearing imperative force). Example (54) illustrates this type of command with the verb *qing3* 'invite.'

(54)   *Qing3   man4   yi1   dianr3   suo1*
        invite   slow   one   bit   say
        'Please, (you) speak slower.'
        * 'Please, (I/he) speak slower.'
        * '(You) request for (me) to speak slower.'
        * '(He) requests for (you) to speak slower.'

The two-verb occurrence of polite commands like "invite say" (54) might be, on first observation, amenable to a subordination analysis. The author concludes, however, that there is no evidence supporting an embedding hypothesis for polite imperatives in Mandarin Chinese.

> Commands formed with polite verbs seem to resist embedding [...]
> Embedding under the verbs we have been using to test for embedding so far,
> yao1qiu2 'request, demand' and quan4 'urge,' yields unacceptable sentences. (Chen-Main 2005: 42)

The following ungrammatical example in (55) serves as illustration.

(55)   *Wo3 yao1qiu2 qing3 ni3 jie3shi4 zhe4 jian4 shi4
        I request invite you explain this-CLASSIFIER matter
        (intended meaning: 'I demand that you please explain this matter.')

This is not to say that the verbs that function as politeness indicators cannot be used in embedded contexts. However, if they are, they receive a literal interpretation (56): "In acceptable sentences that look like embedded polite commands, the polite element is interpreted as a [lexical] verb, not as a polite command element." (p. 42; example 19). The behavior of the two verbs in polite imperatives suggests the alternative analysis that they form a complex predicate, in line with the LPH hypothesis.

(56)   *Wo3 xiang3 qing3 ni3 jie3shi4 zhe4 jian4 shi4*
        I wish invite you explain this-CLASSIFIER matter
        'I wish to invite you to explain this matter.'
        * 'I wish for you to please explain this matter.'

4.6.3.3   On English *do*

Finally, we close with an additional case which supports the complex predicate analysis [v[V]] of imperatives under the LPH assumptions. The argument comes from the use of English *do* when it conveys emphasis/insistence or when it signals a polite request. Han (2000b) notes that, when imperatives are used as antecedents of conditional clauses – an embedded position – emphatic/insistent *do* is banned (57).

(57)   a. do come closer!
        b. ?do come closer and I'll give you 10 pounds.

In a somewhat parallel fashion to Chinese polite imperatives, we note that *do* cannot be interpreted as a politeness indicator in "embedded" imperatives. Thus (58b) cannot be read as meaning that the invitation was polite (cf. 58a); rather, the speaker is using emphasis.[33]

(58)   a. Mary, (please) do come in!
        b. John requested that Mary does come in

The ban on the use of *do* in (57b) and the absence of the polite request in (58b) follow if we assume that *do* in the (a) examples realizes the performative.

4.6.4   *Dedicated auxiliary*

Further evidence comes from prohibitive constructions. It is well known that negative imperatives may be expressed by means of a sort of dedicated construction, such as an "auxiliary" verb unique to imperatives (59a; Zulu), or a prohibitive marker derived from a combination of negation and a (modal) verb, as in the example from Afrikaans (58b; van der Auwera (2010: 6, ex. 11b; 10, ex. 22a), or by verbs with negation lexically built in (e.g., 'not want' or 'be unwilling to': Mandarin Chinese (59c) cf. Chen-Main 2005: 5, ex. 5; Latin (59d) cf. Allen and Greenough 1983: sec. 285, 450, ex. 1).

(59)   a. *musa*   *uku-ngen-a!*
           PROH.AUX   INF-come-INF
           'Don't come in!'
        b. *moeni   dit   vir   hom   gee   nie!*
           PROH   this   for   him   give   NEG
           'Don't give it to him.'

   c. *bu2yao4   dong4!*
      buyao   move
      'Do not move!' / 'Stop moving!'
   d. *noli   putare*
      be.unwilling   suppose.INF
      'do not suppose!' (be unwilling to suppose)

In a sample of close to 600 languages, van der Auwera reports that most languages use prohibitive constructions, followed by languages that negate imperatives, and finally languages that don't (e.g., Romance). An analysis of the imperative clause must recognize the role that additional verbal morphology plays. The LPH identifies prohibitive morphology as independent realization of the performative light verb or as a fused realization of the performative light verb alongside negation.

4.6.5 *Particle imperatives in Badiotto: "point of view"*

Since LPH concerns the imperative sentence type, not just its negation, we need to show that the additional imperative morphology is also seen in the affirmative imperative sentence. We have seen two examples from Ibero-Romance (Panamanian, Salvadorian Spanish). Next, we will reproduce an additional example from Rhaeto-Romance. Badiotto requires that imperative sentences contain certain particles that Poletto and Zanuttini (2003) analyze as point of view. In (60a) the imperative sentence contains the particle *ma*, which indicates that the speaker of the utterance means the imperative to be taken as something that would benefit the addressee. In contrast, in (60b), the particle *mo* is used, indicating that the execution of the imperative expression is given from the point of view of the speaker.

(60)   a. *Màngel   ma   che   spo   crësceste.*
           eat-it   ma   that then   grow (2SG)
           'Eat it and you'll grow.'
     b. *Puzenëieme mo ciamò   i ćialzà!*
           clean-me   mo   yet   the shoes
           'Polish my shoes!' or 'You still have to polish my shoes!'

An interesting aspect of the Badiotto particles is that they are obligatory in the affirmative command only. In the negative command they are optional. The construction is nevertheless referred to as a prohibition, as is customary, since some additional verbal morphology is involved in the expression of the imperative sentence. Similarly, Salvadorian *ve* appears in affirmative and negative commands. The point here is that this type of imperative-specific morphology is perhaps better characterized as belonging to the syntax of the imperative sentence type more generally, as in Badiotto or Salvadorian, and not only to its negation.

Based on semantic considerations, the authors find support in their data for the hypothesis that imperatives in Badiotto are characterized in a syntactic projection lower than CP, namely a dedicated Modal Phrase (ModP), where "*ma* is the specifier of a functional projection which expresses point of view and that is found in the part of the tree which Cinque (1999) identifies as expressing modality" (Poletto and Zanuttini 2003: 186), roughly derived in as (61).

(61)   *Fà-l ma doman!* (29a, p. 165) $[_{CP}[_{C^\circ} f\grave{a} \ldots [_{ModP} ma \ldots [_{TP} doman]]]\ldots]$
       do-it *ma* tomorrow(2sg)
       'do it tomorrow!'

Poletto and Zanuttini's theory of Badiotto's functionally compelling role of Speaker and Hearer is articulated in terms of a dedicated projection (ModP) in the lower (content) phase of the sentences. The particle *ma* must occupy a position which is not the head of ModP or it would block movement of the verb to C, implying a dependency which the verb, but not the particle, must check. Hence ModP encodes the "point of view" of the Speaker and Hearer, a crucial property of Badiotto imperatives which the analysis is silent about as it stands, and hence falls short of providing a fuller account.

Badiotto is another empirical case in the typology of imperative syntax which reclaims the encoding of speech act functions for a descriptively adequate syntax of imperatives under minimalist assumptions. Under LPH assumptions, we argue, a more viable hypothesis is made possible. In brief, we propose an LPH derivation of Badiotto *ma*-imperative, reminiscent of Latin American Spanish double-verb analysis (cf. 4.6.2 above). LPH's v in the content phase is in scopal licensing dependence with IF in the context phase, deriving the referential syntax of the clause without recourse to special projections like ModP or JussiveP (Zanuttini 2008), $[T_{Imp}{}^\circ, 2_\varphi]$ (Jensen 2004b).

(62)   Deriving particle-verb imperatives in Badiotto
       (a) The F-marked *fa-l!* Merges in v; Agree with e^2 Addressee role-2
       (b) <u>a</u> Merges in v, incorporating *-ve*; Agree with e^1 Speaker role-1
       (c) <u>b</u> Merges in F valuing its imperative feature*!*
       $[_{CP} F\ fa\text{-}l! \ [_{vP} e^1 \ [_{v'} \ [_v fa\text{-}l! \ ma \ [_{vP} e^2 \ [_{v'} \ [_v \ [_{vP} \ [_v fa\text{-}l! \ ]]]]]]]]]]$

4.6.6   On do-support
Finally, we will conclude this section with an additional line of argument based on observations reported in the literature about subject position in negated

English imperatives and the distribution of *do-support* and emphatic *do*. A second verbal projection has also been invoked to address variation in the position of the pronoun in negated English imperatives (Pollock 1989; Wilder and Cavar 1994; Platzack and Rosengren 1998; Rupp 2003). A second verbal projection on top of the verb phrase would host *do* in negatives. The optionality in the position of the pronoun, which may appear before or after *don't*, would find its root in the availability of an additional specifier position the subject could move to (63; see also Henry 1995).

(63)   a. Don't you forget!
        b. You don't be late!   (Potsdam 2007: 2, exs. 4a, 5b)

Concerning emphatic *do* and *do-support*, whatever mechanism governs its use, it must apply differently in imperatives. Both are possible with *be* and *have* (the latter in the relevant dialects; 64, 65; 66 cf. van der Wurff 2007b: 10; exs. 35, 36), verbs which would otherwise be incompatible with them.

(64)   Don't be a fool!

(65)   a. Don't have hit your head!
           (parent upon hearing a crash in the kitchen)
        b. Do be here when the band begins to play!

(66)   a. You *don't be/aren't a fool.
        b. You *do be/ARE a fool.
        c. I *don't have (got)/haven't (got) time.

If *do* realizes a higher verbal position in imperatives, a position not present in declaratives and interrogatives, we have cause to observe this asymmetry in imperative sentences.

If indeed imperative expressions contain a performative vP, as the arguments in this section would seem to indicate, it follows that canonical imperatives will feature two vPs (67a) and extended imperatives three (67b).

(67)   a. [CP [$_{vP}$ A [prescribe-v [$_{vP}$ B [*DO P*]]]]]   *Go!*
        b. [CP [$_{vP}$ A [prescribe-v [$_{vP}$ B [cause-v [$_{vP}$ C [*DO P*]]]]]]]   *Let ... go!*

4.7   Summary, projections and concluding remarks

Chapter 4 has developed the "Light" Performative Hypothesis (LPH), a functional speech-act-inspired proposal conceived as a comprehensive syntactic theory for the characterization and derivation of imperative clauses. LPH accounts for utterances where the Addressee is a Performer as well as those where the Addressee is not the Performer (Section 4.2.4), with attendant consequences for a definition of the Person distribution of the Addressee (Section 4.1.5), thereby predicting an extended set of imperative expressions, which are left unaccounted for under more restrictive analyses of imperative clauses. An operator-binding account of the CP(vP) imperative interface is proposed in 4.3.3.1.

The core predictions of the proposal hinge on recasting imperative syntax as a light (functional) performative phase vP, hence overcoming a crucial inadequacy of the original PH and rescuing its conceptual intuition about the nature and use of imperative clauses in context (sections 4.4 and 4.5). This scenario projects, as a virtual conceptual necessity, the encoding of indexical properties in the function phase CP with bound variables in the content phase vP (4.3.3.1). Accordingly, under LPH assumptions, the Speaker is the "logical" (indexical) subject of the utterance, which binds the respective variable in Spec of vP, in chain with the "grammatical" subject of the selected prescription vP, and in irreflexive relation with the thematic role of Addressee. From the Speaker>Addressee thematic dependency relation (4.1.3) the putative Person 1>2 condition on imperative clauses is ultimately derived as a contextually licensed syntactic c-command effect (Section 4.2.5, (Figure 4.1a, b)).

Under LPH, the meaning of the imperative expression can be functionally defined as a "prescription" $F(p)$ (Section 4.2.3 (5)). The syntactic computation of imperative expressions is proposed as a Merge and Agree operation CP(vP), under a computational system where "light" (functional) verbs v are licensed in the functional phase CP. Content verbs V come with the lexicon in the lower phase vP (Section 4.2.4). The former (v) is a closed set defining sentential force (aspects of the speech act) and illocutionary force (participants' role relations). The latter (V) is an open subset of world knowledge. Imperative expressions are compositionally interpreted as asymmetric complex predicates of functional and lexical verbs: [v[V]].

The proposed hypothesis is expected to provide an empirically comprehensive account of imperative expressions as "prescriptions" under a minimally marked (SMT) view of syntax (Chomsky 2008). Beyond syntax, the functional CP phase may provide the appropriate grammatical locus for the functional semantics of imperative expressions interfacing with their grammaticalization.

In the course of this chapter, and more intensively in the last two main sections, the predictions expected from LPH have been tested on new and existing analyses of a range of languages including verbal particle Meso-American

Spanish, Chinese polite two-verb imperatives, Maasai paradigm homophony, Badiotto "point of view" particles, etc.

Chapter 5 will present an in-depth analysis of gender allocutivity in Basque as independent evidence for encoding the Speaker>Addressee relation (4.1.3) in a minimalist approach to universal (internalized) grammar as it concerns the functional syntax of imperative clauses.

5 *Basque allocutive agreement*

5.0   Chapter overview

Verbal agreement in Basque is a morphologically complex system that cross-references subjects, objects and datives for person, number and case. In addition to concord with verbal arguments, the Basque verb agrees with a "fourth" person (as the grammatical tradition would put it): the addressee of the utterance.[1] This phenomenon is known as allocutive agreement (AA). AA is a means to express honorificity in the language. Dialects vary in the number of allocutive morphemes and their interpretation. In eastern dialects, AA encodes familiar/informal address, polite/formal address and, in some cases, affectionate address as well (Alberdi 2003). By contrast, in western dialects, AA is limited to familiar/informal address (absence of AA indicates polite/formal address). Expressing honorificity is common in world languages and includes the use of non-argumental pronouns/verbal inflection for first and second person (ethical datives in Romance, Germanic; certain honorifics in Japanese, Korean, Ryukyuan (Japonic), Beja (Afro-Asiatic), Mandan (Siouan) cf. Antonov 2012, 2013a, 2013b). However, according to Basque linguistics, this particular strategy seems uniquely attested in Basque (Oyharçabal 1993; Hualde and Ortiz de Urbina 2003). In fact, allocutives are obligatory (vs. ethical datives), they are not lexically restricted (vs. Japanese, Antonov 2013a: 4), co-occurrence with a second person argument is banned (vs. all of the above-mentioned languages; see Antonov 2012: 17, table 6), their grammaticalization paths are different (on Japanese and Korean, see Antonov 2013a: 14, 19, 29; on Ryukyuan, see Antonov 2013b), and its syntactic distribution is restricted (vs. the above-mentioned languages, where the empirical description is complete).[2] This chapter documents the use of AA through earlier literature and descriptive grammars, as well as its use in corpora and the Internet.[3]

The distribution of AA varies by dialect but it is generally restricted to root declarative and interrogative clauses. When the verb agrees with a second person argument, AA is not possible. Although AA is a relatively well-known phenomenon within the generative literature, as far as we know, it has not been discussed as an indexical phenomenon in the past, but has been generally viewed as an exotic feature of an isolate.[4] Even within typological work that attempts to integrate Basque allocutivity within honorificity systems, Basque allocutives are admittedly regarded as a more grammaticalized form of non-argumental honorificity (Antonov 2012: 18). Considering that AA references a pragmatic property of language beyond syntax (on generative grammar assumptions), and that the distribution of AA is clause-sensitive, typifying AA as an indexical phenomenon (specifically concerning the role of Speaker, Addressee) seems warranted. Hence, AA joins an ever-growing list of structure-sensitive indexical phenomena that currently lie beyond the scope of narrow morphosyntactic theory.

Within the larger context of the study of structure-sensitive indexicality, AA provides evidence for the representation of a context of utterance in root declarative and interrogative clauses. AA occupies a niche in this literature because the more thoroughly studied indexical phenomena provide evidence for a reported context of utterance (indexical shift, logophoricity: 3.3.1–2). Accordingly, this chapter fills a lacuna in the reassessment of AA as an indexical phenomenon, while providing insights regarding the syntactic organization of the context of utterance across root clauses by direct comparison with the structure of the imperative clause.

The "Light" Performative Hypothesis (LPH, Chapter 4), in its characterization of imperative syntax, provides an extended understanding for the clause-sensitive nature of AA. While some variants are found to also employ AA in exclamative clauses, there is no evidence that imperatives or hortatives are compatible with AA (Oyharçabal 1993; Antonov 2012). This is striking because imperatives and hortatives are root clauses as well. If imperatives and hortatives have the addressee as a syntactic argument, as the LPH proposes, the absence of AA follows from the presence of a second person argument (the same restriction that is observed for AA in other root clauses). At the same time, AA provides independent evidence that the subject of imperatives stands in a predicate-argument relation with the addressee, as the LPH defends.[5]

A comparison of the syntactic distribution of imperatives in the world's languages and AA in Basque reveals striking similarities. AA is also possible in coordination and paratactic environments (it is, in effect, used as a test in the grammatical tradition to ascertain whether a clause is subordinate). In some dialects, AA is exceptionally allowed in the antecedent of conditional clauses. On the assumption that indexicality is represented in the syntax, AA and imperatives can be presumed to observe local licensing conditions in the root context of utterance that prevent them from appearing in reported contexts. Said local licensing conditions could shed light on why indexical shift and logophoricity must operate strictly under reported contexts.

The current chapter begins with an overview of verbal agreement in Basque, paying particular attention to second person morphology when it references verbal arguments (5.1). AA is discussed next (5.2). The distribution of AA across clauses follows (5.3). AA is found in matrix clauses – imperatives and hortatives excepted, but not in dependent clauses. This restriction cannot be explained morphologically (5.4). The second person morphemes indicating AA can reference ordinary arguments in dependent clauses. The absence of AA in imperatives is examined and interpreted in the context of our proposal (5.5). The next section discusses the distribution of AA regarding coordinated and paratactic clauses (5.6). These contexts are similar to those where imperative verb forms are allowed across languages. The current chapter ends with concluding remarks (5.7).

5.1   Overview of verbal agreement in Basque

Basque is an isolate spoken in Spain and France. Its agreement morphology displays obligatory concord for person and number with all arguments to the verb: subject, direct object and indirect object (1). The following three sentences provide a glimpse of the Basque agreement system by showing an intransitive (1a: *heldu* 'arrive'), a transitive (1b: *apurtu* 'break') and a ditransitive verb (1c: *eman* 'give'). Basque being a morphologically ergative or split-intransitive language (depending on the analysis of unergatives as intransitive or transitive predicates, respectively, Alcázar 2008), unaccusative subjects and direct objects bear absolute case (ABS, A), and transitive subjects ergative case (ERG, E). In the indicative, transitive predicates (including unergatives) select auxiliary *ukan* 'have'; unaccusatives *izan* 'be.' Most western Indo-European languages display similar differences in auxiliary selection (Sorace 2000). A key to the glosses can be found in this footnote.[6]

(1)   a. *Haurr-ak*   *heldu*   *d-i-ra*
          children-ABS.PL   arrived   Ø-AUX.BE-PL(A)
          'The children arrived.'
       b. *Haurr-ek*   *platera-k*   *apurtu*   *d-it-u-zte*
          children-ERG.PL   plate-ABS.PL   broken   Ø-PL(A)-AUX.HAVE-3PL(E)
          'The children broke the plates.'
       c. *Haurr-ek*   *amei*   *plater-ak*   *eman*
          children-ERG.PL   mom.DAT.PL   plate-ABS.PL   gave
          d-i-zki-e-te

Ø-PRED-3PL(A)-3PL(D)-3PL(E) [AUX.HAVE]
'The children gave the plates to their mothers.'

The glosses for the auxiliaries in (1) are rich in detail to permit an authoritative discussion of AA.[7]

The next section discusses a special use of second person singular agreement morphemes (i.e., AA). It is therefore fitting to observe second person morphology in a familiar context first. The examples in (2) slightly modify those in (1) to show the morphemes that would represent a second person singular argument: absolutive (2a: *z-*; regardless of grammatical function: subject or object[8]), ergative (2b: *–zu*), dative argument (2c: also *–zu*). Note that for absolutive arguments there is a plural mark (2a). This is because the inflection was historically plural and was later reanalyzed as a singular honorific.

Second person agreement marks that reference a verbal argument: *z-*, *–zu*
(2)   a. *Zu*   *heldu*   *z-a-ra*
        2SG.ABS   arrived   2(A)-Ø-PL(A) [AUX.BE]
        'You arrived.'
      b. *Zu-k*   *platera-k*   *apurtu*   *d-it-u-zu*
        2SG-ERG   plate-ABS.PL   broken   Ø-PL(A)-AUX.HAVE-2SG(E)
        'You broke the plates.'
      c. *Haurr-ek*   *zu-ri*   *plater-ak*   *eman*
        children-ERG.PL   2SG-DAT   plate-ABS.PL   given
        d-i-zki-zu-te
        Ø-PRED-3PL(A)-2SG(D)-3PL(E) [AUX.HAVE]
        'The children gave the plates to you.'

The second person verbal agreement marks *z-*(A) and *–zu*(E/D), alongside the pronouns *zu*(A), *zu–k*(E) and *zu–ri*(D), constitute a neutral or honorific address. Depending on sociolinguistic factors, and their use in particular dialects, these forms could be loosely equivalent to third person pronouns and verbal inflection in Spanish ([*tratar de*] *usted*), Italian ([*dar del*] *Lei* or *Voi*$_{2ppl}$; or the plurality of second person in French (*vouvoiement*). Like Spanish and French, Basque also names this treatment in a similar fashion, making a reference to the pronoun involved: *zu-ka* ('[to address somebody] you-ly'), or *zu-tano*.[9]

To express non-honorific address, Basque employs a different set of second person agreement morphemes and pronouns. These are shown in (3). The pronouns are *hi*(A), *hi-k*(E) and *hi-ri*(D). This treatment is referred to as *hi-ka* or *hi-tano*. The verbal agreement marks indicate gender for ergative and dative arguments (*–k* or medial *–a-* for masculine; *–n* or medial *–na-* for feminine). Absolutive arguments show a silent morpheme *h-* in writing (some dialects aspirate). For clarity, we list the morphemes involved in AA (in later examples) individually in (3'):

<u>Second person agreement marks that reference a verbal argument: *h-*, *–k/–a-*, *–n/–na-*</u>

(3)   a. *Hi   heldu   h-a-iz*
            2SG.ABS   arrived   2-Ø-AUX.BE
            'You arrived.'

       b. *Hi-k   platera-k   apurtu   d-it-u-k*
            2SG-ERG   plate-ABS.PL   broken   Ø-PL(A)-AUX.HAVE-2SG.MASC(E)
            'You broke the plates.'   ('you' is a man (*-k*))

       b'. *Hi-k   platera-k   apurtu   d-it-u-n*
            2SG-ERG   plate-ABS.PL   broken   Ø-PL(A)-AUX.HAVE-2SG.FEM(E)
            'You broke the plates.'   ('you' is a woman (*-n*))

       c. *Haurr-ek   hi-ri   plater-ak   eman*
            children-ERG.PL   2SG-DAT   plate-ABS.PL   given
            d-i-zki-a-te
            Ø-PRED-3PL(A)-2SG.MASC(D)-3PL(E) [AUX.HAVE]
            'The children gave the plates to you.' ('you' is a man (*-a*))

       c'. *Haurr-ek   hi-ri   plater-ak   eman*
            children-ERG.PL   2SG-DAT   plate-ABS.PL   given
            d-i-zki-na-te
            Ø-PRED-3PL(A)-2SG.FEM(D)-3PL(E) [AUX.HAVE]
            'The children gave the plates to you.' ('you' is a woman (*-na*))

(3')   The non-honorific (E/D) morphemes listed individually:
       -k: 2SG.MASC(E/D) in final position
       -n: 2SG.FEM(E/D) in final position
       -a-:   2SG.MASC(E/D) in medial position
       -na-: 2SG.FEM(E/D) in medial position

This concludes our succinct overview. There are extensive discussions of the Basque agreement system, which make it unnecessary to pursue a general introduction to Basque verbal morphology in this chapter. The reader is referred to Rebuschi (1981), Oyharçabal (1993) and Albizu (2002), and to relevant sections of the reference grammars of Hualde and Ortiz de Urbina (2003) and de Rijk (2008). For recent grammars written in Basque, see the multi-volume of *Euskaltzaindia* (1985–2005, Royal Academy of the Basque Language) and Zubiri and Zubiri (2000), among others. Alberdi (1996), also in Basque, is a monograph on Basque honorificity that deals extensively with allocutive agreement.

5.2   Allocutive agreement

This section illustrates and discusses AA, noting dialectal variation (5.2.1) and distinguishing the phenomenon from ethical datives (5.2.2).

The dataset in (1) shows that Basque verbs must agree with all arguments of the verb. In addition, verbal morphology is able to represent agreement with a speech act participant: the Addressee of the utterance.[10] However, this is only possible when no argument of the verb (A, E or D) is second person.[11] In this respect, AA is different from other non-argumental second person honorifics, such as those of Japanese, Korean, Beja and Mandan (see Antonov 2012: 17, table 6), as well as ethical datives more generally (5.2.2), which can co-occur with second person arguments.

AA is expressed in verbal inflection irrespective of the valence of the verb. Accordingly, all the examples in (1) could reference this additional argument by means of second person singular agreement marks – by contrast, the dataset in (2) has second person arguments, and the corresponding AA forms do not exist. The AA forms of (1) are shown in (4), which is repeated from chapter 4 for the reader's convenience. The examples in (4) are the same as (1), but they include AA, which changes the auxiliary. In dialects spoken in Spain this is obligatory when the Speaker wishes to converse with the Addressee in a non-honorific fashion. These dialects are referred to in Basque as the western (or southern) dialects. The dialects spoken in France are named eastern (or northern; the reference point being the Pyrenees). We adhere to this custom in what follows and use the terms eastern and western dialect. Regarding honorificity, the examples in (1) above are honorific or polite neutral addresses (in western dialects) because they are not allocutive forms (eastern dialects have honorific allocutive forms). The second person non-honorific agreement morphemes (E/D) indicate the gender of the Addressee (male –*k* or female –*n*). In (4) the allocutive marks are suffixes, so the medial allomorphs do not show.

Second person agreement marks that reference the Addressee: *-k, -n*

(4) a. *Haurr-ak*   *heldu*   *d-it-u-k*
        Children-ABS.PL arrived Ø-PL(A)-AUX.HAVE-2SG.MASC
        'The children arrived.' (talking to a man(-*k*))

    a'. *Haurr-ak*   *heldu*   *d-it-u-n*
        Children-ABS.PL arrived Ø-PL(A)-AUX.HAVE-2SG.FEM
        'The children arrived.' (talking to a woman(-*n*))

    b. *Haurr-ek*   *platera-k*   *apurtu* *d-it-i-zte-k*
        children-ERG.PL plate-ABS.PL broken Ø-PL(A)-Ø-3PL(E)-2SG.MASC
        'The children broke the plates.' (talking to a man(-*k*))   [AUX.HAVE]

    b'. *Haurr-ek*   *platera-k*   *apurtu* *d-it-i-zte-n*
        children-ERG.PL plate-ABS.PL broken Ø-PL(A)-Ø-3PL(E)-2SG.FEM
        'The children broke the plates.' (talking to a woman(-*n*)) [AUX.HAVE]

    c. *Haurr-ek*   *amei*   *plater-ak*   *eman*
        children-ERG.PL mom.DAT.PL plate-ABS.PL given

z-i-zki-e-te-k[12]
Ø-PRED-3PL(A)-3PL(D)-3PL(E)-2SG.MASC [AUX.HAVE]
'The children gave the plates to their mothers.' (talking to a man(-*k*))

c2'. *Haurr-ek   amei   plater-ak   eman*
children-ERG.PL   mom.DAT.PL   plate-ABS.PL   given
z-i-zki-e-te-n
Ø-PRED-3PL(A)-3PL(D)-3PL(E)-2SG.FEM [AUX.HAVE]
'The children gave the plates to their mothers.' (talking to a woman(-*n*))

A note of clarification on the gloss of (4a) is in order. A close look at the auxiliary glosses in (1a) vs. (4a) reveals that, in unaccusatives, AA must be expressed with *have* instead of *be*. Arguably, this suggests that Basque morphology considers the Addressee as an argument for auxiliary selection.[13] That said, the potential mood has allocutive forms with the auxiliary *be* (de Rijk 2008: 821). Because the auxiliary with AA in intransitives syncretizes in form with the transitive auxiliary (without AA), this could most certainly confuse the reader when comparing (3b) with (4a). In (3b) the auxiliary *dituk/n* expresses the following agreement pattern: 'you[SG]' subject, 'them' object, and the Addressee is not marked. In (4a), the auxiliary *dituk/n* is allocutive, as it expresses the following pattern: 'they' subject, 'you.SG' Addressee. Remember that Basque has absolutive case (unaccusative S, transitive O, ditransitive O) instead of accusative (O), making part of the syncretism we observe here possible.

With respect to the interpretation of allocutive (4) and non-allocutive utterances (1), Hualde, Oyharçabal and Ortiz de Urbina (2003: 243) note that "sentences containing allocutive forms have exactly the same meaning as their corresponding 'plain' [non-allocutive] sentences regarding both propositional content and information structure." Although non-honorific marks indicate, in addition, what the gender of the Addressee is, and that the Addressee is a single person, this seems a fair evaluation: allocutive marks do not change the meaning of the proposition.

Where do the second person marks in (4) come from? Morphologically, this is an obvious question to answer. They are the morphemes ordinarily employed to express second person singular agreement in dative and ergative arguments shown in dataset (3). This includes both the allomorphs used in final position and those used medially (3'). The syncretism is not difficult to handle in a theory of morphology that considers semantic underspecification of morphological exponents, such as Distributed Morphology (Halle 1990, 1997; Halle and Marantz 1993; Embick 2000; Embick and Noyer 2001). If the marks in (3') are specified for person and number only [2SG], but not for case, these will be inserted to realize second person unless some other form is a better match. On the auxiliary assumption that *h-* is further specified for case [2SG, ABSOLUTIVE], the morphemes in (3′) will be selected to realize all other second person arguments and the Addressee. As such, the morphemes in (3′) present two cases of syncretism: (i) case syncretism (E/D) and (ii) an argument/non-argument syncretism. Syncretism is to be expected if (3′) are the elsewhere forms.[14] Furthermore, that AA is restricted to second person singular, barring plural Addressees, can be viewed as an accident, namely an epiphenomenon of morphological specification. On the other hand, the restriction of a single occurrence of second person morphology (i.e., utterances with a second person argument do not have AA forms) is congruent in that there is no need to mark the Addressee twice once it participates in the predicate-argument structure. That said, there are plenty of instances where morphology is repeated elsewhere in world languages (e.g., gender and number agreement in Romance; grammatical case in Basque). Why AA is restricted in this fashion may be a morphological property, but it may also relate to fundamental questions regarding the syntax of agreement.

When the marks in (3′) express an ordinary argument, they are not considered to be allocutive. Accordingly, allocutive agreement requires that no argument of the verb be second person, as advanced above. Regardless of use, argumental or allocutive, the same honorificity value is expressed. Hence, the examples in (4) allow Basque speakers to continue to indicate non-honorific treatment via second person marks even when their interlocutor is not an argument of the verb (by comparison, honorificity in Romance is limited to the participation of the Addressee in predicate-argument structure). This Basque speakers must do. Concord with the Addressee is obligatory in non-honorific addresses. Additionally, coordinated and paratactic clauses must agree in allocutivity (*Euskaltzaindia* 1990: 11–15; see also Adaskina and Grashchenkov 2009: 2–3 on coordination). That is, both verbs in the conjuncts must be allocutive or non-allocutive. By contrast, these restrictions are not apparent in other languages with non-argumental second person honorifics (Antonov 2012, 2013a, 2013b), although, admittedly, exhaustive empirical descriptions are yet to be completed for some of these languages.

In a theoretical model that considers the pragmatic role of the Addressee to be extra-linguistic, that is to say, not represented in syntax, it is not possible to determine where in the clause the Addressee would be. Verbal agreement with an extra-linguistic argument is unexpected. As advanced in the outline of the chapter, we propose to view AA as an indexical phenomenon manifesting in root clauses. AA constitutes direct evidence that the addressee is represented in root clauses. This type of evidence is language specific; AA is rare, if not unique to

Basque. Vocatives, on the other hand, are presumably universal (see Hill 2007, 2010). It is reasonable to assume that AA would respond to an implicational agreement hierarchy, such as the one informally proposed here: addressee > dative > object > subject. The occurrence of AA would then be restricted to languages with the richest form of verbal agreement. Such hierarchy would predict AA to be rare. Because the Addressee functions as an argument for the purposes of verbal agreement, AA suggests that the syntactic categories of the C-I interface may also be verb-like (Speas and Tenny 2003; LPH, see Chapter 4).

5.2.1   *Allocutive agreement in eastern dialects*

We continue with the illustration of AA in eastern dialects, where this phenomenon is more complex than reported for western dialects. In western dialects, allocutivity is restricted to the non-honorific morphemes (3b,c: argumental agreement, 4: allocutive forms). But in eastern dialects, honorific or polite neutral *–zu* (2b,c) is also used allocutively.

Eastern dialects have extended the use to the honorific or polite neutral *–zu* (*–zü* in Souletian Basque), by analogy with non-honorific morphology (*–zü*: 2SG(E/D); see 2b,c). As a result, AA is obligatory if the Addressee is singular, regardless of treatment (Oyharçabal 1993). We follow the lead of Oyharçabal for eastern dialects, comparing AA with examples from Souletian, an eastern Basque dialect. The example in (5), a sentence with the unergative/transitive verb ('do work'), is structured as follows: (5a) shows AA without indicating the gender of the Addressee (honorific/neutral or French *vouvoiement*);[15] (5b) and (5c) show AA indicating the gender of the Addressee (non-honorific or French *tutoiement*); lastly, (d) has no allocutive marks and is therefore unmarked for honorificity. In Souletian, AA is obligatory in formal and informal registers. The absence of allocutive marks denotes that the Addressee is more than one person. To exercise caution, we will not rewrite the auxiliary glosses provided by Oyharçabal. The auxiliary systems may depart considerably or present syncretisms that we are not aware of.

Second person agreement marks that reference the Addressee: *–zü, –k, –n*

(5)   a. *Pettek*   *lan egin*   *dizü*
          Peter.ERG   worked   AUX.3E.ALLOVOUV (Vouvoiement)
          'Peter worked.'

       b. *Pettek*   *lan egin*   *dik*
          Peter.ERG   worked   AUX.3E.ALLOMASC (Masculine tutoiement)
          'Peter worked.'

       c. *Pettek*   *lan egin*   *din*
          Peter.ERG   worked   AUX.3E.ALLOFEM (Feminine tutoiement)
          'Peter worked.'

d. *Pettek   lan egin   dü*
   Peter.ERG   worked   AUX.3E (Non-allocutive)
   'Peter worked.'

In eastern dialects, the morphemes involved in AA are also the same as those employed for argumental second person singular agreement (E/D). Let us take a quick look at these for completeness (6, 7 cf. ex. 9 in Oyharçabal; modified for clarity). In (6) there is a second person (ergative) transitive subject. It is referenced either by *–zü* (2SG; honorific), or *–k* (2SG.MASC)/*–n* (2SG.FEM; non-honorific). (7) shows the same for a second person dative argument. By Ø in the Basque examples Oyharçabal means the 'null' morpheme (on our part, we make use of Ø in the glosses to indicate that a given segment may not be a morpheme).

Second person agreement marks that reference an argument: *–zü, –k, –n*

(6)   a. *Lan egin   dü-zü*
          worked   AUX-2VOUVE
          'You worked.'   ('you' is gender neutral)
       b. *Lan egin   dü-k*
          worked   AUX-2MASC.E
          'You worked.'   ('you' is a man (*-k*))
       c. *Lan egin   dü-n*
          worked   AUX-2FEM.E
          'You worked.'   ('you' is a woman (*-n*))

(7)   a. *Gertatu   Ø-zai-zü*
          happened   3A-AUX-2VOUVD
          'It happened to you.'   ('you' is gender neutral)
       b. *Gertatu   Ø-zai-k*
          happened   3A-2MASC.D
          'It happened to you.'   ('you' is a man (*-k*))
       c. *Gertatu   Ø-zai-n*
          happened   3A-2FEM.D
          'It happened to you.'   ('you' is a woman (*-n*))

As expected, the presence of ergative or dative arguments ('we', 'to me' in (8)) precludes AA in these dialects (Oyharçabal ex. 10).

Second person agreement marks that reference the Addressee: *–zü*

(8)   a. *Lan egin   d-i---zü------gü*
          worked   AUX-ALLOVOUV-1PLE.
          'We worked.' (*Vouvoiement*)
       b. *Zahartzia   hullantü   Ø--zi--ta---zü*
          oldness.NOM approached   3A-AUX-1SGD--ALLOVOUV
          'Aging caught up with me.'[16] (*Vouvoiement*)

There are at least two substantial differences between AA in western and eastern dialects. One is honorificity. Since western speakers have only one honorific value for allocutivity, they refer to allocutivity as non-honorific treatment or *hika*, without regard for whether the mark refers to an argument of the verb or not (we have come across terms like *zeharkako* (indirect) *hika* to name allocutivity in language teaching). The other difference is that in western dialects, but not in eastern ones, AA is also employed in the plural (e.g., Alberdi 2003; see Fontaneda 2008), contrary to the prescriptive tradition. It seems that this innovation is limited to the allocutive use. Thus, when the non-honorific forms refer to an argument, this must be singular. All in all, western dialects distinguish argumental vs. allocutive use in two ways: (i) only non-honorific forms can be allocutive and (ii) only in the allocutive use can these forms be plural.[17]

5.2.2   *Allocutive agreement vs. ethical datives*

Although rare, AA it is not the only case where the Speaker or the Addressee is referenced as non-arguments to the verb (see Franco and Huidobro 2008 on ethical datives in Romance and references therein). The sentence in (9) is an example of our own illustrating a non-argumental first person singular clitic in Spanish. Assume that the speaker is looking for a well-lit spot in a room to read comfortably and notices that the blinds are down. The speaker remarks:

(9)   (yo) me   levanto   la persiana   y así   veo   mejor
      I   ETH.DAT.1SG raise.1SG   the blind   and so see.1SG   better
      'I'll raise [me] the blinds so that I see better.'

The arguments to the verb in (9) are "I" (subject) and "the blinds" (object). However, there is an additional pronoun, *me*, which indicates in this context that the speaker will be positively affected by the action (negative affect is also possible).

De Rijk (2008: 810) also draws this connection between AA and ethical datives. He mentions examples from French and German (10a,b). Beyond Romance and Germanic, Antonov (2012) notes that ethical datives extend to the Northeast Caucasian languages Chechen and Ingush. He also provides interesting examples from Gascon (10c,d), where first and second person forms can be used simultaneously (quoted from Morvay 2002; see references therein).

(10)   a. *Qu'on me l'égorge tout à l'heure*
          'Have his throat cut at once (for me).'   (cf. Grevisse 1980, sec. 634)
       b. *Daß du mir nicht zu spät kommst!*
          'Don't show up late (on me)!'   (cf. *Duden Grammatik ...*)
       c. *te   me   los   copèt   la   coa*
          2:DAT   1:DAT   6:ACC   cut:PST:IND:3   ART:F:SG   tail
          'He cut their tail (*for you *for me).'

d. *te   me   son   partits   sul   pic*
   2:DAT 1:DAT be:PRS:IND:6 go away:PTCP:PL:M on.ART:M:SG top
   'They left immediately (*for you *for me).'

In Antonov's typological view (2012), AA, ethical datives and other second person non-argumental honorifics are grouped together under a broader label of allocutivity (sometimes it is not clear how this label is non-equivalent to honorificity itself). In this continuum, AA would be the most grammaticalized form. Antonov (2012: 6, and fn. 7) suggests that Basque allocutives may have in effect developed from contact with Romance languages, AA being a more grammaticalized form of ethical datives. However, there are important differences between AA and ethical datives, as well as other broadly conceived "allocutive" forms in languages like Japanese or Korean, which we turn to discuss next.

Hualde, Oyharçabal and Ortiz de Urbina (2003: 243) also note similarities between AA and ethical datives. However, they warn that direct comparison is not possible on account of multiple morphosyntactic and semantic differences:

> Allocutivity is different from the so-called "ethical dative" of some
> Romance languages, where the use of the second person dative marker indicates that the addressee is somehow affected or interested in the proposition.
> The use of allocutive forms does not convey any such meaning. It is simply an obligatory feature of the familiar treatment [in western dialects]. [...]
> Moreover, while ethical datives can be used for all persons, allocutivity only registers second person addresses.

De Rijk makes similar observations and further adds that "The ethical dative is an optional stylistic device. Allocutive forms in Basque are compulsory whenever they are possible." (2008: 810). In this respect, AA patterns with imperatives in being restricted to second person reference.

Oyharçabal is careful to distinguish AA from implicative sentences, which seem to be roughly equivalent to ethical datives. Implicative sentences are also possible in Basque (Rebuschi 1982) but, as Oyharçabal shows, said sentences (11a) are in fact compatible with AA (11b; Oyharçabal uses of the *accusative* term in (11) is equivalent to our *absolutive*.

(11)   a. *Semea   gerlara   joana   dut*
          son.ACC   war.ADL   gone.RES   AUX.3A.1E.
          lit. 'I have the son gone to the war.' (Non-allocutive)
       b. *Semea   gerlara   joana   diat*
          son.ACC   war.ADL   gone.RES   AUX.3A.1E.ALLOMASC
          Same translation (Masculine allocutive)

Beyond ethical datives, AA observes incompatibility with argumental second person forms (5.2), to include imperatives (5.3), and strict syntactic distributional properties (5.4). Furthermore, allocutives are not syntactically restricted, nor do they have verbal origin (e.g., Japanese). By contrast, other broadly conceived forms of "allocutivity" do not feature these restrictions.

5.3   Allocutive agreement in matrix clauses

According to the grammatical tradition and generative studies, AA is a matrix phenomenon. What particular root clause must bear AA, on the other hand, varies depending on the source. For instance, *Euskaltzaindia* limits AA to matrix declarative clauses.[18] Oyharçabal (1993), Hualde, Oyharçabal and Ortiz de Urbina (2003) and de Rijk (2008) report that AA is also used in yes/no-questions in western dialects. Alberdi (1996), based on a survey of over 200 speakers, finds AA in matrix wh-questions in western dialects too. We have consulted monolingual corpora, a parallel corpus and the Internet to ascertain the validity of these claims. We have found AA in the contexts claimed in earlier literature, that is, in root declaratives, yes/no-questions and wh-questions. The exception is found in imperatives and hortatives, where AA is not attested. Oyharçabal (1993), assuming that hortatives do not have a syntactic Addressee, noted that hortatives required explanation. Although the domain of AA is expanded to various degrees depending on the consulted source, all sources agree that a basic descriptive generalization to be accounted for is the ban on embedding.

5.3.1   *Yes/no-questions*

Earlier examples of AA illustrated root declaratives. Prescriptive grammars dictate that AA should not be used in yes/no-questions. However, Oyharçabal notes that speakers of western dialects use AA in this context, too (see Etxabe and Garmendia 2003 on Zaldibia Basque for a similar comment; Hualde, Oyharçabal and Ortiz de Urbina 2003).

The following examples from the Internet (12–14) illustrate the use of AA in root yes/no-questions.[19] These pairs illustrate the use of masculine (a) and feminine (b) forms. (12a) is part of a guestbook comment addressed to a man. (12b) is part of a song or poem addressed to a woman. AA is seen in a main verb in (12a) and in an auxiliary in (12b).[20] The non-allocutive form for (12) would have been *n-a-iz* '(I) am' (1SG-Ø-AUX.BE).

(12)   a. *Bañe   ain   txarra   al   n-a-u-k   ba??*
     but   so   bad   yes/no.Q   1SG(A)-Ø-AUX.HAVE-2SG.MASC   so

'But am I that bad?'
www.fotolog.com/kortaberri/33773264

b. *mundu-a   ezagutzeko   gogo-ei   saldu*
   world-ABS.SG   to.know   wish-DAT.PL   sold
   n-a-u-n   ala?
   1SG(A)-Ø-AUX.HAVE-2SG.FEM   or.not
   'Have I given myself away to the desire to see the world?'
   www.fotolog.com/autumns_child/56538504

The following two examples are from a short story (13a), where the question is addressed to a man, and a play (13b), where the character Beke addresses Sofie. The corresponding non-allocutive form for (13) is *n-a-go* '(I) am' [1SG(A)-Ø-BE] (stage level *be*). This is a finite form of *egon* 'be,' which is not an auxiliary for monovalent predicates, and is directly augmented with allocutive marks. Since AA is commonly found in literary sources, it does not appear that speakers are too aware of, or particularly sensitive to the prescription of *Euskaltzaindia* to limit AA to declaratives.

(13) a. *Hain   pottola   n-ego-k   ala?*
         so   fat   1SG(A)-BE-2SG.MASC   or.not
         'Am I so fat?'
         www.susa-literatura.com/liburuak/narr0908.htm

      b. *BEKE: Amets-etan   al   n-ego-n   edo bizirik.*
         BEKE: dream-LOC   yes/no.Q   1SG(A)-BE-2SG.FEM   or alive
                 Mundu ontan?...
                 world this
                 'Am I dreaming or alive, in this world? ...'
         SOFIE: *(sukaldetik sartzen dalarik) Gure etxean, nik uste.*
         SOFIE: '(entering through the kitchen) At home, I think.'
         klasikoak.armiarma.com/idazlanak/L/LabaienAgar006.htm

The last set (14) comes from a recent interview in a newspaper (14a), where the journalist is addressing a man called Joxe Anjel, and a book (14b), where a woman is asked about some homeless people. The corresponding non-allocutive form for (15) is *d-i-ra* '(they) are' (Ø-AUX.BE-PL(A)).

(14) a. *-Eta   beste   bi   anai-ak   ere   joaten   al*
         and   other   two brother-ABS.PL   too   go   yes/no.Q
         d-it-u-k   zuekin?
         Ø-3PL(A)-AUX.HAVE-2SG.MASC   you.PL.with
         'and the other two brothers also go along with you all?'
         www.diariovasco.com/20090319/al-dia-local/joxe-anjel-itsuarekin-jolas-ean-20090319.html

      b. *Aiza-n,   ibili   al*
         listen.IMP-2SG.FEM(E)   be.around   yes.no.Q

Table 5.1 *Use of AA in yes/no-questions and wh-questions*

YES	NO	RARELY	TOTAL/PERCENTAGE
134	70	4	208
64.4%	33.6%	1.9%	100%

> *d-it-u-n*
> Ø-3PL(A)-AUX.HAVE-2SG.MASC
> *gizon   eskale-ak   hemen   barna?*
> men   solicitor-ABS.PL   here   inside
> 'Hey listen, have the beggars been inside here?'
> www.armiarma.com/emailuak/txalaparta/pram04.htm

5.3.2   Wh-questions

Oyharçabal (1993) does not find AA in wh-questions. Alberdi (1996) looks into the syntactic restrictions on AA in a sample of more than 200 speakers. One of his findings is that AA is generally used in matrix yes/no-questions as well as wh-questions. The participants in his study were asked to translate (15) from Spanish or French (Romance, Indo-European) into Basque to determine if they used AA in this context.

(15)   a *¿Ha venido Mikel?/ Est-ce que Michel est venu?*
             'Has Mikel come?'
         b *¿Quién ha venido?/ Qui est venu?*
             'Who has come?'

Table 5.1 shows the results (Alberdi 1996: 284). The majority of speakers in his sample use AA in questions. Additionally, Alberdi notes that 60 of the 70 speakers who reject AA in questions happen to be speakers of eastern dialects.

The next examples from the Internet show AA in wh-questions (16–17). The examples in (16) are all addressed to a man and the ones in (17) to a woman (the non-allocutive form would have been: *da* AUX.BE.3SG 'is').

The question in (16a) is self-addressed or rhetorical, and it is found in a short story by a local aspiring writer that is featured on the web page of the town hall of Orio (Spain). The example in (16b) comes from an interview in a reputable magazine with a long tradition ([*Zeruko*] *Argia*, since 1919). The last question is part of a comment that reportedly quotes a novel (16c).

(16)   a. *Ring-ring! Telefonoa? Nor ote   d-u-k?*   – *Bai...*
             ring-ring! telephone? Who MIR   Ø-AUX.HAVE-2SG.MASC yes
             'Who is it?' Yes...' [or 'Who could it be?']
             www.oriora.com/Udala/Euskara/Gazteliteratura/1996/Salsamendi

b. *Eta nor*   *atera-tzen* *d-u-k?*   *Inor*   *ez!*
  and who.ABS come-IMP Ø-AUX.HAVE-2SG.MASC someone.ABS NEG
  'and what [young soccer players] break through? No one!'
  www.argia.com/argia-astekaria/866/tontoak-ailegatzen-dira-gora

c. *-Baina* *Pernando,* *nor*   *hil* *d-u-k?*
  but   Pernando who.ABS die Ø-AUX.HAVE-2SG.MASC
  'But Pernando, who has died?' (ringing the church bells)
  -Karidadea, herri hontan karidadea hil da.
  'Charity, charity has died in this town.'
  sustatu.com/1053504707

On the other hand, (17a) is a passage where two women converse from the Basque translation of Miguel de Unamuno's *Abel Sánchez* (1917). (17b) is an excerpt from the play *Ibañeta* (Piarres Larzabal 1968), where a he-bear talks to a she-wolf.[21] Finally, (17c) is taken from a play for children of 9 years and older to perform at school.

(17)   a. *Bere aitorlearena izango dun.*
        'It must be her confessor's.'
        Nor   *d-u-n?*   *– Etxeberria jaun-a.*
        Who.ABS Ø-AUX.HAVE-2SG.FEM Etxeberria mister-ABS.SG
        'Who's him? – Mr. Etxeberria.'
        www.armiarma.com/unibertsala/unamuno/unamuno29.htm

     b. HARTZA: *Nor*   *d-u-n*   *neska* *hori?*
        he-bear who.ABS Ø-AUX.HAVE-2SG.FEM girl   that
        'HE-BEAR: who is that girl?'
        OTSANDA: *Ez duk neska… Ezkondua duk…*
        'SHE-WOLF: it's not a girl[she's not single]…she is married…'
        klasikoak.armiarma.com/idazlanak/L/LarzabalIbaneta002.htm

     c. ELVIRA: *Zer*   *Oneka,*   *nor*   *d-u-n*
        Elvira   what   Oneka who.ABS Ø-AUX.HAVE-2SG.FEM
        'ELVIRA: what's up Oneka, who is'
        ma [sic] maiteminduta haukan gazte misteriotsua?
        'the mysterious young boy you are in love with?'
        www.idazten.com/index.php?option=com_content&view=article&id=98
        2:antzerkia&catid=48:antzerkia&directory=476

5.4   Restrictions on allocutive agreement

Earlier we mentioned that AA is not found with second person arguments or, in the absence of a second person singular argument, when the addressee is plural. A second restriction is that AA is not found in complement clauses, indirect questions and relative clauses. As far as Basque morphology is concerned, AA in dependent clauses would not be a problem. The same morphemes (2b,c, 3′) reference second person arguments in finite dependent clauses.

Oyharçabal provides examples of AA being unavailable in relatives (18), subjunctive clauses (19) and indirect questions (20; cf. exs. 25–27).

(18) a. *[Lo egiten   duen]*   *gizona   Manex   dun*
          sleeping   AUX.3E.COMP   man   John   COP.3A.ALLOFEM
          'The man [who is sleeping] is John.'

      b. **[Lo egiten   dinan]*   *gizona   Manex*
          sleeping   AUX.3E.ALLOFEM.COMP   man.the   John
          dun
          3A.COP.ALLOFEM
          Same translation

(19) a. *Ez   dinat*   *nahi   [gerta   dakion]*
          NEG   AUX.1E.ALLOFEM   want   happen   3A.AUX.3D.COMP
          'I don't want it to happen to him.'

      b. **Ez   dinat*   *nahi   [gerta*
          NEG   AUX.1E.ALLOFEM   want   happen
          diakionan]
          3A.AUX.3DALLOFEM.COMP
          Same translation

(20) a. *Ez   dakinat*   *[zer   gertatu   den]*
          NEG   know.1E.ALLOFEM   WHAT.NOM   happened   3A.AUX.COMP
          'I don't know what it is.'

      b. **Ez   dakinat*   *[zer   gertatu*
          NEG   know.1E.ALLOFEM   what.NOM   happened
          dunan]
          3A.AUX.ALLOFEM.COMP
          Same translation

Alberdi's survey covers whether AA is used in relatives (21) and indirect questions (22 cf. 1996: 285; exs. and tables (e), (g)). The informants translated the sentences from Spanish or French. Tables 5.2 and 5.3 summarize the results of the study, namely whether the verb is expressed in allocutive form.

(21)   *El que ha llegado ahora es mi cuñado/ Celui qui est arrivé maintenant est mon beau frère.*
        'The one that has arrived now is my brother in law.'

(22)   *No sé si vendrá/ Je ne sais pas s'il viendra*
        'I don't know if he will come'

The majority of speakers in his sample do not use AA in relatives and indirect questions (>85%). The minority who use AA (<13%) belong to the same

Table 5.2 *Use of AA in relative clauses (suffixal complementizer: –n)*

YES	NO	MAYBE	TOTAL/PERCENTAGE
26	178	2	202
12.5%	85.5%	1.4%	100%

Table 5.3 *Use of AA in indirect questions (suffixal complementizers: –n (if) and –nentz (whether))*

YES	NO	MAYBE	TOTAL/PERCENTAGE
23	183	3	208
11.1%	88.4%	1.4%	100%

dialectal and demographic group: they are speakers of western dialects under 45 years of age. This group tends to use AA in both matrix and dependent clauses (see below).

In completive clauses (23, 24) and temporal clauses (25: p. 285; exs. and Tables (a), (b), (d)), the same pattern is repeated. The majority group (E: all ages, W: >45 years old) limits its use to matrix clauses. The minority group (W: <45 years old) uses AA in matrix and dependent clauses.

(23)   *Ha dicho que vendrá tarde/Il a dit qu'il viendra tard.*
         'He has said <u>that he will be late</u>.'

(24)   *No creo que venga/ Je ne crois pas qu'il vienne.*
         'I don't think <u>that he will come</u>.'

(25)   *Cuando venga, dile que me llame/ Quand il viendra, dit lui de m'appeler.*
         '<u>When he comes</u>, tell him to call me.'

Dialectal differences do explain two observed facts for Alberdi: (i) the extension of AA to matrix questions in western dialects, and (ii) the extension to the honorific paradigm in eastern dialects (by full analogy with the morphology (E/D) and syntactic distribution (matrix declaratives) of the non-honorific AA system). Regarding the use of AA in dependent clauses, Alberdi reasons that it cannot be attributed to a different dialectal evolution in the minority group (W: <45yrs). He proposes instead that the extension could be due to different factors. One is hypercorrection. Speakers may think that they should logically apply AA in finite clauses, matrix or otherwise. Another is "ignorance" (cf. *ezjakintasuna*; that is, language attrition in native speakers or use of Basque

Table 5.4a *Use of AA in completive clauses (suffixal complementizer: –la)*

YES	NO	MAYBE	TOTAL/PERCENTAGE
22	186	1	209
10.5%	88.9%	0.4%	100%

Table 5.4b *Use of AA in completive clauses (suffixal complementizers: –nik, –n and –la)*

YES	NO	MAYBE	TOTAL/PERCENTAGE
13	193	–	206
6.3%	93.6%	–	100%

Table 5.5 *Use of AA in temporal clauses (suffixal complementizers: –nean (when), –larik (while))*

YES	NO	MAYBE	TOTAL/PERCENTAGE
20	180	2	206
9.9%	89.1%	0.9%	100%

as a second language), which is the explanation that Alberdi favors. In western dialects, non-honorific morphology is fading away, and AA along with it. Speakers may be hesitant about where to use AA. Simplification of honorific paradigms and generalization of the syntactic domain likely signals language attrition or language learning.

More recently, scholars have directed their attention to western dialects (Guipuzcoan) that seem to allow AA in embedded clauses (de Rijk 2008; Adaskina and Grashchenkov 2009: 2). According to Adaskina and Grashchenkov (2009: 2), said uses in their data abide by the obligatory allocutive agreement rule observed in coordinated clauses; that is, if a root verb form is allocutive so must the embedded form be (mismatches are ungrammatical). If that is the case, native speakers may not be reflecting a prescriptive zeal (overcorrection) or language attrition/incomplete acquisition, as Alberdi (1996) entertains. From the perspective of indexicality being represented in syntactic structure, should these uses in embedded clauses be legitimate, they may represent an extension of the syntactic domain of AA from root CPs (*context of utterance*) to embedded CPs (*reported contexts*). This is a natural explanation if AA is viewed as an indexical phenomenon (cf. 4.3.3). Other indexical phenomena that concern both root CPs and embedded CPs include indexical shift (3.3.1) and conjunct-disjunct systems (3.3.3).

5.5   Absence of allocutive agreement in imperative clauses

With particular reference to imperatives, Oyharçabal (1993) is the only source we have consulted that discusses this aspect. Oyharçabal assumes that AA is not possible. The reason for this is that a second person counts as argumental. Consequently, the second person singular marks that we see in (26: western Basque) are to be interpreted as non-allocutive. They refer to the subject argument (ergative)[22] (see Antonov (2012: 3) for a similar argument).

(26)   a. *egin   eza-zu!*
           done   AUX.EZAN-2SG(E)
           'do it!'
        b. *egin   eza-k!*
           done   AUX.EZAN-2SG.MASC(E)
           'do it!'
        c. *egin   eza-n!*
           done   AUX.EZAN-2SG.FEM(E)
           'do it!'

Antonov (2012: 3) briefly mentions this distributional aspect, and considers it a criterion of allocutivity in his broader sense. However, since none of the languages surveyed in his works are incompatible with second person arguments, it is not clear how we can tell, for these particular languages, whether non-argumental second person honorifics are indeed banned in imperatives as they are in Basque.

Regarding hortatives, these are problematic for Oyharçabal's account. AA is expected with first or third person. This is not the case (27).

(27)   a. *jan   d-eza-gu-n!*
           eat   Ø-AUX.EZAN-1PL(E)-COMP?
           'Let's eat (it)!'
        b. *hurbil   bekizkit!*
           get.closer   AUX.3(A).PL(A).1SG(D)
           'Let them get close to me!'
           (Saltarelli 1988: 305–06)

Oyharçabal proposes an analysis of AA as an operator generated as an adjunct to TP, which later has to be licensed by movement to C at LF. When

C is filled, movement is prevented, and the allocutive operator is not licensed. Oyharçabal's proposal achieves broad empirical coverage, as it accounts for the absence of AA in subordinate contexts. Additionally, the analysis builds on the absence of AA in matrix wh-questions in his data, although yes/no-questions undermine an operator analysis in western dialects, and so does the availability of AA in wh-questions, where two different operators would be competing for licensing.

To account for the absence of AA in hortatives, Oyharçabal proposes that C is filled in first and third person forms:

> The contrast only concerns imperative forms where the subject DP is 3d [sic.] person; cf. Etor bedi / *bedik hire laguna "Let come your friend!" [sic.] If it is 2d[sic.] person, allocutive form is excluded following the general incompatibility of allocutivity with argumental 2d person agreement (*zatoztek tenoreko! Come in time! (with an [sic.] 2d person plural)). If it is 1st person, it appears with a Complementizer-type suffix [-en] and this excludes allocutive marking [...]. Maybe the prefix b- found in these forms (as in bedi [3SG]) is a complementizer-type element. (fn. 11) [emphasis in the original]

This idea is plausible on the auxiliary assumptions that (i) *b-* is a prefixal complementizer in third person commands and, as a corollary of the analysis, that (ii) *–(e)n* should be a suffixal complementizer in first person commands.

Oyharçabal suggests that first and third person imperatives *imply* an addressee, but the addressee is not an argument. For this reason, AA must be prevented. Under LPH, hortatives are "prescriptions," like imperatives (4.2.3, ex. 5), but their structure differs from imperatives in that they feature a causative vP (4.2.5, Figures 4.1a, b). AA is not possible in hortatives because the addressee is also structurally represented as the external argument of the causative verb (see Chapter 4, Figure 4.1b). For further discussion in the context of LPH, see 4.3.5.

5.6   Parallelisms between allocutive agreement and imperatives

The distribution of AA is similar to that of imperatives. While AA is banned in subordinate clauses, it is obligatory in (i) coordinated clauses and (ii) paratactic clauses (cf. *Euskaltzaindia*; Oyharçabal 1993). Additionally, (iii) speakers exceptionally use AA in one particular subordinate clause: the protasis of conditional clauses (Alberdi 1996). See 4.5.4 for conditional sentences and their paratactic, not hypotactic, hierarchical status.

These are precisely the contexts where we can observe imperative verb forms cross-linguistically (see van der Wurff 2007b and references therein).

AA and imperative clauses thus present parallel syntactic behavior in that they appear to share the same licensing environments. We propose to account for these similarities by an analysis of AA where indexicality is encoded in syntax (cf. 4.3.5).

5.6.1 Allocutive licensing as a test of parataxis

Euskaltzaindia proposes AA as a test to determine if a given clause is paratactic or subordinate (*Euskaltzaindia* 1990: 11–15). Coordination requires AA in both conjuncts (28a). In (28b) the causal relation implied in (28a) is rendered explicit by subordination with enclitic –*lako* 'because,' barring AA (cf. *Euskaltzaindia* 1990: 15, ex. 35)

(28) a. *Horrela   esan   d-i-a-t*
        so   said   Ø-Ø-2SG.MASC-1SG(E) [AUX.HAVE]
      eta   horrela   d-u-k.
      and   so   Ø-AUX.HAVE.3SG(E)-2SG.MASC
      'I said so and that's the way it is.' (talking to a man(-*a*-, -*k*))
  b. *Horrela   esan   d-i-a-t,*
        so   said   Ø-Ø-2SG.MASC-1SG(E) [AUX.HAVE]
      horrela de-lako   */*d-u-a-lako*
      and   so AUX.BE.3SG(A)-COMP   Ø-AUX.HAVE.3SG(E)-2SG.MASC-COMP
      'I said so because that's the way it is.' (talking to a man(-*a*-, *-*k*))

In contrast to subordination (28b), parataxis requires AA (29, cf. *Euskaltzaindia* 1990: 12, ex. 25). In (29a), the second clause is simply juxtaposed to the first and a causal relation is inferred. In (29b), the second clause is subordinated by *bait* 'because,' a proclitic, and AA is precluded.

(29) a. *Lasai   egon, neska,   laster   etorriko   d-u-n.*
        relaxed been girl   soon   come.FUT Ø-AUX.HAVE.3SG(E)-2SG.FEM
      'Take it easy, girl, he will come soon.' (talking to a woman(-*n*))
  b. *Lasai   egon, neska,   laster   etorriko   bait*
        relaxed been girl   soon   come.FUT because
      da   */*d-u-n.*
      AUX.BE.3SG(A) Ø-AUX.HAVE.3SG(E)-2SG.FEM
      'Take it easy, girl, because he will come soon.'

This test directly applies to causal clauses with the suffix –*eta* 'and' (30 cf. *Euskaltzaindia* 1990: 157, ex. 187, 188; also adversative clauses with the connective *baina*). The following examples from *Euskaltzaindia*'s grammar are root questions/exclamatives with AA followed by causal –*eta*, also with AA.[23] These examples stand in sharp contrast to the ones in (28b) and (29b), where the causal markers prevent embedding.

Table 5.6 *Use of AA in causal clauses (complementizers:* bait-, –lako*)*

YES	NO	MAYBE	TOTAL/PERCENTAGE
12	178	6	198
6.1%	90.8%	3%	100%

(30) a. *Nola etorriko   d-u-k   bada,*
      how come.FUT   Ø-AUX.HAVE.3SG(E)-2SG.MASC   well
      'How could he come!?' (talking to a man(-*k*))
      ama   hil   z-a-i-o-k   eta
      mom.ABS.SG   die   Ø-Ø-PreD-3SG(D)-2SG.MASC [AUX.BE]   and
      '[considering that] his mom passed away' (talking to a man(-*k*))
   b. *Nola ez   d-i-k,   bada,   jakingo,*
      how NEG   Ø-PreD-2SG.MASC   well   know.FUT
      'Well, how couldn't he know?!' (talking to a man(-*k*))
      beti ikas-ten   ari   d-u-k   eta
      always study-IMP   PROG   Ø-AUX.HAVE.3SG(E)-2SG.MASC   and
      '[considering that] he is always studying' (talking to a man(-*k*))

As noted, causal clauses with the complementizer *bait-* or –*lako* reject AA.
This is further corroborated by Alberdi's survey (34 cf. 1996: 285; table (f)).
Table 5.6 is once again subject to the majority vs. minority group distinction
alluded to before.

(31)   *No ha venido porque no le han llamado/ Il n'est pas venu parce qu'ils
       ne l'ont pas appelé.*
       'He did not come because they did not call him.'

It is worth noting that –*eta* is also used in a well-known paratactic context
for Indo-European languages: the absolute participial construction (Kayne
1989; Belletti 1990), which Basque also has (32, Alcázar and Saltarelli 2007a,
2007b, 2008a). However, we cannot see AA in absolutes since the construction
is non-finite in Basque.

(32)   *Maria hel-du-ta,   Gianni   lasaitu   zen*
       Maria arrive-PER-AND   Gianni   relaxed   was
       'Maria [having] arrived, Gianni was relieved.'

The conjunction is also seen in absolutes in Ancient Greek, Hittite (Bauer
2000: 270, 283–84) and English, bringing validity to coordination as a source
of parataxis. For English, Visser (1966) notes that the absolute past participial
construction may be followed by *and* + main sentence (33; "This usage must
not be confounded with that in which before the past participle an auxiliary is
omitted or should be supplied from the preceding syntactical unit" p. 1278).

(33)   a. The battle done, and they within our power shall never see his pardon.
(William Shakespeare, *King Lear* (1605): V, I, 67)
   b. Given certain factors, and sound brain should always evolve the same
fixed product.
(Oliver Wendell Holmes, *The Autocrat of the Breakfast-Table* (1587), I, 12)

According to Visser, this use has survived in present-day Irish English.

For Adaskina and Grashchenkov (2009), AA is "a marker of some special discourse register placed in Force head of CP (Rizzi 1997)" (p. 2). They thus analyze AA outside the broader context of structure-sensitive indexical phenomena. One of the properties they seek to account for in their analysis is the requirement that coordinated clauses agree in allocutivity. This particular aspect of AA can be elucidated by appealing, as they do, to the Law of Coordination Likes (Williams 1978), which assumes that XPs must agree in features. Such a principle is consistent with the SMT. If AA is, as we contend, an indexical phenomenon, the requirement that coordinated and paratactic clauses agree in allocutivity is a significant argument that indexicality is part of syntactic computation, as LPH defends. If a mismatch of allocutive and non-allocutive forms leads to ungrammaticality, then allocutivity is a syntactically represented and active feature that is computed during coordination. Hence, *Euskaltzaindia*'s test for parataxis is, in effect, an argument for indexicality in syntax.[24]

5.6.2   *Imperatives in paratactic clauses*
Like AA, imperative verbs, too, may appear in clauses that may be analyzed as paratactic (see 4.5.4).[25] A frequent case is that of appositive relative clauses. The following examples are from Latin (34a), Ancient Greek (34b) and English (35a is from the Elizabethan period cf. van der Wurff 2007b: 23, ex. 69; 24, exs. 70, 71; and references therein). These examples are repeated here from Chapter 2 for the reader's convenience.

(34)   a. *multas   ad   res   perutiles   Xenophontis libri sunt;*
            many   for things   very-useful Xenophon's books are
            *quos   **legite**   studiose*
            which read.IMP.PLU   carefully
            'Xenophon's books, which you should read carefully, are most useful for
            many things' (Cicero, Cat. M 59; Hopper and Trauggot 1993: 175)
       b. *krateres   eisin [...]   on   krat'   **erepson***
            mixing-bowls are   whose   brims   crown.IMP.2SG
            'There are mixing bowls, whose brims you must crown.'
            (Soph. *Oed. Tyr.* 473; Rivero and Terzi 1995: 316 n.5)

(35)   a. Thursday next is Saint Iames day, against which time **prepare** thy selfe
            to goe with me to the faire.
            (T. Deloney, c.1600, *The Gentle Craft* 207.31–33: Ukaji 1978: 114–17)

 b. Space has sadly precluded any discussion of Wittgenstein's positive
  views on epistemology, for which **see** Wittgenstein (1969a)
  (British National Corpus, J. Dancy, *Introduction to Contemporary*
  Epistemology, Oxford: Blackwell, 1992, 1425).

5.6.3 Imperatives and allocutives in the protasis of conditional clauses
Alberdi notices a solitary exception to the embedding ban, for which he can
offer no explanation. AA surfaces in the protasis of conditional clauses (36; see
4.5.2 on reproachatives and 4.5.4 on conditionals).

(36) *Si <u>viene</u>, quiero verle/ <u>Si il vient</u> je veux le voir.*
   '<u>If he comes</u>, I want to see him'

  The use in this context extends beyond the minority group. Excluding two
of the three eastern dialects in his sample, the percentage increases to 57.6 per-
cent (75/130). Among western speakers older than 45 years of age, 23.7 per-
cent use AA in the protasis. In this last group, as with eastern dialects, AA in
embedded clauses is rejected across the board as well.

  From a comparative perspective, the above characteristic is welcome.
Imperative clauses also serve as the protasis of conditional clauses in familiar
languages (37: English and Spanish, 38: Latin cf. Allen and Greenough 1983:
403). This exception can be resolved if the conditional use of the imperative
arises from a semanticized implicature in *imperative* and *imperative sequences*
(with Boogaart 2004). This conditional use is juxtaposed or paratactic and,
over time it is reanalyzed as a subordinate clause. If some Basque conditional
clauses originate as a coordinated clause, as some absolute constructions do,
the variability in acceptability for AA may be explained in relation to the stage
of reanalysis.

(37) a. Leave me and you will never see your children again.
   b. *Abandóname y te juro que no verás a tus hijos nunca más.*

(38) a. *cras petito, dabitur*
    '[if you] ask tomorrow, it shall be given you.'
   b. *Haec reputent, videbunt*
    'Let them consider this[if they consider this], let them see.'
   c. *Roges Zenonem, respondeat*
    'If you should ask Zeno, he would answer.'

  Beyond matrix clauses, AA is obligatory in coordinated and paratactic
clauses. These facts corroborate the hypothesis that imperative clauses and
AA have a similar distribution. Under the LPH (Chapter 4) the restriction of
imperatives to root clauses is formalized in the c-command licensing relation

Table 5.7 *Use of AA in the protasis of conditional clauses (prefixal complementizer:* ba-*)*

YES	NO	MAYBE	TOTAL/PERCENTAGE
76	130	2	208
36.5%	62.5%	0.9%	100%

between C and prescriptive v. It is conceivable that the similar syntactic distribution of imperatives and allocutives could be accounted for by comparable local licensing relations.[26]

5.6.4   Putative exceptions to the embedding ban on imperatives

Kaufmann (2012) reports two types of contexts where embedded imperatives occur (39: p. 206, ex. 32). She deals with the possible analysis of examples from Scandinavian under predicates such as *say/tell* and subject to "double access" readings. In the first type, the matrix clause is also an imperative. In the second, the matrix clause is an explicit performative utterance that seems to be interpreted as an imperative. Examples of each type are given in (40a: p. 206, ex. 28 from Rögnvaldsson 1998; 40b: p. 206, ex. 29 from Erdmann 1886).

(39)   a. IMPERATIVE that you IMPERATIVE
        b. I ({must, want}) {allow, advise, ask,...} (you) that you IMPERATIVE

(40)   a. *Nu' ger   pu' svo mannlega   ath pú   rek   pá*
           now act.IMP you so manly   that you drive.IMP   them
           brottu   svo adh vith   pörfnumst eigi allra   góthra hluta
           away   so   that we   lack   not all   good   things
           'Now act so manly that you drive them away, so that we don't lack all
           good things.' (Old Icelandic, Þorvaldsp áttur viþhförla)
        b. *ik   bimunium   dih,   [...] daz du   niewedar ni   gituo*
           I.NOM   implore   you.ACC that you   never   not do.IMP
           'I implore you never to do this again.'

Kaufmann concludes that "we could think of the embedded imperative as performing a speech act with respect to the actual context [utterance context] and with respect to the reporting context which happens to be identical to the actual one" (p. 207). However, it is not clear that we must assume that there exist two clauses in these particular contexts. Giorgi (2010) assumes that verbs of saying and believing in Italian are not real verbs, and thus arguably give rise to mono-clausality in such contexts (see 4.3.2.2). The same caveat applies to Kaufmann's analysis of verba dicendi in Modern High German.

In spoken registers of Modern High German, in contrast to (40), context harmony is partial with verba dicendi: neither the speaker nor the tense of the reported context need be the same as in the utterance context. The only requirement that is left is that the addressee be the subject of the embedded imperative (41: Kaufmann 2012: 211).[27]

(41)   The **addressee constancy restriction** (ACR)
        Imperative embedding in Modern High German is possible only if the
        person spoken to in the reported context is identical to the addressee in the
        utterance situation CA.

The above examples are questionable as embedded imperatives in consideration of the aforementioned caveat but, above all, because the illocutionary force of the main predicate is that of an imperative. For a genuine embedded imperative case, one would like to find examples of a different speech act (e.g., a declarative) where an imperative is embedded. This is not the case of (39–40). Arguably, the first case (39a) is a sequence of two imperative utterances, while the second case (40) is an IDI or overt performative construction (see Chapter 4, 4.5.4).

5.7   Conclusion

This chapter has presented the phenomenon of Basque AA. An examination of verbal morphology reveals that AA morphemes are the same as ergative/dative morphemes. There are dialectal variations in the number of AA morphemes and in their syntactic distribution across main clauses. Overall, AA is restricted to root, coordinated or paratactic clauses. The main predicate cannot have a second person argument. Imperatives and hortatives do not feature AA.

Other scholarly hypotheses have analyzed AA as a stand-alone phenomenon (Oyharçabal 1993; Adaskina and Grashchenkov 2009). With particular reference to hortatives, they fall short of accounting for why AA would be absent. We have shown that AA has a similar syntactic distribution to that of imperatives. Imperatives are not exceptional in that they have a second person argument, their subject. Under LPH, hortatives are causative imperatives. It is thus expected that AA will not exist because the Addressee is construed as the causative subject. The syntactic distribution of AA parallels that of imperatives across languages. We have proposed to account for the root nature of allocutives via local licensing conditions. For an LPH analysis in comparison with other mainstream hypotheses aiming to capture the indexical nature of the addressee, see 4.3.5.

Conclusion

This volume studies the ontology of the imperative clause, one of the three major syntactic types that have been found to be typologically universal in languages of the world (Sadock and Zwicky 1985). Research on the "meaning" of the imperative is approached in direct interface with the speech acts of communication as intended in the course of human activities (Austin 1962; Searle 1969). The driving thesis of this study is the following: categories of the speech act, specifically Speaker and Addressee, are conceptually necessary for an adequate generative syntactic description of the imperative clause and toward a more advanced understanding and formalization of clause typing (Portner 2004; Baker 2008; Giorgi 2010). The thesis of this study is articulated and tested under a minimalist hypothesis (Chomsky 1995–2008) with a functional view of performatives and their access to indexicality in morphosyntactic computation. The proposal, the light performative hypothesis (LPH, Chapter 4), is preceded by an extensive review of new typological data on imperatives in languages of the world (Chapter 2) and a critical survey of competing hypotheses and proposals (Chapter 3). Beyond a strict analysis of imperatives and as an extended test of the proposed hypothesis on encoding the Addressee in a CP(vP) syntactic component, this volume closes with a presentation and discussion of the unique phenomenon of allocutive agreement in Basque (Chapter 5). Upon this phenomenon, which grammaticalizes the Addressee in declaratives but not in imperatives, this volume offers the reader the critical option to arrive at his/her own conclusion about the nature and feasibility of an "indexical syntax" in the future of generative grammar.

Notes

1 Introduction

1 In this introduction, when we refer to the communicative function of a basic sentence type, we mean its *literal* meaning. Beyond the literal meaning of basic sentence types lie the addressee's interpretations of the communicative intent of the speaker, or what is commonly known as *indirect speech acts* (see Levinson 1983: Ch. 5; 2.5 in this book). For example, a declarative can be used in place of an imperative if the speaker says "It feels cold in here" and the addressee infers that the communicative intent of the declarative is an order or suggestion. We seek to establish the non-controversial position that basic sentence types can be identified by their core or literal meaning and by the morphosyntactic properties that associate with each clause type (e.g., Sadock and Zwicky 1985, among many). In our narrative, this serves to background the upcoming discussion of the morphosyntax of the imperative type, which constitutes a departure from both declarative and interrogative clauses in that there appear to be pragmatic constraints that affect the interpretation of the imperative.

2 This will not be an exhaustive list but a representative sample. Additional imperative-specific characteristics will be presented later in this introduction and in the course of the succeeding chapters (especially Chapter 2).

3 On these grounds, it could be argued that the imperative is underspecified or defective in its morphosyntax, and that, for this very reason, pragmatics plays an important and necessary role in its interpretation. Yet imperatives may be rather complex (finite) forms, as we will see in 1.1.2 and Chapter 2.

4 By way of comparison, in the study of control clauses [John persuaded Bill PRO$*_{J/B}$ to go], research lines converge on whether control is the result of movement or agreement, and whether control and raising can be reduced to the same property (Davies and Dubinsky 2006). The only consensus in the generative studies of imperatives concerns the restriction to consider imperative second person forms only. Said restriction emerges as a practical methodological compromise to reduce the complexity of the inquiry, rather than as a vetted result of earlier work.

5 We consider alleged cases of imperative embedding as parataxis (adjunction or coordination clauses, hence not as hypotaxis (embedding, i.e., selected as a complement by a superordinate verb). Thus, their syntactic analysis does not affect the assumed matrix nature of imperative clauses (see 2.3.1, 4.1.2, end. 7).

6 Alarcos Llorach notes that in imperatives negation cannot negate the speech act itself, but only the verb (1994: 213). On the logical incompatibility of negative imperatives see Reichenbach (1947: 342).

7 With Aikhenvald (2010), we assume that the meaning of the prescription varies in the strength of the command or power dynamics/relative social standing between speaker and addressee. For instance, a prepositional infinitive in Spanish cannot be used as an imperative form if the addressee is in a position to refuse an order. Nor can this form be used to request or grant permission. The semantic choices in imperative verb forms afforded by complex morphological paradigms seem comparable to choices in causatives. We leave this matter for future research.

2   Imperatives across languages

1 See also Zanuttini (1997) on linguistic variation within Romance.

2 In addition, König and Siemund (2007) is an extension of Sadock and Zwicky's original survey on sentence types in 51 languages.

3 In an extended typological view, imperative expressions include hortatives (e.g., "let me/them go!"). Hortatives share with imperatives most of their morphosyntactic and semantic characteristics. It thus seems fitting to view hortatives as a type of imperative (see 1.1.2, 1.2). However, while imperatives are universal, hortatives are not attested in all languages. For this reason, a larger section of the current chapter is dedicated to canonical imperatives, that is, second person forms.

4 We disambiguate the universality of the (notion) imperative as an I-language speech act expression from an E-language clause type.

5 Outside the passive, Aikhenvald notes no restrictions in the formation of imperatives in valence-changing derivations.

6 Birjulin & Xrakovskij and Aikhenvald provide examples that can be interpreted as (evil) wishes ("Slip down and break your leg!", Aikhenvald 2010: 150; in-text example). But they do not draw a generalization whereby wishes systematically escape the requirement that the action be controllable. Such generalization would seem to apply to the languages we are most familiar with: Basque, English, Italian and Spanish.

7 See Potsdam (1998) for a semantic explanation related to exceptional cases of imperatives in English. See also Farkas (1988) on the semantic criteria that valid antecedents of PRO, the elided subject of non-finite complements, as well as imperative subjects, should meet.

8 There are comparable predicate restrictions in other syntactic domains, some of which have been analyzed as syntactic. For instance, agentive intransitive predicates (unergatives cf. Perlmutter 1978a and b; Burzio 1986) are barred from particular clauses in certain languages. In Romance, they are excluded from absolute constructions and reduced relatives (Belletti 1992; Alcázar and Saltarelli 2008a). While in other languages, such as Basque – and in Old Italian for absolutes (Egerland 1996), unergatives are acceptable in the same environments. It is plausible that cross-linguistic variation in these cases results from differences in clause structure. According to Alcázar and Saltarelli, Romance participial constructions lack a vP, the projection where an agentive subject would be introduced, while Basque and Old Italian participials have such a vP.

In connection with this, consider an observation that Aikhenvald (2010) makes. Some languages exhibit surrogate analytical forms that allow uncontrollable actions

to be coerced into imperative readings. For example, Tukang Besi employs an
agentive verb *go* ((i) cf. p. 151, exs. 4.66a, 4.66c and references therein).

(i)   a. **Moturu!*
         'Sleep!'
      b. *Wila moturu!*
         'Go and sleep!'

Data such as (i) is promising, because it suggests that the semantic restriction
can be related to structural properties of the imperative clause. Specifically, the
projection introducing an agentive predicate must be present/active or morphologically realized.

9 But see 2.3–4 on first and third person subjects.
10 Earlier analyses (1.1.2) generally assume that the nature of imperatives is responsible for at least some of its quirks (e.g., restrictions in person and tense), thus escap-
   ing (or not requiring) formal analysis in syntax. In his review article, van der Wurff
   (2007b: 81) concludes that some aspects of imperative syntax may be irreducible:
   "perhaps the presence of an [IMP] feature in the highest functional projection or an
   inherent specification for second person" (brackets in the original).
11 This expectation is, of course, true only if we assume the speech act thematic role
   of Addressee as the primitive category for a syntactic computation of imperatives
   clauses (rather than morphological Person). A Person-based analysis would otherwise be confronted with the use of the morphological third person reverential strategy in Italian: *la finisca* [3SG.SUBJ] *Lei* [3SG.FEM] *la zuppa! per favore* 'YOU finish
   the soup! Sir.' Both third person morphologically and pronominal 3FEM are sociolinguistic conventions, in dialect alternation with second person plural, heeding
   to a speaker intended reverential speech act. Needless to say, morphological *third
   person* and *feminine* do not affect the indexical meaning of the imperative clause.
   On these empirical facts and higher order considerations our proposal (Chapter 4)
   encodes the indexical [Speaker>Addressee] relation under a speech act perspective
   of syntactic computation to the exclusion of morphological Person. These preliminary remarks suggest, provisionally, a reconsideration of the notion that "morphology drives syntax" or the converse.
12 Potsdam (1998) has demonstrated for English that this type of noun phrase behaves
   as a subject (4b; see Iatridou 2008: 5–8 for a review).
13 In passing (via Rudolf P. de Rijk), Ross also noted the phenomenon of Basque allocutive agreement (see Chapter 5), which represents a non-argumental addressee,
   also to convey honorificity.
14 As noted, other person values for imperative subjects will be discussed in 2.3–4.
15 While this generalization holds, it is important to specify that there exist contexts
   where English would generally allow the omission of subjects on the basis of person: first person subjects may be omitted in declaratives and second person subjects
   in interrogatives (Speas and Tenny 2003).
16 Unlike D&I, however, neither imperatives nor hortatives can express allocutive
   agreement. There exists language-internal evidence that this can be taken as a sign
   that the addressee participates in the predicate-argument structure of the verb for
   imperatives and hortatives (see Chapter 5).

17 These languages support the view that pro could be the underlying subject of the imperative, since strong agreement features could license pro.

18 Aikhenvald (2004) provides interesting examples for English.

19 This reading is not available in Uruguayan Spanish (Brenda Laca, p.c.).

20 See also n.10 for independent assessment of imperatives as "deictic signs."

21 Note that in Spanish the lexical verb *decir* (Declarative) selects either the indicative as a verb 'say, tell' or the subjunctive as a verb of 'request, insist (Imperative)'. Arguably, the imperative force +SUBJ in (22c) is externalized as an analytic (lexical) imperative (Speaker>Addressee), which seems to be supported by the (lexical) declarative +IND *te digo que vienes a comer* 'I am telling you that you are coming for lunch.'

22 So far, neither one of the "putative" cases in Latin (24a) and Greek (24b) is obviously selected as a complement of a higher lexical verb. Unfortunately, the claims of "embedding" have been made on syntactically unanalyzed data or without a clear theory of imperative clauses on which to validate the cases. Examples bundled in a text (24) neither prove nor disprove that the imperative verb is in a root clause. An analysis is needed to assess that the imperative verb in the clauses is "dependent" on a higher predicate verb by which it is selected as an argument clause. The same reasoning applies for the English examples (25). More compelling is the so-called "conditional" imperative which (like Bosque's "retrospective" (counterfactual) imperative, are in need of further analysis and an explicit theory of imperatives. Needless to say, prior questions must be clarified: (a) "what is the operational definition of "dependent" clause?" (b) "what is the operational imperative clause (beyond the morphological form of the verb)?" As obvious as the query may seem, claims of "embedding" regarding (23–25) rest on the answers to (a&b). (cf. Chapter 4).

23 While indirect speech is also mentioned, all too often these forms turn out to be subjunctives (e.g., Slovenian, see Hill 2010: 7, fn. 5).

24 Editorial directional conventions. In addition to "see" *(!), "cf." is an abbreviation of Latin *confer* (to be sure, the imperative form of *conferre* 'bring together') used to refer to other material that may provide additional information or arguments.

25 There is an extensive literature concerned with whether the past tense form is really an imperative form (vs. an aorist for Russian: Gronas 2006). The question seems to be raised for all languages with such a use. It is unexpected to find what appears to be an imperative form reanalyzed as – of all things – a past tense.

26 In our view, a more likely anchor to this path of grammaticalization (i.e., the imperative reanalyzed as a marked past tense) is the indexical interpretation of the imperative verb form. The closest analog to the imperative verb form used as a past tense is arguably the historical present. While the historical present does not share the pragmatically and/or aspectually marked features salient in its analog, both forms convey vivid renditions of the past which are present-like. This may be a reason why imperatives are recruited as marked past tenses.

27 Note that the exclamation point (!) is used in English at the end of emphatic declarations, interjections or commands. Singularly, commands (imperatives) are speaker>addressee "prescriptions": (Chapter 4)
    (a) Directive (imperative) speech act: 'Leave!'; (Chapter 4)
    (b) Exclamatory speech act: 'What a beautiful day!' 'The war is over!' 'No!'; Salutatory/Wishing speech act: 'Hello!' 'Have a good summer!'

28 Unless it is reflexive: 'let yourself go!'
29 In these examples, the addressee is not necessarily the performer of the action, because the speaker does not know who will open the door among the addressees, and because the speaker does not know who will taste the soup. An independent representation of the addressee and performer seems warranted; hence the use of an expression that appears to be a hortative. If that is the case, the semantic difference lies in the addition of a third participant: the performer, following B&X, with the attendant dissociation between addressee and performer.
30 The semantic maps proposed by van der Auwera et al. illustrating these markedness relations are far more complex and fine-grained than the example just given.
31 Why this hierarchy is not brought forward as an argument for the unity of imperative-hortative paradigms we cannot ascertain from the text.
32 A plausible scenario for suppletion to accidentally work differently in these languages could be conceived. Assume that the hortative contains some sort of causative auxiliary that happens to have suppletive forms. The imperative, by contrast, would not have the causative auxiliary. The markedness counterexamples would have been brought about by reanalysis of a lexical or causative verb as a hortative auxiliary. This is simply a means to illustrate how language change could introduce exceptions to the hierarchy.
33 Similarly, Haverkate (1976) proposes different semantic distributions for the prepositional infinitive, the infinitive and the imperative in Spanish.
34 The above authors appear to take a general interpretive approach to the treatment of exclamations, rather than the narrower production-based imperative expression as a singular speech act of the human faculty of language (Katz and Postal 1964). The diverging research orientation in the study of human language has been resurrected in a recent discussion in *Language* (2012) 88.1 on "What is the faculty of language? Two views."
35 Only second person singular imperative forms are considered in this set.
36 A mixed group containing dedicated and non-dedicated forms that is also restricted to second person singular forms.
37 Contemporary studies on the distribution of negation in imperative clauses have documented a wide, but patterned, range of morphosyntactic grammaticalization across the languages of the world. The variation is aligned along three robust types: prohibitives, negation of imperative verbs, and surrogates (cf. 2.6.2). A biolinguistic interest in the development of these homologues asks a prior question in the compatibility between logical negation and imperative force, a question informally broached by Alarcos Llorach (1994: sec. 213; cf. Chapter 1, n.6), their logical validity formulated in Reichenbach (1947: 342). Our syntactic computation will be illustrated in (4.2.4). The general conclusion in analyzing imperatives is that (negative (imperative expressions) $\sim(f(p))$ are logically meaningless. The scope of negation can only be the content $f(\sim p)$. Under this enhanced perspective, a path leading to an explanatory understanding of the variable syntactic development of the three major homologues appears to be closer at hand.

3   Foundations for an analysis of the imperative clause

1 "Recent inquiries into these questions in the case of language has come to be called 'the minimalist program' MP, but there has been so much misunderstanding, even within professional circles, that it is perhaps worth reiterating that it is a *program*, not a *theory*, and a program that it is both traditional in its general flavor and pretty much theory-neutral, insofar as the biolinguistic framework is adopted" (Chomsky 2007: 4).

2 Other scholars argue that, in some received lines of research, minimalist principles may not be applicable when the properties under study are potentially intrinsic to language (although this would be, arguably, a research result of embracing minimalist principles, better defining the dividing line between language and external cognitive systems, that is). For example, Pesetsky and Torrego (2011) reflect on the difficulty of relating the minimalist tenets beyond grammatical case: "These principles themselves look quite specific to syntax and morphology, with little apparent connection to external cognitive systems (not to mention general properties of organic systems)" (p. 52). On the other hand, in Government and Binding, head movement derives complex words syntactically, such as verbs inflected for tense and agreement, which would move to higher projections hosting these features (V+T+Agr). Concerning the working hypothesis that head movement could be excluded from the set of core syntactic operations, further simplifying the structure building process, Roberts's review (2011) finds that the competing minimalist proposals (vs. P&P theory, which also embraces economy and simplicity) do not stand as a generalized alternative to head movement (as a virtual conceptual necessity). While the minimalist program may have made strides in the relation between syntax and semantics, its application to the other interfaces (phonetics and phonology and, for some, morphology cf. Distributed Morphology, Halle and Marantz 1993) has been comparatively less studied (Samuels 2011).

3 Minimalism (vs. unbridled non-economy-driven programs of linguistic analysis) is consistent with virtual conceptual necessity. Referential dependencies may very well be one of these strictly syntactic phenomena. Only competing theories of reference will point to better solutions under minimalism. One possible example comes to mind: a strictly syntactic account of irreflexivity (protect*myself/yourself/*himself) in imperative clauses appears to be difficult to justify without appeal to the C-I context interface (cf. Chapter 4).

4 The brain has been growing since the australopithecines *c*.3.5 million years ago. Deacon (1997: 353) argues that the growth of the brain, particularly the development of the neocortex of the frontal lobes, reflects the evolutionary pressure to select individuals that possess greater capacity for symbolic processing (better language processing). On the other hand, Bjorklund, Cormier and Rosenberg (2005: 157–59) take a different view. They propose that the growth of this same area relates in part to evolutionary pressure to inhibit behavior that leads to unwanted social outcomes – assuming the presence of a primitive theory of faculty of mind, as in present-day chimpanzees (Premack and Woodruff 1978; Call and Tomasello 2008). In contrast to the former two, Lieberman (2002) advances the alternative view that subcortical structures are more important for language. While the first two views are compatible,

and could be argued to strengthen one another, the ability of the brain to commit large structures to multiple cognitive tasks precludes direct assessment of these proposals – much in the same way as linguistic deficits acquired in aphasias baffle linguistic analysis from traditional disciplinary divisions, since multiple areas of language production and comprehension are affected simultaneously. The appeal of these proposals is that they relate brain growth to the development and refinement of unique human abilities.

5   The only exception that we know of is certain adjectival psych-predicates in Japanese (*nikurasi–i* 'hate,' *kanasi–i* 'sad,' *natukasi–i* 'remember with nostalgia,' ...), which require a first person subject in declaratives and a second person subject in interrogatives (Kuroda 1965; Kuno 1973; Tenny 2006).

6   See Stalnaker (1978) and Heim (1983) for a different implementation based on the common ground between the speaker and the addressee.

7   Schlenker (1999, 2003) proposes an important modification to the Kaplanian view in allowing context-shifting operators, on the observation that indexical elements can be interpreted locally in dependent clauses in some languages (see 3.1). Evidence for this phenomenon was initially anecdotal, but there is now an ever-growing body of languages with indexical shift (Speas 1999; Bianchi 2003; Anand and Nevins 2004; Anand 2006, 2009).

8   It is not readily clear what the Logophoric Centre implies in terms of the nature of the categories of sentential computation and how it would account for imperatives. Suggestion (4), however, regarding deixis is consistent with Weinreich's (1966) logical reasoning that imperatives and deictics interact. Empirically, this intuition is realized in Tariana and Trio (cf. Chapter 2), where imperative clauses mark proximal, distal and dislocative morphemes on the imperative verb of the "prescription." In a parallel and common way, deixis is observed in demonstrative determiner phrases, such as in Marsican spatial demonstratives. C-I access to spatial indexicals, then, is justified both in verbal and in nominal clauses. Implementation of (4) in syntax would converge with studies in other related human sciences, such as the philosophy of language (Kaplan 1977, 1989). Unfortunately, the suggestion is difficult to articulate specifically with respect to the syntactic computation of the imperative clause (cf. Chapter 4).

9   Sigurðsson seems to use the term *logophoric* as in the phenomenon of indexical shift (3.1), where indexicals are interpreted relative to the utterance context or a reported context. In such a language, the sentence "John told Mary I saw you" could be interpreted as direct speech or indirect speech: "John$_i$ told Mary$_k$ that he$_i$ saw her$_k$" (e.g., Zazaki, Turkic: Anand and Nevins 2004). The term "logophoric" has a more restricted use when referring to a special class of pronouns in African languages that is limited to indirect speech. If English had a class of logophoric pronouns (say, "hem" for "he" and "herm" for "her"), the sentence "John$_i$ told Mary$_k$ that hem$_i$ saw herm$_k$" would be an example of the use of logophoric pronouns (see Sells 1987; Culy 1994). For real examples and discussion, see 3.2.

10 This representation of clause structure is put forward as a minimal set of features that UG must have, which, Sigurðsson clarifies, may need to be further subdivided or enriched with additional features in future research.

11 On reflection, Sigurðsson's proposal is quite novel, hence difficult to evaluate as to how it would account for the properties of the imperative clause (1.1).

12 It is appropriate to interject in this discussion that under human language dynamics, speech acts occur singularly as intentional of the thinker/speaker and timed at speaker's time and place (physical or virtual). If so, then deixis must also be speaker-oriented. So, if a speaker in California is communicating on the telephone with an addressee in Illinois, deixis is invariant. Deixis switches with speaker switch. Nevertheless, the grammaticalization of deixis may vary cross-linguistically: proximate/distal/dislocative. See Chapter 2: Tariana and Trio are languages that morphologically mark deixis on the imperative verb.

13 See Bianchi (2010) on the roots of syntactic theories of indexicality in philosophy of language and semantics and for interpretation of Kaplanian and Stalnakerian elements in the syntactic proposals currently available.

14 Bianchi presents her theory without offering specific directions about how her Logophoric Centre can be broken down into particular syntactic projections and what their relative ordering might be.

15 While quite compelling, Bianchi's proposal is yet to be understood with respect to a syntactic theory of the imperative expression and derived clause types (Chapter 1), which is the topic and thesis (Chapter 4) of this treatise.

16 On the assumed extended domain of syntax to I-language (intentional-conceptual) in its interface to E-language (articulatory-perception).

17 This generalization extends to the other indexicals.

18 It is also possible in direct discourse for "I" to refer to both the "speaker of the reported context" and the "speaker of the utterance context" when quoting self (i):

(i) I_i said: "I_i am too easy with my daughter."

19 We thank an anonymous referee for bringing to our attention the more widespread distribution of languages with indexical shift.

20 This is also possible under Speas and Tenny's (2003) proposal and our own account of the imperative, since the speaker and addressee are introduced in distinct structural layers.

21 Kaufmann (2012) presents cases of embedded imperatives where the reported context must be equivalent to the utterance context, which appears to be the opposite property.

22 Schlenker (2004) proposes a richer treatment of the context of utterance with the addition of a context of thought as a means to address the intricacies of free indirect discourse (Banfield 1982; Doron 1991; Speas 1999) and the historical present. See also Recanati (2004 and references therein) for a similar proposal.

23 Since we do not deal with imperatives in subordinate contexts, this question falls outside the scope of our treatise.

24 Areal features could be interpreted as an argument for the polygenesis of language.

25 Meaning differences and ambiguities can be subtle. For instance, the use of *omen* in a pragmatic context compatible with reported information and speaker uncertainty makes it difficult to elicit what the communicative purpose of the speaker is. The interpretative conflict in the analysis of logophoricity – is a point of view expressed

in indirect discourse? must a point of view be expressed in indirect discourse? – may have arisen from precisely the potential ambiguity of these elements.

26 In our reading of the literature on indexical shift we did not come across examples that contradicted Culy's (12) and Huang's hierarchy (13) for logophoricity.

27 Hale (1980: 99): "Alternatively one might say that the conjunct-disjunct form of a true question anticipates that of its answer" (i.e., 'Did you…?' 'Yes, I…').

28 In this respect, the LPH (Chapter 4) recasts the PH, arguably inspired by Austin. However, it is not the case that Ross's (1970: 223 (5)) performative verbs in the more abstract underlying deep structure were "necessarily abstract" verbs. They were lexical performatives with specific subcategorization features on which the transformational rule (Performative Deletion, cf. p. 249) would operate. In LPH, the performative is a "light" v in a complex predicate relation with the lexical imperative V: [v[V]].

29 Regarding the addressee formalized as an indirect object in sap, it is difficult to explain why the addressee always grammaticalizes as the subject in imperative clauses.

30 If the approximation to Ross's PH (1970) is correct, then Speas and Tenny's (2003) proposal runs the risk of a similar criticism as that which led to the demise of that theory in the 1970s.

31 This is a crude representation for purposes of illustration. Unaccusatives (50c) may have an inactive higher layer. Unergatives (17a) may also have an inactive base layer. On the Unaccusative Hypothesis/Burzio's Generalization, to which these structures respond, see Perlmutter (1978a and b), Burzio (1986), Levin and Rappaport-Hovav (1995), Sorace (2000) and Legate (2003), among others.

4   The syntax of imperative clauses: a performative hypothesis

1 The syntax of imperative clauses is assumed to be the externalization of a forward-feeding production model of the faculty of language (cf. Jackendoff vs. Seuren debate in *Language* (2012: 174–79). The inspiration relates to the dynamics of human mental activities from a speech-act perspective (Austin 1962; Searle 1969, 1979). Under this perspective, the role of context in imperative expressions is central to the thesis of this chapter.

2 "Light" (functional v) vs. "heavy" (lexical V) verbs have raised unsettled theoretical issues (cf. Cardinaletti and Giusti 2001; Butt 2003; Megerdoomian 2008; Saltarelli and Alcázar 2010). In this chapter, Larson's (1988) split-vP is articulated as "little" vP(VP) under a phase theory of syntax (Chomsky 2001, 2008). The function of light performative v is licensed as a selection of C; accordingly, the illocutionary force defining the directive speech act is thus grammaticalized as the imperative clause type. The light (performative) verb v is in the leftmost higher periphery of the content phase vP. It projects aspect and event information encoding the Speaker, which functions in LPH as the thematic role of the external argument. Hence, functional light verbs (like v) differ in argument structure from lexical verbs V, with which they form a syntactically complex predicate: [v[V]]. It should be noted that in

contrast with syntactic light verbs (v), the concept "light verb" has been widely used as a function in complex lexical V: Persian *zædæn* 'to hit' in *hærf zædæn* (lit. letter hit) 'speak, talk' (Family 2006: 54), or a class of complex unergative predicates in Basque such as *egin* 'to do' in *hitz egin* (lit. 'word do/make') 'speak'.

3 Thematic role is here used as the semantic notation of the way entities function in the speech act, as opposed to theta role, the syntactic notation of the way entities function in the sentence.

4 The term "performative" is used as an interpretation of what the philosopher John Austin (1962: 5, fn. 2) refers to as utterance types, "much as the term imperative" is in contrast with "constative," uttered to make a statement. We extend the use of the term to contrast a "light" (functional) verb v and a lexical verb V (cf. Alcázar and Saltarelli 2010). Under LPH, light performatives are properties of the imperative CP function phase, which may or may not be realized in the content vP phase. Nevertheless, "light" v are discernible and amenable to inquiry when uttered or performed in a speech act across human languages. Typologically, a performative property may be realized as a lexical verb, a "light" verb, a syntactic turn, a particle, a prefix, a paradigm inflection, a prosodic choice, etc. The LPH in the Austinian spirit is syntactically couched in a strong minimalist thesis (SMT) (Chomsky 2008): CP(vP). The imperative clause is characterized as a (functional) property F (CP) associated with a light verb v (vP) under phase theory.

5 In LPH, the functional dependence C... v is a licensing relation, sensitive to c-command (cf. Safir 2005).

6 The ability of an element to activate a functional head (Cinque 1999).

7 An imperative is a root clause in the sense that it is a direct intentional expression by the Speaker with the function to do, not to say, something to someone (Reichenbach 1947: 336). Accordingly, imperative clauses are syntactically not "selected" by a superordinate lexical verb V. In this sense they are matrix clauses.

8 See Alcázar and Saltarelli (2012). In spite of tacit agreement on this issue (Katz and Postal 1964; Sadock and Zwicky 1985), instances of imperative verb forms in non-restrictive or appositive relative clauses (NRRC) in Latin and Ancient Greek texts raise empirical questions (van der Wurff 2007b: 23). Such putative examples of "embedding" remain, however, difficult to justify without a confirmation of the syntactic status of NRRC, or a formal theory of the imperative against which to evaluate the claims. More compelling evidence are the cases in Old Scandinavian reported by Platzack (2007: 181–82). They fall into two classes (1) indirect discourse imperatives (IDI) "watch that," "I ask you that," and complex predicates (2) 'try-Imp lift-Imp,' 'hasten-Imp light-Imp.' Both IDI (1) as analytic imperatives (cf. 4.3.4) and (2) double-verb complex predicates (cf. 4.6.2) are not unexpected under the LPH hypothesis. The latter type (2) occurs in Salvadorian Spanish. IDIs are, under LPH, the analytic (fully externalized) grammaticalization of an imperative clause: "I order you to leave(!)" which can be uttered as an imperative in the context of "...or I'll call the police." The same may be uttered as reported speech: in the context "..., John said." Note that the imperative interpretation with so-called IDI must comply with the [Speaker1>Addressee2] relation (4.1.3).

9   (p.119) a function *f* is called *irreflexive* if *(x) f(x,x)* is always false,

i.e., *(x) ~((f(x,x))*
(p.118) an *asymmetrical* function, i.e., a function which, when it holds between two arguments, excludes the validity of its converse (Allwood et al. 1995:8):
$\forall x \sim R(x, x)$ irreflexive
$\forall x \, y \, (R(x, y) \rightarrow \sim (R(y, x))$ asymmetric

10   The (ir)reflexivity and (a)symmetry principles are also observed in the lexicalization of biological kinship systems ("mother/father of," "son/daughter of vs. brother/sister of") and in other aspects of grammatical computation "x is taller/shorter than y" vs. "x is as tall/short as y." The universal relevance of (4.1.3 (2a,b)) is necessary and sufficient from a speech act view of syntax.

11   Parallel domains of reference vP, nP in complex demonstratives (Saltarelli 2011, DSM6.Ms.

12   "Extended 'let' imperatives include 'hortatives'." Under LPH, the imperative–hortative system is unitarily accounted for by the universal dependency Speaker>Addressee (4.1.2). The restriction also follows from the pragmatics of the speech act, necessarily wanting for an account of the grammar of referentially reflexive imperatives "protect *myself, yourself, *him/*herself" (cf. also 4.1.2).

13   LPH distinguishes between functional (indexical) and content (lexical) meaning. Sentences (a) and (b) below would have the same lexical meaning but different functional meaning in the context in which they are uttered (cf. Delfitto and Fiorin 2011).

   (a)   I request that you leave (said John).
   (b)   (i)   I request that you leave! (or I'll call the police)
         (ii) Leave! (or I'll call the police)

14   Katz and Postal (1964) introduce pre-sentential markers (Q for questions and I for imperatives) to align syntactic structures and semantic rules of interpretation. Coincidentally, the proposed semantics of I is defined along a similar paraphrase. Katz and Postal coin the more general acronym RIM (request, insist, demand).

15   See a similar description of the Ewe imperative paradigm by Agbodjo and Litvinov (2001: 397; table 2).

16   Canonical imperative derivation (LPH). See 4.6.2 for complex predicates in Salvadorian Spanish.

$$[_{CP} \; F_i ven(ga)! \; [_{vP} \; e^1 \; [_{v'} \; [_{v} \; {}_i ven(ga)! \; [_{vP} \; B \; [_{v'} \; [_{v} \; {}_i ven(ga)! \; [_{VP} \; [_{V} \; {}_i ven(ga)! \;]]]]]]]]$$

17   Under LPH assumptions, familiar tree diagrams (4.2.5 (Figure 4.1a,b)) are not intended as a formal representational model of syntax but rather as informal illustrations of a derivational computational model (Chomsky 1995).

18   Modern English has, apparently, the post-position option (V_{imp} Neg P …): "Ask not what the government can do for you, but …" (JFK, President), in addition to the common (DO-Neg V_{imp} P): "Don't ask what the government can do for you, but …" Under LPH assumptions, DO is, arguably, the externalization of the "light" verb v in the content phase vP licensed by IF in the functional phase CP.

19   For Reichenbach (1947, §57) pragmatic moods, as speaker's "instruments," cannot be negated.

assertive mood: (a) $\vdash (\sim p)$, but not (b) $\sim(\vdash (p))$
interrogative mood: (a) $?\,(\sim p)$, but not (b) $\sim(\,?\,(p))$
imperative mood: (a) $!\,(\sim p)$, but not (b) $\sim(\,!\,(p))$

If substantiated, the incompatibility debate over negative true imperative clause (TNI) reduces to an issue of the logical validity of TNIs; that is, negative imperative expressions are "meaningless" (Reichenbach 1947: 442 (11)). Accordingly, all imperative (mood) clauses are of form $!(p)$ or $!(\sim p)$, where the exclamative sign is the imperative(functional) meaning and p is the lexical (denotative) meaning of the expression. Hence, following Reichenbach, there is no negative functional meaning of the imperative, rather there is a true/false meaning of the denotative content, that sub-clause we have been calling the "prescription." Conceptually, however, LPH imperative clauses are interpreted as complex predicates: [v[V]] of functional force and lexical content. The LPH derivation of imperative clauses (cum positive prescription) (4.2.6.2 (6a)) and imperative clauses (cum negative prescription or prohibitions) (4.2.6.2 (6b)) is illustrated.

20 Cf. Zeijlstra (2006) for the "ban" on TNI.
21 An account of allocutive agreement in Basque, as morphosyntactic grammaticalization of morphemes ($-k/-n$) in reference to the speech act context of utterance requires access to Speaker's knowledge, namely to the biological gender of the Addressee in a given intentional expression. An optimal biolinguistic perspective of morphosyntax (Di Sciullo and Boeckx 2011) would encode event structure coordinates in syntax under SMT minimalism. Some prospective options on the nature and locality of event structure in syntax (Megerdoomian 2008; Baker 2008; Giorgi 2010) will be the subject of future research on indexical syntax.
22 We note a few special cases where ABB is chosen over AB. When the Addressee is in a position of self-restraint, the Speaker may command the Addressee to abandon that position, as in "let yourself go!" or the Spanish polite formula *¡mándese entrar!* 'feel free to come in!' (lit. order yourself to come in). If the Speaker lacks the will to do something, an ABB also seems suitable: "make yourself go to the gym!" For ease of exposition, we have opted not to include this type in Table 4.1.
23 In the relation X>Y, X "dominates" Y syntactically and thematically. The same relation applies to Person. Arguably, the use of natural numbers 1, 2 are notational mnemonics for the equivalent speech act thematic relation, rather than independent category of grammar consistent with SMT.
24 Harris (1998), commenting on Rivero and Terzi (1995), claims that "a satisfactory account of semantic, syntactic and morphological mismatches in Spanish imperatives must appeal to a Morphology module of grammar; real explanation is beyond the reach of purely syntactic analysis." While agreeing on the diversity in grammaticalization of Spanish imperative expressions, we aim to demonstrate that the proverbial devil is not in morphology (viz. *¡ve-te/*me/*le!* 'go (away)!') but rather in the functional meaning of syntax with access to the indexical properties of the intentional context of imperative expressions, generally recoverable under the perspective of a speech act hypothesis (4.1 and 4.2).
25 Note the use of the infinitive form of the verb in Italian when referencing a virtual Addressee (as opposed to an actual one) in signs: *Chiudere (*chiudi/*chiuda) la porta! Grazie.* 'Shut the door! Thank you.'

26 Note, however, that in canonical hortatives (speaker and addressee included) the δ-relation 1>2 is complied with in an arguably exceptional way in Spanish canonical imperatives: *¡vamonos!* 'let's go' (you, me, everyone).

27 It may be appropriate to comment that Zanuttini's (2008) JussiveP is an innovation in the functional architecture of derivational syntax, while seemingly at odds with other C-selected functions such as event time. JussiveP is, consequently, a departure from SMT. Moreover, decoupling the Addressee from its ontological Addressor (Speaker) fails to recognize the δ-relation as a distinguishing thematic aspect of imperative clauses, with attendant descriptive consequences.

28 LPH has little to say about counterfactual constructions in Syrian Arabic using "an ordinary imperative lexical verb combined with the perfect of *kan* 'to be'" (cf. van der Wurff 2007b: 46) except in connection with examples, cited also for Dutch and Spanish. We feel that this statement is legitimate, short of a specific context hypothesis of the functional meaning of the imperative against which a comparative appraisal could be entertained.

29 Part of the material presented in this section is adapted from Alcázar and Saltarelli (2010, 2012, to appear).

30 There are two discrepancies between Italian and Spanish in the position of clitics. (i) In polite affirmative commands. Spanish takes enclitics *escríbalo/*lo escriba* vs. Italian that takes pro-clitics **scrivalo/lo scriva*. A possible account of the difference may be feasible if we assume philological evidence in favor of a further historical stage in the demise of the Tobler-Mussafia Law for Italian clitics in this context. If substantiated, its grammaticalization would block Rivero's V-to-C to a position lower than C (as well as substantiate Kayne's CliticCl-to-silent Aux). But what about raising in polite affirmative imperatives? In a tentative LPH version of Italian clitic climbing, the clitic head may have markedly acquired probe status in polite commands, hence merging as phase category at PF. (ii) A second discrepancy concerns informal negative commands with infinitive. Italian allows pre-infinitive clitics *non lo mangiare* (38d), but Spanish does not **no lo comer* (40d). Both (i) and (ii) receive a unitary historical account as a shift in the probe status of the Italian clitic head, under LPH as well as under Kayne's Original Cl Climbing rule (OCC.) Under Rivero and Terzi's V-Raising hypothesis of (i) and (ii), however, a unitary account would be complicated. Once again, LPH recaptures core properties of OCC, enhancing its descriptive and explanatory viability. This footnote anticipates material that follows.

31 A second person singular (etymologically plural) form of address that is characteristic of Latin American Spanish of the Southern Cone and Central America.

32 Homophony is often the epiphenomenal result of phonological evolution. For example, Latin vidēte (Imp) and vidētis (Ind) merge into It. *vedete*(!) 'you look/look'!(Imp/Ind), as the result of historical vowel lowering and final C deletion. The opposite may result through morphosyntactic split, whereby the same function marker acquires different realizations in different clause types. This is the case of negation in Latin, where *nē/nōn* are respectively grammaticalized imperative/declarative functional types. Other examples of functional homophony

are found in Korean (Han and Lee 2002, 2007), where the negative marker *mal* negates imperatives as well as questions and declaratives, but only if the proposition expresses deontic modality.

33 Note that *do* can also be used to express strong commands (Richard Kayne, p.c.).

5   Basque allocutive agreement

1 Agreement implies a two-place probe/goal relation between the verb realizing the allocutive morpheme and the donor head. LPH suggests that the donor is a variable (4.3.5).

2 But see Ross (1970) on Thai speaker particles.

3 This chapter expands on the data and analysis presented in Alcázar and Saltarelli (2012).

4 Thanks to Myriam Uribe-Etxebarria for suggesting a possible correlation between imperatives and Basque allocutivity.

5 The subject of this monograph is the imperative clause type. Demonstrating or refuting whether other sentence types feature a performative v is beyond the scope of our research.

6 Case/verbal agreement: ABS/A absolutive, ERG/E ergative, DAT/D dative; number: SG singular, PL plural; gender: FEM feminine, MASC masculine; AUX auxiliary; other: PRED pre-dative; COMP complementizer; NOM nominal form; THMV thematic vowel.

7 A quick note on the glosses: Ø means that the segment is possibly not a morpheme but is there for phonological reasons; PreD means pre-dative (1c), a segment that normally appears before dative agreement markers. Further information could have been added as well. For instance, with reference to these auxiliary forms, absolutive plural is expressed by *–ra* (subject case: intransitives), *–it-* (object case: transitives), and *–zki-* (object case: ditransitives). But this and other facets of morphological analysis are not relevant for the discussion at hand.

8 The *z-* suffix also represents second person when the absolutive argument is the object of a transitive verb (e.g., the auxiliary for 'he sees you' would be *z-a-it-u* 2(A)-Ø-PL(A)-AUX.HAVE; the plural morpheme is a historical relic, as noted in the text). Ditransitives do not have second person absolutive arguments. They are restricted to third person.

9 In western dialects it is possible to shift to the third person as a high honorific. This treatment is also named after the pronoun: *berori-ka*. It appears to be out of use. Many consider *berorika* to be a calque from Spanish.

10 *Euskaltzaindia* talks about a fourth person mark in the verb (*Euskaltzaindia* 1987b: 392).

11 Second person singular arguments encode honorificity. Second person plural morphemes, on the other hand, have no distinction in honorificity. Second person plural forms have no allocutive uses either. For lack of comparative data, we speculate that AA is restricted to second person singular due to a language-specific restriction in the morphology; namely, that the AA morpheme is specified for this person and number value.

12 In (4c) there is a change from *d* to *z* (spirantization, according to Hualde, Oyharça-
    bal and Ortiz de Urbina 2003). Outside allocutive forms, this is also observable in
    present vs. past pairs.

13 An alternative possibility is that this is a case of syncretism, as in present-day Span-
    ish and English (vs. Basque and Italian), where there are no auxiliary distinctions
    based on the valence of the predicate.

14 For a similar Distributed Morphology analysis, see Albizu (2002).

15 Alberdi (1996) notes an additional allocutive morpheme: *–xu* or *–xü* (a palatalized
    version of *–zu/zü*; e.g., Low Navarre, eastern Basque). Palatalization is a form of
    consonantal symbolism (CS). In Basque, CS is used to express relative size and
    speaker attitude (positive or negative), as in other languages with CS (see Nichols
    1971). The use of diminutive/augmentative morphemes in Romance is function-
    ally equivalent. According to de Rijk (2008: 14–5), CS is most commonly applied
    to sibilants and dentals in Basque. The allocutive morpheme *–xu/xü* appears to
    express affection towards the Addressee (small children, nuclear family). Alberdi
    reports that, in some dialects, palatalization occurred first in the allocutive form,
    and then the CS form extended to the stand-alone pronoun and argumental uses.

16 We modified the English translation in (8b) to make it idiomatic.

17 It seems that there is considerable diversity in the use of non-honorific forms. Sal-
    aburu, in the introduction to Alberdi (1996), writes that in his dialect women would
    not use *hika*, that he would not know how to construct the auxiliaries for the femi-
    nine forms, and that he was shocked to hear women speaking other dialects use or
    master masculine and feminine forms.

18 Although one finds examples with matrix interrogatives and exclamatives here and
    there when AA is not being discussed (e.g., see 5.6.1).

19 The examples in this section come from various corpora and the Internet. *Ere-
    duzko Prosa Gaur* (Contemporary Reference Corpus of Written Basque) is
    a monolingual corpus consisting of books (287, 13m. words, 2000–2006) and
    press (the newspaper *Berria*, 10m. words, 2004–2006; and the supplement *Her-
    ria*, 2m. words, 2001–2005). The corpus is available online through the Univer-
    sity of the Basque Country (www.ehu.es/euskara-orria/euskara/ereduzkoa/). The
    University began a new project designed to compile a written corpus of scien-
    tific prose named *Zientzia Irakurle Ororentzat* (For all Science Readers). At the
    time of writing it contains seven books. It is accessible online: www.ehu.es/ehg/
    zio/. The *Consumer Eroski Parallel Corpus* consists of magazine articles writ-
    ten originally in Spanish and then translated to Basque (1998–2006). The size
    of the Spanish–Basque section is approximately 2m. words (the corpus contains
    Spanish–Catalan and Spanish–Galician sections as well). The corpus is avail-
    able for consultation online through the University of Vigo (sli.uvigo.es/CLUVI/
    index_en.html). An updated version of the corpus is accessible through the Eroski
    Foundation (corpus.consumer.es). The original magazine *Consumer Eroski* can
    be found at revista.consumer.es.

20 As noted in the previous section for auxiliary *izan* 'be,' individual-level *be*, when
    used as a main verb, also resorts to *have* for allocutive forms.

21 The she-wolf replies that the woman is *not* a girl using AA. Traditional grammars
    prescribe that AA should not be used with negation or with emphatic affirmation.
    Nonetheless, de Rijk notes that "allocutive forms do occur with the affirmative

prefix *ba-* and the negative particle *ez*" (2008: 810). Yes/no-exclamatives, discussed in the next section, are another example of AA used with negation.

22 *Ezan* is the non-indicative counterpart of auxiliary *ukan* 'have.'

23 A quick note on the auxiliary form in (30b) is necessary. Both verbs are transitive (know, study; 3SG(E) subject and 3SG(A) object), therefore the same allocutive form (*d-i-k*) should be used in both cases. However, the verb 'study' is expressed with a particular progressive construction (the *ari* construction), which detransitivizes the auxiliary (Alcázar 2003). Yet since the allocutive form of auxiliary *izan* 'be' is a transitive proxy, the allocutive form is *d-u-k*. The *ari* construction makes the verb lose in valence. Then AA would seem to make it gain in valence due to the syncretism alluded to earlier in the text.

24 Regarding Adaskina and Grashchenkov's (2009) analysis more generally, we disagree on the characterization of the phenomenon at an empirical level, in that Adaskina and Grashchenkov claim that AA also manifests with second person arguments.

25 Typically, unlike other root initial clauses, imperatives are not found in "embedded" (recursive) syntactic environments (i.e., selected as an argument by a superordinate lexical predicate). A syntactic test question for (34a) might be: what lexical verb is [*quos legite studiose*] a complement of? and in what function?

26 Imperatives and allocutives are indexical phenomena restricted to root clauses. Other indexical phenomena are restricted to (particular) dependent clauses instead, for example, logophoric pronouns (3.3.2) and logophoric uses of conjunct-disjunct person marking (3.3.3). See Schlenker (2003) and Anand and Nevins (2004) for proposals to ascribe the syntactic distribution/interpretation of indexical phenomena to the utterance and/or reported context.

27 This is reminiscent of the interpretation of indexicals. When an indexical is syntactically licit in root and dependent clauses, as indexical pronouns are in English ("I," "you"), their evaluation may nevertheless be restricted in some languages. Amharic indexicals can be interpreted relative to either an utterance or reported context in suitable dependent clauses (Schlenker 1999, 2003).

References

Adaskina, Y. and P. Grashchenkov 2009. "Verb morphology and clause structure in Basque: allocutive." Paper presented at *Morphology of the World's Languages*, University of Leipzig, June 11–13.

Agbodjo, K. H. and V. P. Litvinov 2001. "Imperative sentences in Ewe," in *Typology of Imperative Constructions*, V. S. Xrakovskij (ed.). Munich: Lincom Europa, pp. 390–404.

Aikhenvald, A. Y. 2004. *Evidentiality*. Oxford University Press.

2010. *Imperatives and Commands*. Oxford University Press.

Aikhenvald, A. Y. and R. M. W. Dixon 1998. "Dependencies between grammatical systems," *Language* 74: 56–80.

Alarcos Llorach, E. 1994. *Gramática de la Lengua Española*. Madrid: Espasa Calpe.

Alberdi Larizgoitia, J. 1996. *Euskararen Tratamenduak: Erabilera*. Bilbao: Euskaltzaindia.

2003. "Hika tratamenduaren balore sozio-afektiboak," www.erabili.com/zer_berri/muinetik/1057320285.

Albizu, P. 2002. "Basque verbal morphology: redefining cases," in *Erramu Boneta: Festschrift for Rudolf P. G. de Rijk*, X. Artiagoitia, P. Goenaga and J. A. Lakarra (eds.). Bilbao: University of the Basque Country, pp. 1–19.

Alcázar, A. 2003. "Two paradoxes in the interpretation of imperfective aspect and the progressive," *Journal of Cognitive Science* 4(1): 79–105.

2008. "Against an ontological commitment to unergative verbs," in *Proceedings of the 40th Meeting of the Chicago Linguistics Society: The Main Session*, R. Edwards, P. Midtlyng, C. Sprague and K. Stensrud (eds.). Chicago Linguistic Society, pp. 1–15.

2011. "Information source in Spanish and Basque: a parallel corpus study," in *Linguistic Realization of Evidentiality in European Languages*, G. Diewald and E. Smirnova (eds.). Berlin: Mouton de Gruyter, pp. 131–56.

Alcázar, A. and M. Saltarelli 2007a. "The quirky case of participial clauses," in *Romance Languages and Linguistic Theory 2005: Selected Papers from 'Going Romance' 2005, Utrecht*, S. Baauw, F. Drijkoningen, I. van Ginneken and H. Jacobs (eds.). Amsterdam: John Benjamins, pp. 1–18.

2007b. "Participial constructions: Zanuttini's Hypothesis revisited." Paper presented at *81st Annual Meeting of the Linguistic Society of America* (Anaheim).

2008a. "Argument structure of participial clauses: the unaccusative phase," in *Selected Proceedings of the 10th Hispanic Linguistics Symposium*, J. Bruhn de Garavito and E. Valenzuela (eds.). Somerville, MA. Cascadilla Proceedings Project, pp. 194–205.

2008b. "A minimalist return to the abstract performative hypothesis." Paper presented at *Propositions: Ontology, Semantics and Pragmatics*. University of Venice, Ca'Foscari (Italy). November 17.

2010. "In support of a syntactic analysis of double agreement phenomena," in *Romance Languages and Linguistic Theory 2008: Selected Papers from 'Going Romance' 2008, Groningen*, R. Bok-Bennema, B. Kampers-Manhe and B. Hollebrandse (eds.). Amsterdam: John Benjamins, pp. 1–16.

2012. "Why imperative sentences cannot be embedded," in *Building a Bridge Between Linguistic Communities of the Old and New World: Current Approaches to the Study of Tense, Aspect, Mood and Modality Across Languages*, Ch. Nishida and C. Russi (eds.). New York: Rodopi, pp. 1–23.

To appear. "Untangling the imperative puzzle," *Proceedings of the 44th Meeting of the Chicago Linguistics Society: the Main Session*. Chicago Linguistic Society.

Allen, J. H. and J. B. Greenough 1983. *New Latin Grammar*. New York: Caratzas.

Allwood, J., L.-G. Andersson and Ö. Dahl 1995. *Logic in Linguistics*. Cambridge University Press.

Alpatov, V. M. 2001. "Imperative in Modern Japanese," in Xrakovskij (ed.), pp. 106–25.

Anand, P. 2006. *De de se*. Doctoral dissertation, Massachusetts Institute of Technology.

2009. "The cross-linguistic manifestations of de se expressions," *Arché/CSMN Minicourse and Workshop: De Se Attitudes*. CSMN, University of Oslo, June 6.

Anand, P. and A. Nevins 2004. "Shifty operators in changing contexts," in Watanabe and Young (eds.), pp. 20–37.

Antonov, A. 2012. "Verbal allocutivity in a crosslinguistic perspective." Unpublished manuscript.

2013a. "Grammaticalization of allocutivity markers in Japanese and Korean in a cross-linguistic perspective," in *Shared Grammaticalization: With Special Focus on Transeurasian Languages*, M. Robbeets and H. Cuyckens (eds.). Amsterdam: John Benjamins.

2013b. "Verbal allocutivity in Ryukyuan." Paper presented at *Workshop on Historical and Comparative Linguistics of the Japanese and Ryukyuan languages*. Kyoto University, February 19–20.

Austin, J. L. 1962. *How To Do Things with Words*. Oxford: Clarendon Press.

Auwera, J. van der 2005. "Prohibitives: why two thirds of the world's languages are unlike Dutch," in *Proceedings of the Fifteenth Amsterdam Colloquium, December 19–21, 2005*, P. Dekker and M. Franke (eds.). Amsterdam: University of Amsterdam.

2006. "Why languages prefer prohibitives," *Journal of Foreign Languages* 1: 2–25.

2010. "Prohibition: constructions and markers," in *Contrasting Meaning in Languages of the East and West*, D. Shu and K. Turner (eds.). Tübingen: Narr, pp. 443–75.

Auwera, J. van der, N. Dobrushina and V. Goussev 2004. "A semantic map for imperative-hortatives," in *Contrastive Analysis in Language. Identifying Linguistic Units of Comparison*, D. Willems, B. Defrancq, T. Colleman and D. Noël (eds.). Basingstoke : Palgrave Macmillan.

2008. "Imperative-hortative systems," in *The World Atlas of Language Structures Online*, M. Haspelmath, M. S. Dryer, D. Gil and B. Comrie (eds.). Munich: Max Planck Digital Library, Ch. 72.

Auwera, J. van der and L. Lejeune, with U. Passuwany and V. Goussev 2005a "The morphological imperative," in Haspelmath, Dryer, Gil and Comrie (eds.), pp. 286–89.

Auwera, J. van der and L. Lejeune, with V. Goussev 2005b. "The prohibitive," in Haspelmath, Dryer, Gil and Comrie (eds.), pp. 290–93.

Azkue, R. M. 1925. *Morfología Vasca*. Bilbao: La Gran Enciclopedia Vasca.

Baker, M. 2008. *The Syntax of Agreement and Concord*. Cambridge University Press.

Baldi, P. 1999. *The Foundations of Latin*. Berlin: Mouton de Gruyter.

Banfield, A. 1982. *Unspeakable Sentences: Narration and Representation in the Language of Fiction*. Boston, MA: Routledge & Kegan Paul.

Bauer, B. 2000. *Archaic Syntax in Indo-European*. Berlin: Mouton de Gruyter.

Bauer, W. 1993. *Maori (Descriptive Grammars)*. London: Routledge.

Belletti, A. 1990. *Generalized Verb Movement*. Turin: Rosenberg and Sellier.

1992. "Agreement and case in past participle clauses," in *Syntax and Semantics*, Vol. 26, T. Stowell and E. Wehlri (eds.). New York: Academic Press, pp. 21–44.

(ed.) 2004. *Structures and Beyond: The Cartography of Syntactic Structures*, Vol. III. Oxford University Press.

Berwick, R. and N. Chomsky 2011. "The biolinguistic program: the current state of research," in Di Sciullo and Boeckx (eds.), pp. 19–41.

Beukema, F. and P. Coopmans 1989. "A Government-Binding perspective on the imperative in English," *Journal of Linguistics* 25: 417–36.

Bianchi, V. 2003. "On finiteness as logophoric anchoring," in *Temps et Point de Vue/ Tense and Point of View*, J. Guéron and L. Tasmovski (eds.). Paris: Université Paris X Nanterre, pp. 213–46.

2010. *The Person Feature and the 'Cartographic' Representation of the Context*. Manuscript, University of Sienna (extended handout).

Birjulin, L. A. and V. S. Xrakovskij 2001. "Imperative sentences: theoretical problems," in Xrakovskij (ed.), pp. 3–50.

Bjorklund, D. F., C. Cormier and J. S. Rosenberg 2005. "The evolution of theory of mind: big brains, social complexity, and inhibition," in *Young Children's Cognitive Development: Interrelationships Among Executive Functioning, Working Memory, Verbal Ability and Theory of Mind*, W. Schneider, R. Schumann-Hengsteler and B. Sodian (eds.). Mahwah, NJ: Erlbaum, pp. 147–74.

Bobaljik, J. D. 2008. "Missing persons: a case study in morphological universals," *The Linguistic Review (special theme issue Examples of Linguistic Universals)* 25(1–2): 203–30.

Boeckx, C. (ed.) 2011. *The Oxford Handbook of Linguistic Minimalism*. Oxford University Press.

Boeckx, C. and N. Hornstein 2004. "Movement under control," *Linguistic Inquiry* 35: 431–52.

2006a. "Control in Icelandic and theories of control," *Linguistic Inquiry* 37: 591–606.

2006b. "The virtues of control as movement," *Syntax* 9: 118–30.

2007. "Pronouns in a minimalist setting," in *The Copy Theory of Movement*, N. Corver and J. Nunes (eds.). Amsterdam: John Benjamins, pp. 351–85.

Bolinger, D. 1967. "The imperative in English," in *To Honor Roman Jakobson: Essays on the Occasion of His Seventieth Birthday*, Vol. 1 of Janua Linguarum. The Hague, Paris: Mouton, pp. 335–62.

Bond, O. 2006. "A broader perspective on point of view: logophoricity in Ogonoid languages," in *Selected Proceedings of the 35th Annual Conference on African Linguistics*, J. Mugane, J. P. Hutchison and D. A. Worman (eds.). Somerville, MA: Cascadilla Proceedings Project, pp. 234–44.

Boogaart, R. 2004. "'Meet het en je weet het': van gebod naar voorwaarde," in *Taal in Verandering*, S. Daalder, T. Janssen and J. Noordegraaf (eds.). Münster: Nodus Publikationen, pp. 23–36.

Borer, H. 1989. "Anaphoric Agr," in *The Null Subject Parameter*, O. Jaeggli and K. Safir (eds.). Dordrecht: Kluwer, pp. 69–109.

Bosque, I. 1980. "Retrospective imperatives," *Linguistic Inquiry* 11: 415–19.

Brandstetter, C. and D. Rus (eds.). 2005. *Georgetown Working Papers in Theoretical Linguistics 4*. Washington DC: Department of Linguistics, Georgetown University.

British National Corpus. 1992. J. Dancy, *Introduction to Contemporary Epistemology*. Oxford: Blackwell, p. 1425

Burzio, L. 1986. *Italian Syntax*. Dordrecht: Reidel.

Butt, M. 2003. "The light verb jungle." Harvard Working Papers in Linguistics.

Bystrov, I. S. and N.V. Stankevič 2001. "Imperatives in Vietnamese," in Xrakovskij (ed.), pp. 461–74.

Call, J. and M. Tomasello 2008. "Does the chimpanzee have a theory of mind? 30 years later," *Trends in Cognitive Sciences* 12: 187–92.

Canac-Marquis, R. 2003 "Asymmetry, syntactic objects and the mirror generalization," in *Asymmetry in Grammar*, A. Di Sciullo (ed.). Amsterdam: John Benjamins, pp. 65–94.

Cardinaletti, A. and G. Giusti 2001. "Semi-lexical motion verbs in Romance and Italian," in *The Function of Content Words and the Content of Function Words*, N. Corver and H. Riemsdijk (eds.). Berlin and New York: Mouton de Gruyter.

Chen-Main, J. 2005. "Characteristics of Mandarin imperatives," in Brandstetter and Rus (eds.), pp. 1–51.

Chierchia, G. 1989. "Anaphora and attitudes de se," in *Language in Context*, R. Bartsch, J. van Benthem and van Emde Boas (eds.). Dordrecht: Foris, pp. 1–31.

Chomsky, N. 1965. *Aspects of the Theory of Syntax*. Cambridge, MA: MIT Press.

1986. *Barriers*. Cambridge, MA: MIT Press.

1995. *The Minimalist Program*. Cambridge, MA: MIT Press.

2001. "Derivation by Phase," in *Ken Hale: A Life in Language*, M. Kenstowicz (ed.). Cambridge, MA: MIT Press, pp. 1–52.

2004. "Beyond explanatory adequacy," in Belletti (ed.), pp. 104–31.

2007. "Approaching UG from below. In *Interfaces + recursion = language?*" in U. Sauerland and H.-M. Gärtner (eds.). Berlin: Mouton de Gruyter, pp. 1–29.

2008. "On phases," in *Foundational Issues in Linguistic Theory: Essays in Honor of Jean-Roger Vergnaud*, R. Freidin, C. P. Otero and M. L. Zubizarreta (eds.). Cambridge, MA: MIT Press, pp. 133–66.

2010. "Some simple Evo Devo theses: how true might they be for language?," in Larson, Deprez and Yamakido (eds.), pp. 45–62.

Cinque, G. 1999. *Adverbs and Functional Heads: A Cross-Linguistic Perspective.* Oxford University Press.

2002. *Functional Structure in DP and IP: The Cartography of Syntactic Structures*, Vol. I. Oxford University Press.

2004. "Restructuring and functional structure," in Belletti (ed.), pp. 132–91.

Clark, B. 1993. "*Let* and *let's*: procedural encoding and explicature," *Lingua* 90: 173–200.

Clark, H. H. 1996. *Using Language.* Cambridge University Press.

Clements, G. N. 1975. "The logophoric pronoun in Ewe: its role in discourse," *Journal of West African Languages* 2: 141–77.

Comrie, B. 1985a. *Tense.* Cambridge University Press.

1985b. "Causative verb formation and other verb-deriving morphology," in *Language Typology and Syntactic Description*, Vol. III. Grammatical Categories and the Lexicon, T. Shopen (ed.). Cambridge University Press.

Corver, N. and H. Van Riemsdijk (ed.) 2001. *Semi-Lexical Categories.* Berlin: Mouton De Gruyter.

Creissels, D. 2008. "Remarks on so-called 'conjunct/disjunct' systems," in *Proceedings of Syntax of the World's Languages III.* In press.

Culicover, P. W. 1976. *Syntax.* New York: Academic Press.

Culy, C. 1994. "Aspects of logophoric marking," *Linguistics* 32(5): 1055–1094.

1997. "Logophoric pronouns and point of view," *Linguistics* 35: 845–59.

Curnow, T. J. 2002a. "Conjunct/disjunct marking in Awa Pit," *Linguistics* 40(3): 611–27.

2002b. "Three types of verbal logophoricity in African languages," *Studies in African Linguistics* 31(1/2): 1–25.

Daiber, T. 2008. "Metaphorical use of the Russian imperative," *Russian Linguistics* 33(1): 11–35.

Davies, E. 1986. *The English Imperative.* London: Croom Helm.

Davies, W. D. and S. Dubinsky 2006. "The place, range, and taxonomy of control and raising," *Syntax* 9(2): 111–17.

Deacon, T. 1997. *The Symbolic Species: The Co-evolution of Language and the Brain.* New York: W. W. Norton & Company.

Deal, A. R. 2008. "Events in space," in *Proceedings of SALT 18.*

DeLancey, S. 1986. "Evidentiality and volitionality in Tibetan," in *Evidentiality: The Linguistic Coding of Epistemology*, W. Chafe and J. Nichols (eds.). Norwood NJ: Academic Press, pp. 203–13.

1992. "The historical status of the conjunct/disjunct pattern," *Acta Linguistica Hafniensa* 25: 39–42.

1997. "Mirativity: the grammatical marking of unexpected information," *Linguistic Typology* 1: 33–52.

2001. "The mirative and evidentiality," *Journal of Pragmatics* 33: 369–82.

Delfitto, D. and G. Fiorin 2011. "Person features and pronominal anaphora," *Linguistic Inquiry* 42(2): 193–224.

Dessalles, J.-L. 2007. *Why We Talk: The Evolutionary Origins of Language.* Oxford University Press.

2010. "Review of *The Evolution of Human Language: Biolinguistic Perspectives,*" *Language* 87(2): 411–14.

Diaconescu, R. C. 1999. *Romanian Imperatives from the Perspective of Generative Grammar.* Ph.D. dissertation, University of Ottawa.

Dickinson, C. 1999. "Semantic and pragmatic dimensions of Tsafiki evidential and mirative markers," in *Chicago Linguistic Society 35: Papers from the Panels*, S. J. Billings and J. P. Boyle (eds.). Chicago Linguistic Society, pp. 29–44.

Di Sciullo, A. M. and C. Boeckx (eds.) 2011. *The Biolinguistic Enterprise: New Perspectives on the Evolution and Nature of the Human Language Faculty.* Oxford University Press.

Dixon, R. M. W. 2000. "A typology of causatives: form, syntax and meaning," in *Changing Valency*, R. M. W. Dixon and A. Aikhenvald (eds.). Cambridge University Press, pp. 30–83.

Doron, E. 1991. "Point of view as a factor of content," in *Proceedings of the 1st Semantics and Linguistic Theory Conference, held April 19–21, 1991 at Cornell University*, S. K. Moore and A. Z. Wyner (eds.), pp. 51–64.

Drummond, A., D. Kush and N. Hornstein 2011. "Minimalist construal: two approaches to A and B," in Boeckx (ed.), pp. 396–426.

Egerland, V. 1996. *The Syntax of Past Participles. A Generative Study of Nonfinite Constructions in Ancient and Modern Italian.* Lund University Press.

Embick, D. 2000. "Features, syntax and categories in the Latin perfect," *Linguistic Inquiry* 31: 185–230.

Embick, D. and R. Noyer 2001. "Movement operations after syntax," *Linguistic Inquiry* 32: 555–95.

Ervin-Tripp, S. M. 1976. "Is Sybil there: some American English directives," *Language in Society* 5: 25–66.

Etxabe, K. and L. Garmendia 2003. *Zaldibiako Euskara: Bertako bizimodua, ohiturak eta pasadizoak.* Zaldibia Town Hall: Zaldibia.

Euskaltzaindia 1985. *Euskal gramatika: lehen urratsak-I.* Iruñea: Euskaltzaindia – Nafarroako Gobernua.

1987a. *Euskal gramatika: lehen urratsak-I (eraskina).* Bilbao: Euskaltzaindia.

1987b. *Euskal gramatika: lehen urratsak-II (aditza).* Bilbao: Euskaltzaindia.

1990. *Euskal gramatika: lehen urratsak-III (lokailuak).* Bilbao: Euskaltzaindia.

1994. *Euskal gramatika: lehen urratsak-IV (juntagailuak).* Bilbao: Euskaltzaindia-EHU.

1999. *Euskal gramatika: lehen urratsak-V (mendeko perpausak-1).* Bilbao: Euskaltzaindia-EHU.

2005. *Euskal gramatika: lehen urratsak-VI (mendeko perpausak-2).* Bilbao, Euskaltzaindia.

Faarlund, J. 1985. "Imperatives and control: first person imperatives in Norwegian," *Nordic Journal of Linguistics* 8: 149–60.

Family, N. 2006. "Light verb constructions in Persian." Paris. www.risc.cnrs.fr/Theses_pdf/2006_family.pdf.n

Farkas, D. F. 1988. "On obligatory control," *Linguistics and Philosophy* 11(1): 27–58.

Fontaneda, G. 2008. "Hitano zena." www.erabili.com/zer_berri/muinetik/1210664497.

Fortuin, E. L. J. 2000. *Polysemy or Monosemy: Interpretation of the Imperative and Dative-Infinitive Construction in Russian*. Amsterdam: ILLC Dissertation Series.

Franco, J. and S. Huidobro 2008. "Ethical datives, clitic doubling and the theory of *pro*," in *Selected Proceedings of the 10th Hispanic Linguistics Symposium*, J. Bruhn de Garavito and E. Valenzuela (eds.). Somerville, MA: Cascadilla Proceedings Project, pp. 215–24.

Freidin, R. and H. Lasnik 2011. "Some roots of minimalism in generative grammar," in Boeckx (ed.), pp. 1–26.

Gili Gaya, S. 1961. *Curso superior de sintaxis española*. Barcelona: Vox.

Giorgi, A. 2010. *About the Speaker: Towards a Syntax of Indexicality*. Oxford University Press.

Grevisse, M. 1969. *Précis de Grammaire Française*. Gembloux: Duculot.

Gronas, M. 2006. "The origin of the Russian historical imperative," *Russian Linguistics* 30(1): 89–101.

Gruzdeva, E. J. 2001. "Imperative sentences in Nivkh," in Xrakovskij (ed.), pp. 59–77.

Guasti, M. T. 1993. "Verb syntax in Italian child grammar: Finite and nonfinite verbs," *Language Acquisition* 3: 1–40.

Hagège, C. 1974. "Les pronoms logophoriques," *Bulletin de la Société de Linguistique de Paris* 69: 287–310.

Hale, A. 1980. "Person markers: finite conjunct and disjunct verb forms in Newari," in *Papers in South-East Asian Linguistics*, No 7, R. L. Trail (ed.) Canberra: Pacific Linguistics, pp. 95–196.

Hale, K. and J. Keyser 1998. "The basic elements of argument structure," in *Papers from the UPenn/MIT roundtable on Argument Structure and Aspect*, H. Harley (ed.). Cambridge, MA: MIT Press, pp. 73–118.

    1999. "Bound features, merge and transitivity alternations," in *Papers from the UPenn/MIT Roundtable on the Lexicon*, L. Pylkkänen, A. van Hout and H. Harley (eds.). Cambridge, MA: MIT Press, pp. 49–72.

Halle, M. 1990. "An approach to morphology," in *Proceedings of NELS 20*, J. Carter, R.-M. Déchaine, B. Philip and T. Sherer. Amherst: University of Massachusetts, GLSA, pp. 150–84.

    1997. "Distributed morphology: impoverishment and fission," in *PF: Papers at the Interface*, B. Bruening, Y. Kang and M. McGinnis (eds.). Cambridge, MA: MIT Press, pp. 425–49.

Halle, M. and A. Marantz 1993. "Distributed morphology and the pieces of inflection," in *The View from Building 20: Essays in Linguistics in Honor of Sylvain Bromberger*, K. Hale and S. Jay Keyser (eds.). Cambridge, MA: MIT Press, pp. 111–76.

Han, C.-H. 2000a. *The Structure and Interpretation of Imperatives: Mood and Force in Universal Grammar*. New York: Garland.

2000b. "The evolution of *do*-support in English imperatives," in *Diachronic Syntax: Models and Mechanisms*, S. Pintzuk, G. Tsoulas and T. Warner (eds.), pp. 275–95. Oxford University Press.

2001. "Force, negation and imperatives," *The Linguistic Review* 18: 289–325.

Han, C.-H. and C. Lee 2002. "On negative imperatives in Korean." *Proceedings of the 16th Pacific Asia Conference on Language, Information and Computation*. The Korean Society for Language and Information.

2007. "On negative imperatives in Korean," *Linguistic Inquiry* 38(2): 373–95.

Hargreaves, D. 1990. "Indexical functions and grammatical sub-systems in Kathmandu Newari," in *Papers from the Annual Regional Meeting, Chicago Linguistic Society* 26(1), pp. 179–93.

1991. "The conceptual structure of intentional action: data from Kathmandu Newari," *Proceedings of the Annual Meeting of the Berkeley Linguistics Society* 17, pp. 379–389.

2005. "Agency and intentional action in Kathmandu Newari," *Himalayan Linguistics* 5: 1–48.

Harley, H. 2011. "A minimalist approach to argument structure," in Boeckx (ed.), pp. 427–48.

Harris, J. 1998. "Spanish imperatives," *Journal of Linguistics* 34: 27–52.

Harris, J. and M. Halle 2005. "Unexpected plural inflections in Spanish: reduplication and metathesis," *Linguistic Inquiry* 36: 195–222.

Haspelmath, M., M. S. Dryer, D. Gil and B. Comrie (eds.) 2005. *The World Atlas of Language Structures*. Oxford University Press.

Hauser, M. D., N. Chomsky and W. T. Fitch 2002. "The faculty of language: what is it, who has it, and how did it evolve?," *Science* 298: 569–79.

2010. "The faculty of language: what is it, who has it, and how did it evolve?" in *The Evolution of Human Language*, R. K. Larson, V. Déprez and H. Yamakido (eds.) Cambridge University Press.

Haverkate, H. 1976. "Pragmatic and linguistic aspects of the prepositional infinitive in Spanish," *Lingua* 40: 223–45.

Heim, I. 1983. "On the projection problem for presuppositions," in *Proceedings of the Second West Coast Conference on Formal Linguistics*, D. Flickinger, M. Barlow and M. Westcoat (eds.). Stanford University Press, pp. 114–25.

Henry, A. 1995. *Belfast English and Standard English: Dialect Variation and Parameter Setting*. Oxford University Press.

Hill, V. 2007. "Vocatives and the pragmatics-syntax interface," *Lingua* 117(12): 2077–105.

2010. "The status of Romanian *ia* in imperative clauses," *Balkanistica* 23: 75–92.

Hopper, P. 1991. "On some principles of grammaticalization," in *Approaches to Grammaticalization*, Vol. I, E. C. Traugott and B. Heine (eds.). Amsterdam: John Benjamins, pp. 17–36.

Hopper, P. and E. C. Traugott 1993. *Grammaticalization*. Cambridge University Press.

Hornstein, N. 2001. *Move! A Minimalist Theory of Construal*. Malden, MA: Blackwell.

Hornstein, N., J. Nunes and K. Grohmann 2005. *Understanding Minimalism*. Cambridge University Press.

Hualde, J. I. and J. Ortiz de Urbina (eds.). 2003. *A Grammar of Basque*. Berlin: Mouton de Gruyter.

Hualde, J. I., B. Oyharçabal and J. Ortiz de Urbina 2003. "Allocutive forms," in Hualde and Ortiz de Urbina (eds.), pp. 242–46.

1991. "A neo-Gricean pragmatic theory of anaphora," *Journal of Linguistics* 27: 301–55.

1996. "Logophoricity: logophoric pronouns in African languages and long-distance reflexives in East Asian languages." Unpublished manuscript, University of Reading.

Huang, Y. 2003. "Switch-reference in Amele and logophoric verbal suffix in Gokana: a generalized neo-Gricean pragmatic analysis," in *Reading Working Papers in Linguistics 7*, M. Georgiafentis, E. Haeberli and S. Varlokosta (eds.), pp. 53–76.

Hyman, L. and B. Comrie 1981. "Logophoric reference in Gokana," *Journal of African Languages and Linguistics* 3: 19–37.

Iatridou, S. 2008. "De modo imperativo." Lecture Notes: ENS, Paris September 16–19.

Isac, D. and E. Jakab 2004. "Mood and force features in the languages of the Balkans," in *Balkan Syntax and Semantics*, O. Miseska Tomic (ed.). Amsterdam: John Benjamins, pp. 315–38.

Jaeggli, O. and K. J. Safir 1989. "The null subject parameter and parametric theory," in *The Null Subject Parameter*, O. Jaeggli and K. J. Safir (eds.). Dordrecht: Kluwer Academic Publishers, pp. 1–44.

Jackendoff, R. 2011. "What is the human language faculty? Two views," *Language* 87(3): 586–624.

2012. "Response to Seuren," *Language* 88(1): 177–78.

Jensen, B. 2004a. "Syntax and semantics of imperative subjects," *University of Tromsø Working Papers on Language and Linguistics* 31(1): 150–64.

2004b. "Imperative clause structure." Unpublished manuscript, University of Cambridge.

Kamp, J. A. W. 1981. "A theory of truth and semantic representation," in *Formal Methods in the Study of Language* (Part I), J. Groenendijk, T. Janssen and M. Stokhof (eds.). Amsterdam: Mathematical Centre Tracts, pp. 277–321.

Kany, C. E. 1944. "Impersonal dizque and its variants in American Spanish," *Hispanic Review* 12(2): 168–77.

1951. *American Spanish Syntax*. University of Chicago Press. 2nd edn.

Kaplan, D. 1977/89. "Demonstratives," in *Themes from Kaplan*, J. Almog, J. Perry and H. Wettstein (eds.). Oxford University Press, pp. 481–563.

1979. "On the logic of demonstratives," *The Journal of Philosophical Logic* 8: 401–12.

1989. "Afterthoughts," in *Themes from Kaplan*, J. Almog, J. Perry and H. Wettstein (eds.), pp. 565–614.

Katz, J. J. and P. M. Postal 1964. *An Integrated Theory of Linguistic Descriptions*. Cambridge, MA: MIT Press.

Kaufmann, M. 2012. *Interpreting Imperatives*. Dordrecht: Springer.

Kayne, R. 1989. "Facets of Romance past participle agreement," in *Dialect Variation and the Theory of Grammar*, P. Benincà (ed.). Dordrecht: Foris, pp. 85–103.

1992. "Italian negative infinitival imperatives and clitic climbing," in *Hommages à Nicolas Ruwet*, L. Tasmowsky and A. Zribi-Hertz (eds.). Ghent: Communication and Cognition, pp. 300–12.

2008. "Toward a syntactic reinterpretation of Harris and Halle (2005)." Paper presented at *Going Romance*, University of Groningen (Holland), December 12, 2008.

Keenan, E. L. and B. Comrie 1977. "Noun phrase accessibility and universal grammar," *Linguistic Inquiry* 8(1): 63–99.

Klee, C. A. and A. Lynch 2009. *El español en contacto con otras lenguas*. Georgetown University Press.

Koopman, H. 2001. "On the homophony of past tense and imperatives in Kisongo Maasai," in *UCLA Working Papers in Linguistics 6, Papers in African Linguistics 1*, H. Torrence (ed.), pp. 1–13.

Koopman, H. and D. Sportiche 1982. "Variables and the bijection principle," *The Linguistic Review* 2: 139–60

König, E. and P. Siemund 2007. "Speech act distinctions in grammar," in *Language Typology and Syntactic Description*, T. Shopen (ed.). Cambridge University Press, pp. 276–324.

Kuno, S. 1973. *The Structure of the Japanese Language*. Cambridge, MA: MIT Press.

Kuroda, S.-Y. 1965. "Causative forms in Japanese," *Foundations of Language* 1: 30–50.

Kuzmenkov, E. A. 2001. "Imperative verb forms in Mongolian," in Xrakovskij (ed.), pp. 98–105.

Laka, I. 1990. *Negation in Syntax: On the Nature of Functional Categories and Projections*. Doctoral dissertation, Massachusetts Institute of Technology.

Landau, I. 2000. *Elements of Control: Structure and Meaning in Infinitival Constructions*. Dordrecht: Kluwer.

2004. "The scale of finiteness and the calculus of control," *Natural Language and Linguistic Theory* 22: 811–77.

2008. "Two routes of control: evidence from case transmission in Russian," *Natural Language and Linguistic Theory* 26: 877–924.

Larson, R. K. 1988. "On the double object construction," *Linguistic Inquiry* 19: 335–91.

Larson, R. K., V. Déprez and H. Yamakido (eds.) 2010. *The Evolution of Human Language: Biolinguistic Perspectives*. Cambridge University Press.

Legate, J. A. 2003. "Some interface properties of the phase," *Linguistic Inquiry* 34(3): 506–15.

Levin, B. and M. Rappaport-Hovav 1995. *Unaccusativity: At the Syntax Semantics Interface*. Linguistic Inquiry monographs 26.

Levinson, S. C. 1983. *Pragmatics*. Cambridge University Press.

Lieberman, P. 2002. *Human Language and Our Reptilian Brain: the Subcortical Bases of Speech, Syntax and Thought*. Harvard University Press.

Lipski, J. M. 1994. *Latin American Spanish*. London: Longman.

Lyons, J. 1977. *Semantics. Vols. 1–2*. Cambridge University Press.

Maiden, M. 2006. "On Rumanian imperatives," *Philologica Jassyensia* 1: 47–59.

Mastop, R. 2005. "Event-based imperatives," in *Proceedings of the 14th Amsterdam Colloquium*, P. Dekker and R. van Rooij (eds.). Amsterdam: ILLC.

Mauck, S., M. Pak, P. Portner and R. Zanuttini 2005. "Imperative subjects: a cross-linguistic perspective," in Brandstetter and Rus (eds.), pp. 135–52.

Megerdoomian, K. 2008. "Parallel nominal and verbal projections," in *Foundational Issues in Linguistic Theory*, R. Freidin, C. Otero and M. L. Zubizarreta (eds.) Cambridge, MA: MIT Press.

Mithun, M. 1999. *The Languages of Native North America*. Cambridge University Press.

Morvay, K. 2002. "Gora euskara,euskaldunon hizkuntza! (reflexions sobre els procediments expressius del basc," in *Hommage à Jacques Allières: Romania et Vasconia*, Vol. I, Domaines basque et pyrénéen, M. Aurnague and M. Roché (eds.), pp. 183–94.

Newmeyer, F. J. 1986. *Linguistic Theory in America*. Orlando, FL: Academic Press. Second edition.

Nichols, J. 1971. "Diminutive consonant symbolism in Western North America," *Language* 47: 826–48.

Nuyts, J. 2001. *Epistemic Modality, Language, and Conceptualization. A Cognitive-Pragmatic Perspective*. Amsterdam: John Benjamins.

Orozco, R. and G. R. Guy 2008. "El uso variable de los pronombres sujetos: ¿qué pasa en la costa Caribe colombiana?," in *Selected Proceedings of the 4th Workshop on Spanish Sociolinguistics*, M. Westmoreland and J. A. Thomas (eds.). Somerville, MA: Cascadilla Proceedings Project, pp. 70–80.

Oyharçabal, B. 1993. "Verb agreement with nonarguments: on allocutive agreement," in *Generative Studies in Basque Linguistics*, J. I. Hualde and J. Ortiz de Urbina (eds.). Amsterdam: John Benjamins, pp. 89–114.

Pak, M., P. Portner and R. Zanuttini 2008. "Agreement in promissive, imperative, and exhortative clauses," *Korean Linguistics* 14: 157–75.

Pantcheva, M. 2009. "First phase syntax of Persian complex predicates: argument structure and telicity," *Journal of South Asian Linguistics* 2(1): 53–72.

Perlmutter, D. M. 1978a. "Impersonal passives and the unaccusative hypothesis," *Proceedings of the Fourth Annual Meeting of the Berkeley Linguistics* Society, Berkeley Linguistics Society, 157–89.

1978b. "The unaccusative hypothesis and multiattachment: Italian evidence," paper presented at the Harvard Linguistics Circle, May 9.

Pesetsky, D. and E. Torrego 2011. "Case," in Boeckx (ed.), pp. 52–72.

Pinker, S. and R. Jackendoff 2005. "The faculty of language: what's special about it?," *Cognition* 95: 201–36.

Platzack, C. 2007. "Embedded imperatives," in van der Wurff (ed.), pp. 181–203.

Platzack, C. and I. Rosengren 1998. "On the subject of imperatives: a Minimalist account of the imperative clause," *Journal of Comparative Germanic Linguistics* 3: 177–224.

Plungian, V. A. 2001. "The place of evidentiality within the universal grammatical space." *Journal of Pragmatics* 33(3): 349–57.

Poletto, C. and R. Zanuttini 2003. "Marking imperatives: evidence from central Rhaetoromance," in C. Tortora (ed.), *The Syntax of Italian Dialects*. Oxford University Press, pp. 175–206.

Pollock, J.-Y. 1989. "Verb movement, Universal Grammar, and the structure of IP," *Linguistic Inquiry* 20: 365–424.

Portner, P. 2004. The semantics of imperatives within a theory of clause types," in *Proceedings of Semantics and Linguistic Theory 14*, K. Watanabe and R. B. Young (eds.). Ithaca, NY: CLC Publications, pp. 235–52.

Portner, P. and R. Zanuttini 2003. "Decomposing imperatives." Paper presented at *IX Giornata di Dialettologia*, Padua, June 26, 2003.

Potsdam, E. 1998. *Syntactic Issues in the English Imperative*. New York: Garland.

2007. "Analysing word order in the English imperative," in van der Wurff (ed.), pp. 111–28.

Premack, D. and Woodruff, G. 1978. "Does the chimpanzee have a theory of mind?" *Behavioral Brain Sciences* 1: 515–26.

Proeme, H. 1984. "Over de Netherlandse imperativus," *Forum der Letteren* 25: 241–48.

Quer, J. 2005. "Context shift and indexical variables in sign languages," in *Proceedings from SALT 15*, E. Georgala and J. Howell (eds.). Ithaca, NY: CLC Publications, pp. 152–68.

Ramchand, G. 2011. "Minimalist semantics," in Boeckx (ed.), pp. 449–71.

Rebuschi, G. 1981. "Autour des formes allocutives du basque," *Iker* 1, 307–22. Bilbao: Euskaltzaindia.

1982. *Structure de l'énoncé en Basque*. Département de Recherches linguistiques, Université de Paris 7; new edition, SELAF, Paris (1984).

Recanati, F. 2004. "Indexicality and context-shift," Paper presented at *Workshop on Indexicality, Speech Acts and Logophors*, Harvard University, November 20.

Reichenbach, H. 1947. *Elements of Symbolic Logic*. New York: Macmillan & Co.

Reuland, E. J. 2001. "Primitives of binding," *Linguistic Inquiry* 32(3): 439–92.

2005. "Agreeing to bind," in *Organizing Grammar: Linguistic Studies in Honor of Henk van Riemsdijk*, H. Broekhuis and N. Corver (eds.). Berlin: Mouton de Gruyter, pp. 505–13.

Rice, C. 2003. "Dialectal variation in Norwegian imperatives," in *Proceedings of the 19th Scandinavian Conference of Linguistics*, A. Dahl, K. Bentzen, and P. Svenonius (eds.). *Nordlyd* 31(2): 372–84.

Rice, K. 1986. "Some remarks on direct and indirect speech in Slave (Northern Athapaskan)," in *Direct and Indirect Speech*, F. Coulmas (ed.). Berlin: Mouton de Gruyter, pp. 47–76.

de Rijk, R. P. G. 2008. *Standard Basque: A Progressive Grammar*. Cambridge, MA: MIT Press.

Rivero, M. L. 1994. "Negation, imperatives and Wackenagel effects," *Rivista di Linguistica* 6: 39–66.

Rivero, M. L. and A. Terzi 1995. "Imperatives, V-movement, and logical mood," *Journal of Linguistics* 31: 301–32.

Rizzi, L. 1997. "The fine structure of the left periphery," in *Elements of Grammar: A Handbook of Generative Syntax*, L. Haegeman (ed.). Dordrecht: Kluwer, pp. 281–337.

2004. *The Structure of CP and IP: The Cartography of Syntactic Structures Volume 2*. Oxford University Press.

Roberts, I. 2011. "Head movement and the minimalist program," in Boeckx (ed.), pp. 195–219.

Ross, J. R. 1970. "On declarative sentences," in *Readings in English Transformational Grammar*, R. A. Jacobs and P. S. Rosenbaum (eds.). Waltham, MS: Ginn and Co, pp. 222–72.

Rupp, L. 2003. *The Syntax of Imperatives in English and Germanic: Word Order Variation in the Minimalist Framework*. Basingstoke: Palgrave Macmillan.

Sadock, J. 1969. "Hypersentences," *Papers in Linguistics* 1: 283–370.

   1974. *Toward a Linguistic Theory of Speech Acts*. New York: Academic Press.

Sadock, J. and A. Zwicky 1985. "Speech act distinctions in syntax," in *Language Typology and Syntactic Description*. Vol. I: Clause Structure, T. Shopen (ed.). Cambridge University Press, pp. 155–96.

Safir, K. 2005. "Person, context and perspective," *Rivista di Linguistica* 16: 107–53.

Saltarelli, M. 1988. *Basque*. London: Croom Helm Descriptive Grammar Series.

   2011. "Marsican spatial demonstratives: towards a grammaticalization of indexical reference." *Conference on Italian Dialects 6*. Cambridge (UK).

Saltarelli, M. and A. Alcázar 2010. "The sentential force of light verbs in southern Italian dialects." Paper presented at the *5th Cambridge Italian Dialect Syntax Meeting*. Freie Universität of Berlin, July 2.

Salustri, M. and N. Hyams 2003. "Is there an analogue to the RI stage in the null subject languages?" *Proceedings of the 27th annual BUCLD*, 692–703.

   2006. "Looking for the universal core of the RI stage," in *The Acquisition of Syntax in Romance Languages*, V. Torrens and L. Escobar (eds.). Amsterdam: John Benjamins, pp. 159–82.

Samuels, B. 2011. "A minimalist program for phonology," in Boeckx (ed.), pp. 574–94.

Sauerland, U. and H.-M. Gärtner 2007. *Interfaces + Recursion = Language: Chomsky's Minimalism and the View from Syntax-Semantics*. Berlin: Walter de Gruyter.

Schauber, E. 1979. *The Syntax and Semantics of Questions in Navajo*. California: Garland Pub.

Schlenker, P. 1999. *Propositional Attitudes and Indexicality: A Cross-Categorial Approach*. Doctoral Dissertation, Massachusetts Institute of Technology.

   2003. "A plea for monsters," *Linguistics and Philosophy* 26: 29–120.

   2004. "Context of thought and context of utterance (a note on free indirect discourse and the historical present)," *Mind and Language* 19(3): 279–304.

Searle, J. R. 1969. *Speech Acts: An Essay in the Philosophy of Language*. Cambridge University Press.

   1979. *Expression and Meaning: Studies in the Theory of Speech Acts*. Cambridge University Press.

Segurola, I. 1992. "Gizon, gizarte, gizagaixoo," *Euskaldunon Egunkaria*, 1992–430, p. 26.

Sells, P. 1987. "Aspects of logophoricity," *Linguistic Inquiry* 18(3): 445–79.

Sepännen, A. 1977. "The position of *let* in the English auxiliary system," *English Studies* 58: 515–29.

Seuren, P. 1996. *Semantic Syntax*. Oxford University Press.

   2009. *Language in Cognition* (Language from within Vol. I). Oxford University Press.

2012. "A reaction to Jackendoff discussion note," *Language* 88(1): 174–76 and 179.

Shklovsky, K. and Y. Sudo In press. "Indexical shifting in Uyghur," in *Proceedings of NELS 40*.

Sigurðsson, H. Á. 1990. "Long distance reflexives and moods in Icelandic," in *Modern Icelandic Syntax*, J. Maling and A. Zaenen (eds.). New York: Academic Press, pp. 309–46.

2004. "The syntax of person and speech features," in *The Syntax and Interpretation of Person Features*, V. Bianchi and K. Safir (eds.), *Rivista di Linguistica* 16(1): 219–51.

Silva-Corvalán, C. 1982. "Subject expression and placement in Mexican-American Spanish," in *Spanish in the United States: Sociolinguistic Aspects*, J. Amastae and L. Elías-Olivares (eds.). Cambridge University Press, pp. 93–120.

Sorace, A. 2000. "Gradients in auxiliary selection with intransitive verbs," *Language* 76(4): 859–90.

Speas, M. 1999. "Person and point of view in Navajo direct discourse complements," in *University of Massachusetts Occasional Papers in Linguistics 23: Papers from the 25th Reunion*, P. DeLacy and A. Nowak (eds.).

2004. "Evidentiality, logophoricity and the syntactic representation of pragmatic features," *Lingua* 14(3): 255–76.

Speas, M. and C. Tenny 2003. "Configurational properties of point of view roles," in *Asymmetry in Grammar*, A. DiSciullo (ed.). Amsterdam: John Benjamins, pp. 315–43.

Squartini, M. (ed.) 2007a. *Evidentiality between lexicon and grammar. Rivista di Linguistica* 19(2).

2007b. "Investigating a grammatical category and its lexical correlates," in Squartini (ed.), pp. 1–6.

2008. "Lexical vs. grammatical evidentiality in French and Italian," *Linguistics* 46(5): 917–47.

Stalnaker, R. 1978. "Assertion," *Syntax and Semantics* 9: 315–32.

Stechow, A. von 2002. "Feature deletion under semantic binding: tense, person, and mood under verbal quantifiers." Paper presented at the annual meeting of the *North East Linguistic Society*, Tübingen, November 2002.

Stegnij, V. A. 2001. "Imperative constructions in Klamath," in Xrakovskij (ed.), pp. 78–97.

Sudo, Y. In press. "Person indexicals in Uyghur indexical shifting," in *Proceedings of Berkeley Linguistics Society 36*.

Tenny, C. 2006. "Evidentiality, experiencers, and syntax of sentience in Japanese," *Journal of East Asian Linguistics* 15: 245–88.

Ukaji, M. 1978. *Imperative Sentences in Early Modern English*. Tokyo: Kaitakusha.

Uriagereka, J. 2011. "Derivational cycles," in Boeckx (ed.), pp. 239–59.

Veselinova, L. N. 2005. "Suppletion according to tense and aspect," in Haspelmath, Dryer, Gil and Comrie (eds.), pp. 322–25.

Visser, F. Th. 1963. *An Historical Syntax of the English Language. I Syntactical Units with One Verb*. Leiden: E. J. Brill.

1966. *An Historical Syntax of the English Language. II Syntactical Units with One Verb (Continued)*. Leiden: E. J. Brill.

1969. *An Historical Syntax of the English Language. III. First Half. Syntactical Units with Two Verbs*. Leiden: E. J. Brill.

Watanabe, K. and R. B. Young (eds.) 2004. *Proceedings of the 14th Conference on Semantics and Linguistic Theory*. Ithaca, NY: CLC Publications.

Weinreich, U. 1966. "On the semantic structure of language," in *Universals of Language*, J. Greenberg (ed.), 2nd edn. Cambridge, MA: MIT Press.

Wilder, C. and D. Cavar 1994. "Word order variation, verb movement and economy principles," *Studia Linguistica* 48: 46–86.

Willet, T. 1988. "A cross-linguistic survey of the grammaticization of evidentiality," *Studies in Language* 12: 51–97.

Williams, E. 1978. "Across the board rule application," *Linguistic Inquiry* 9: 31–43.

Willie, M. A. 1989. "A comparison of indirect speech constructions in two Athabaskan languages." Paper presented at the *4th Meeting of the Pacific Linguistics Conference*, at Eugene, Oregon.

Wurff, W. van der (ed.) 2007a. *Imperatives in Generative Grammar*. Amsterdam: John Benjamins.

　2007b. "Imperative clauses in generative grammar: an introduction," in Wurff (ed.), pp. 1–94.

Xrakovskij, V. S. (ed.) 2001. *Typology of Imperative Constructions*. Munich: Lincom Europa.

Zanuttini, R. 1991. *Syntactic Properties of Sentential Negation: A Comparative Study of Romance Languages*. Doctoral dissertation, University of Pennsylvania.

　1994. "Speculations on negative imperatives," *Rivista di Linguistica* 6(1): 67–89.

　1996. "On the relevance of tense for sentential negation," in *Parameters and Functional Heads*, A. Belletti and L. Rizzi (eds.) *Essays in Comparative Syntax*. Oxford University Press, pp. 181–207.

　1997. *Negation and Clausal Structure: A Comparative Study of Romance Languages*. Oxford University Press.

　2008. "Encoding the Addressee in the syntax: evidence from English imperative subjects," *Natural Language and Linguistic Theory* 26(1): 185–218.

Zanuttini, R. and P. Portner 2000. "The characterization of exclamative clauses in Paduan," *Language* 76(1): 123–32.

　2003. "Exclamative clauses: at the syntax-semantics interface," *Language* 79(1) 39–81.

Zeijlstra, H. 2006. "The ban on true negative imperatives," in *Empirical Issues in Syntax and Semantics 6*, O. Bonami and P. Cabredo Hofherr (eds.), pp. 405–24.

Zhang, S. 1990. *The Status of Imperatives in Theories of Grammar*. Doctoral dissertation, University of Arizona.

Zubiri, I. and E. Zubiri 2000. *Euskal Gramatika Osoa*. Bilbao: Didaktiker.

Zwicky, A. M. 1988. "On the subject of bare imperatives in English," in *On Language: Rhetorica, Phonologica, Syntactica – A Festschrift for Robert P. Stockwell from His Friends and Colleagues*, C. Duncan-Rose and T. Vennemann (eds.). London: Routledge, pp. 437–50.

Index of languages

Index of authors

Index of subjects